The Limits of the Green Economy

T0271873

Projecting win-win situations, new economic opportunities, green growth and innovative partnerships, the green economy discourse has quickly gained centre stage in international environmental governance and policymaking. Its underlying message is attractive and optimistic: if the market can become the tool for tackling climate change and other major ecological crises, the fight against these crises can also be the royal road to solving the problems of the market. But how 'green' is the green economy? And how social or democratic can it be?

This book examines how the emergence of this new discourse has fundamentally modified the terms of the environmental debate. Interpreting the rise of green economy discourse as an attempt to reinvent capitalism, it unravels the different dimensions of the green economy and its limits: from pricing carbon to emissions trading, from sustainable consumption to technological innovation. The book uses the innovative concept of post-politics to provide a critical perspective on the way green economy discourse represents nature and society (and their interaction) and forecloses the imagination of alternative socio-ecological possibilities. As a way of repoliticising the debate, the book advocates the construction of new political faultlines based on the demands for climate justice and democratic commons.

This book will be of interest to students and scholars of environmental politics, political ecology, human geography, human ecology, political theory, philosophy and political economy.

Anneleen Kenis is a post-doctoral researcher at the Divisions of Bio-economics and Geography at KU Leuven, Belgium. Her research interests include ecological citizenship, climate change, activism, air pollution, democracy, post-politics, feminism, and more broadly, political ecology.

Matthias Lievens is a post-doctoral researcher at the Centre for Ethics, Social and Political Philosophy at KU Leuven, Belgium. His research interests include representation, ideology, democracy, the concept of the political, sovereignty and constituent power, and more broadly, continental political theory.

Routledge Studies in Environmental Policy

"This is an important and timely book. Kenis and Lievens present an incisive analysis of the productive plasticity of the contemporary environmental-political discourse that is epitomized by the concept of the 'green economy.' Reading it, for me, felt like scratching an intense itch."

Sherilyn MacGregor, Keele University, UK

"This beautifully written and engaging book was badly needed. Kenis and Lievens help us understand why the 'green economy' as currently rolled out will worsen rather than alleviate global social and environmental ills but also point to a realistic way forward. *The Limits of the Green Economy* needs to be read widely and acted on as a matter of urgency."

Bram Büscher, Wageningen University, The Netherlands

"In this timely book, Kenis and Lievens reveal the 'green economy' – a vision of lush, eco-balanced affluence engineered through smart markets and ethical enterprise – to be a strategic mirage, a pied-piper panacea that co-opts even critical spirits into a politics of complicity with hegemonic power. Against the faux consensus they rehabilitate conflict; against quotidian capitalism they reach out to 'the commons.' Anyone with an interest in a habitable future on Earth should read this book."

Gareth Dale, Brunel University London, UK

"With an intransigent analytical power and incisive surgical precision, this book reveals the limits of the green economy. The alternative political road Anneleen Kenis and Matthias Lievens aim to open up requires imaginative power, scientific insight in both natural and social processes (and their inter-action), a rare intellectual courage, and especially an unwavering fidelity to the truth that things can and should be different."

Erik Swyngedouw, University of Manchester, UK

"This book not only provides us with the most authoritative critique of the 'green economy' written so far, but also invites us to think in original and novel ways about the environmental field."

Guy Baeten, Lund University, Sweden

The Limits of the Green Economy

From reinventing capitalism to repoliticising the present

Anneleen Kenis and Matthias Lievens

Routledge
Taylor & Francis Group

LONDON AND NEW YORK

First published 2015
by Routledge
2 Park Square, Milton Park, Abingdon, Oxfordshire OX14 4RN

and by Routledge
711 Third Avenue, New York, NY 10017

First issued in paperback 2017

Routledge is an imprint of the Taylor & Francis Group, an informa business

Some of the material in this work is based on the authors' book *De mythe
van de groene economie: Valstrik, verzet, alternatieven*, published by EPO
Uitgeverij, Belgium, 2012.

British Library Cataloguing-in-Publication Data

A catalogue record for this book is available from the British Library

Library of Congress Cataloging-in-Publication Data

Kenis, Anneleen.
    The limits of the green economy : from re-inventing capitalism to
re-politicising the present / Anneleen Kenis and Matthias Lievens.
        pages cm
    ISBN 978-1-138-78170-2 (hardback) — ISBN 978-1-315-76970-7
(ebook) 1. Capitalism—Environmental aspects.
    2. Environmentalism—Economic aspects. 3. Economic
development—Environmental aspects. I. Lievens, Matthias. II. Title.
HC79.E5K42145 2015
    333.72—dc23   2014038936

ISBN 13: 978-1-138-05568-1 (pbk)
ISBN 13: 978-1-138-78170-2 (hbk)

Typeset in Goudy
by Apex CoVantage, LLC

Contents

Foreword

Apocalypse now? From the marketisation to the politicisation of the environment

Franklin D. Roosevelt once stated empathically that books are weapons. If I go to the bookshop or surf to Amazon.com, I am far from convinced that this is the case, especially when it comes to books about 'the environment'. Only rarely one stumbles upon a book that really stimulates reflection, disrupts common-sense understanding, undermines apparent certainties, turns ecological doom and gloom into creative engagement and at the same time encourages thought about new forms of social-ecological imagination and political action. This book is one of those rare exceptions. Anneleen Kenis and Matthias Lievens combine uneasy truths and thorough analysis with a clarion call for decisive political action. At the same time, the book moves beyond both the apocalyptic tone and moralistic pedantry that is often associated with critical social-economic and ecological literature, and the limited approach of indicating all too easy solutions. This book does not promise a golden and sustainable future, as words cannot provide such guarantees. They can only indicate a direction.

With an intransigent analytical power and incisive surgical precision, this book reveals the limits of the green economy. The alternative political road the authors aim to open up requires imaginative power, scientific insight in both natural and social processes (and their interaction), a rare intellectual courage and especially an unwavering fidelity to the truth that things can and should be different. Social-ecological change and transformation is not a pipe dream, it is an acute necessity.

This is the emancipatory message, which resounds forcefully throughout this book and radically ruptures contemporary hegemonic environmental thinking. The dominant argumentation of 'green economy' pundits maintains that merely greening the existing socio-economic relations will bring a sustainable solution. Ecologising the economy would be necessary and sufficient to evade a pending ecological Armageddon while permitting the untroubled continuation of civilisation as we know it for a while longer. It is precisely the premise of this biblical promise of a coming ecological catastrophe in the near future that should be rejected completely. Confronted with cataclysmic images of imminent ecological disaster, which predominate the ecological and climate discourse, and whose ultimate goal is precisely to make sure that the disaster does *not* take place (if *we* take the right measures), the only correct answer seems to be 'don't worry' (Al

Gore, Prince Charles, green boys and girls, environmental civil servants), your disaster scenario is factually correct, social-ecological Armageddon *will not only* take place, it *is* already taking place. Many already live *in* the apocalypse, in those places where the intertwining of environmental change and social conditions have already reduced living conditions to 'bare life'. Socio-ecological entanglements have already reached the 'point of no return'. It is already *too late* to do something about nature. It has always already been *too late*. It is precisely by accepting this reality that a new politics can emerge.

Another theme that runs through this book is the eventual recognition of the Death or the End of Nature. This is not to suggest there would be no more ecological and physical-material relations between humans and non-humans. On the contrary, the intertwining of social and 'natural' processes is now so intense that Nature as the merely external condition of existence for human beings has come to an end. There is no longer a form of Nature that is not influenced by social, cultural and economic relations. It is precisely as a result of developments of the last few centuries that this entanglement has become so intense. The historical-geographical dynamic of capitalism and its global spread has banned the very existence of an external nature. Scientists who acknowledge this irreversible dynamic have invented a name for it, the Anthropocene. 'Welcome to the Anthropocene' has become an often heard slogan to inform us that a new geological era has started. Whereas until recently earthly processes proceeded only very slowly and irrespective of human interventions at the Earth's surface or in the atmosphere, human beings have now become co-producers of a deep geological time itself.

Paul Crutzen, a Nobel Prize-winning chemist, invented the term about ten years ago to refer to what comes after the Holocene, the relatively moderate geo-climatic period in which agriculture, cities and complex human civilisations came into being. The Anthropocene heralds the period since the beginning of industrialisation, and therefore capitalism, which brought a qualitative change in the geo-climatic dynamic on Earth as a result of the ever-intensifying interaction between human beings and their physical conditions of existence. The Anthropocene is therefore nothing else than a geological name for a capitalism WITH nature. Ocean acidification, changes in biodiversity, genetic migration and new genetic combinations, climate change, large infrastructures which influence the geodetic dynamic, new materials, global and often unexpected new disease carriers and so on and so forth resulted in ever more complex entanglements of 'natural' and 'social' processes whereby human beings became active agents in the co-production of the Earth's future history. The Anthropocene is just another name to indicate the End or the Death of Nature. This cannot be undone, however hard we try. Time is irreversible. There is no ideal, lost place, time or ecology, no Arcadia to which we can return. Eden has never existed. The past is foreclosed forever, but the future – now including the future of a thoroughly socialised nature – is radically open. It is within this historically and geographically specific configuration that not only the possibility, but also the necessity for a real politicisation of the environment arises, that choices have to be made and different socio-ecological entanglements have to be produced.

The Anthropocene displaces the terrain of the political as merely inter-human activity to the environment as a whole, including those processes which until now were left to (the laws of) nature. Non-human actants and processes are now engaged in a process of politicisation. And this should be recognised in its radical materiality. The Anthropocene opens a perspective whereby different nature-realities and social-ecological interactions can be imagined and realised. The political struggle about the nature, direction and development of these interactions and about the process of egalitarian social-ecological co-production of the commons of life is what a progressive politicisation of the environment envisages. Yes, the apocalypse is already here, but that is not a reason for despair or panic. Let us fully recognise the emancipatory possibilities of an apocalyptic life!

Many people would concur with the view that the climate crisis will fundamentally not be solved by hegemonic approaches of the 'green economy', by making capital compatible with – if not cashing in on – ecology; they note that energy costs are rising, social inequalities increase, rigid nationalisms emerge everywhere and the marketisation of everything is being paid for at an extravagant ecological and social cost. Many people know that things *can* and *should* be different; however, like me, they do not know what to do or how to get there. We share this gnawing and uncanny feeling that hopeless attempts by economic and political elites to translate the ecological and social *catastrophe* which surrounds us into a manageable ecological and social *crisis* do not solve the problems but push them into the future or to other places. Indeed, does the dominant rhetoric of the elite not state that 'the situation is serious but not catastrophic'? Is their neoliberal recipe book not the guarantee that the disaster will not occur? Don't they claim that the crisis can be overcome with a bit of goodwill and effort: social unity will be restored, economic growth will recover and ecological problems will be addressed sustainably? 'Hold on for a while, rescue is coming!'

Don't you have the surreptitious feeling that something is wrong about this rhetoric of those who (sometimes literally) want to conserve the existing situation at all cost; that the ecological and social crisis cannot be made manageable with the help of mere technical and organisational adaptations; that the attempts of the elite to reduce the catastrophe to a crisis which only requires 'good' and 'ecological' management only enlarges the anxiety, increases insecurity, and especially, worsens the catastrophe which many already experience?

What would happen if we threw off the fear? If we resolutely accepted that the ecological, social and economic apocalypse is already here, that it no longer needs to be announced as a dystopian promise for an avoidable future (if only the right measures are taken today)? What if we really would believe that things can not only change, but have to?

Yes but, you might think. After all, there is no catastrophe, we don't live in the apocalypse. It was a good wine year, the summer was a bit disappointing but the holidays were sunny, the financial crisis is being addressed without too much pain for me and my siblings, sustainable environmental technologies are stimulated, the hybrid car really drives smoothly, waste is being reduced, and the new Ikea catalogue promises sustainable entrepreneurship. Furthermore, the green parties are not doing badly in the polls. You're right. The catastrophe is not for most of you or for me. Crisis, yes, but talking about catastrophe appears a bit overdone.

But perhaps we should not forget the words of the Italian Marxist Amadeo Bordiga: 'when the ship goes down, so too do the first class passengers'. This slogan is often adopted by ecologists of a variety of stripes or colours. We are all in the same boat. Bill Gates, Al Gore, the inhabitants of sinking islands and even Prince Charles today share the opinion of this notorious communist. But on closer inspection, Amadeo was desperately wrong. See the blockbuster movie *Titanic* once again. A large share of the upper-class passengers found a lifeboat; the others, well, they were stuck in the underbelly of the beast. The social and ecological catastrophe is indeed not here for everyone; the apocalypse is uneven. And this is where the ultimate truth of our current predicament is situated. Remember the images of the earthquake in Haiti a few years ago, or the devastation wrought by Hurricane Katrina in New Orleans: hundreds of thousands of homeless people, hundreds of deaths, dysentery and malaria spreading fast, exaggerated reports about thieves who stole paltry possessions to stay alive, shortages of drinking water. The earthquake was not the consequence of human interventions in nature, the hurricane perhaps. But what we know very well is that the socio-ecological catastrophe is not caused by the earthquake or the hurricane. It was there long before disaster struck. Nature was not responsible for the post-apocalyptic post-human landscape after the quake. Most Haitians, together with all the others who balance on the verge of survival, have always already lived in the apocalypse, before, during and after the quake. Racial prejudices, dire living conditions and a precarious socio-ecological existence were also the lot of the poor in New Orleans. Or think about the incalculable number of environmental refugees. We have a rough idea about the number that is reaching European shores via the Mediterranean, but we have not a clue about the countless migrants, except through occasional harrowing stories of sunken boats, that fail to make it to the continent, and become fish fodder. It is precisely the combination of ecological, social and economic relations which pushes them, often with desperately little means, to leave their home countries. They, too, fled a catastrophe. Our apocalyptic times are perversely uneven, whereby the survival pods of the elites are fed and sustained by the disintegration of life-worlds elsewhere.

Consider, for example, how the socio-ecological conditions in Chinese mega-factories, like Foxconn, where our iPhone, iPod, iPad and other gadgets indispensable for 'normal' life are assembled, make nineteenth-century European cities look like socio-ecological utopias. The social and ecological catastrophe which international elites imposed upon Greece to make sure the European neoliberal model could be sustained shows that the collapse of daily life is reserved for certain people, while the others can go on as usual. If nuclear power plants close tomorrow, the lights will continue burning on Putin's gas. Despite Pussy Riot. Tar sands exploitation and 'fracking' (a highly harmful process to win gas from certain geological layers) protect us from the disaster of 'peak oil', the approaching decrease of exploitable oil reserves.

A natural and ecological disaster shows in all its sharpness what we have already known for a long time, namely, the politically powerless and economically weak are paying the price. The apocalypse is always theirs, and only theirs. While the biblical apocalypse of Saint John announced the final judgement which offered paradise to the chosen few and damned the bad ones, the social-ecological apocalypse separates the elite from the powerless and excluded. Perhaps something must be done about the lifeboats. For some, the solution is to seal them off hermetically, to protect them with electric fences and impenetrable walls, to strengthen militarised forces to secure the perimeter of their own little paradise. The zombies of the apocalypse, the hordes at the gates, the motley crew which demands its share of nature, the rebels who ask a new order: they represent the reality of catastrophe today. And this reality should be taken seriously. We all share in it. Eco-warrior, advocate of nuclear energy, incorrigible Malthusian and inventor of the Gaia hypothesis James Lovelock summarised the possible consequences of the uneven apocalypse very eloquently and soberly:

> . . . what if at some time in the next few years we realise, as we did in 1939, that democracy had temporarily to be suspended and we had to accept a disciplined regime that saw the UK as a legitimate but limited safe haven for civilisation. Orderly survival requires an unusual degree of human understanding and leadership and may require, as in war, the suspension of democratic government for the duration of the survival emergency.[1]

The emergency situation evoked by Lovelock is not there to make sure everyone survives. It is supposed to be the consequence of the demographic explosion–cum–ecological disintegration of the global South as a result of which hordes of eco-zombies will crowd at the gates of the egalitarian social-ecological paradise at the other side of the Channel. An autocratic leadership and the suspension of democracy are precisely needed to keep the gates firmly shut. This might appear a somewhat exaggerated perspective. But is this not exactly what happened over the last years? Perhaps not so much with regard to climate change (very little has happened on that terrain), but surely with regard to attempts to reduce the economic-financial catastrophe to a manageable crisis. All other problems were shoved aside. Draconian austerity measures were imposed which especially affected the weakest, massive public means were and are mobilised to keep financial institutions afloat, migration is being managed with all possible repressive means. Despite profound and previously unseen protest, only one set of recipes was applied to restore the existing financial-economic order. The elite indeed will, if necessary, use all means available to maintain its status and position.

But does in the generalised forms of resistance reside not only the hope, but the absolute certainty, that change is possible and needed? At the end of this book, Anneleen Kenis and Matthias Lievens suggest that the way ahead carries two names, democracy and the commons. They even suggest, rather provocatively, that the political project that combines those two terms might carry the name 'communism'; 'a communism of the commons'. This suggestion breaks so strongly with the currently hegemonic logic and recipes that many will sceptically respond: how can the democratic management of the commons ever be realised? How can the egalitarian and collective management of the commons be organised in the current neoliberal climate which includes the privatisation of nature, the individualisation of daily life and the fragmentation of the political and ideological landscape? Of course, the critique of the hegemonic project of the green economy is valid, and another approach is necessary, but should we – faced with the coming catastrophes – not rather opt for practical solutions, which maybe do not really question the *status quo*, but are at least a bit more realistic and feasible today?

Furthermore, the term 'communism' probably – and rightly – evokes the horror of the twentieth century (the Stalinist terror, the ecological disaster, the social inequality), or at least the term refers to a radical failure of what was once presented as a utopian solution for society's ills. Perhaps 'communism' is indeed not a good name to refer to a democratic ecological project of the commons. Perhaps it is better to reserve the term 'socialism' or 'communism' for the elitist and undemocratic mobilisation of the commons for personal gain and the reinforcement of the elite's power position. In February 2009, *Newsweek*, not immediately the most radical magazine, stated on its cover 'We are all socialists now'. The title evidently referred to the $1.5 trillion of public money which President Barack Obama pumped into the banking system to save Wall Street and to prevent a (foretold apocalyptic) planetary financial meltdown. Shortly afterwards, other countries, including the European Union, would follow suit. Trillions of euros, part of the common capital, of our commons, were mobilised to provide the sputtering profit motor with new oil. Is there a better example to show that socialism is a real possibility, that collective means, the commons, can massively and collectively be used to reach a particular social goal, in this case the maintenance of elite positions, the avoidance of the apocalypse for the elite on the back of the weakest? Despite the Spanish Indignados, the Greek outraged, and many Occupy! movements which demand 'Real Democracy Now', the assembled elites continue undisturbed, realising their collective phantasmagorical utopia.

Is a better example possible that the commons can indeed be used collectively (in this case the collective of the 1% – still a significant number)? That a communism of the elites is precisely the political name for the current neoliberal practice? Putin's Russia is a good example of the appropriation of the commons by an oligarchic ultra-minority. As Marx stated long ago, history unfolds as a drama (the real socialism of the twentieth century) and repeats itself as a farce (the real socialism of the elites today). What the socialist movement of the twentieth century mostly failed to realise (the nationalisation of the banks) is being achieved by the elite in a very short lapse of time, in the name of the recovery of capitalism. It appears indeed that the collective management of the commons as such is not the problem. It is certainly not a naive or utopian proposal. The question is rather one of its management – by whom and for whom?

Where resides the problem then? What is it that we don't dare to face? What withholds us from tackling the unequal social-ecological apocalypse? The answer is implicit in what precedes. The collective management of the commons, of the environment, is not the problem, but rather the undemocratic character of the current type of management. This does not relate to the shortcomings of the institutional and electoral machines of daily policymaking (parliaments, regular elections, public administration, political parties, etc.), but to the basis of a democratic society itself. The foundation of democracy is that everyone is supposed to be equal. Democratic equality is not a sociologically verifiable given – we all know that each concrete society knows many clearly observable inequalities – but an axiomatic principle. The democratic is precisely the axiomatic acceptance of the equality of everyone and the recognition of the egalitarian capacity to govern in a concrete context, which is always marked by social and ecological inequalities. That is the truth which is put forward time and again by resistance movements, Indignados, the Arab Spring, the women's, workers' and environmental movements. That is why the truth of democracy is not a universal standard. Its universal truth (we are all equal in principle) is carried by the particular group who is wronged as its equality is mis- or unrecognised. That is why we can state that Al Gore, Richard Branson, the president of the European Central bank, and Angela Merkel are undemocratic, while environmental refugees, climate justice activists, resistance movements against the privatisation of the commons and Occupy! activists, through their political action, reveal the scandal of institutionalised democracy and the necessity of an egalitarian restructuration of political, social and ecological relations. In this sense, they precisely indicate what really matters in these apocalyptic times. Let's join them. Translating the egalitarian demand in concrete social-ecological equality is the stake of a real politicisation of the environment. And this requires intellectual courage, social mobilisation and new forms of political action and organisation. We have nothing to lose but our fear.

Erik Swyngedouw

Note

1 Lovelock J. (2009). "The Fight to Get Aboard Lifeboat UK." *The Sunday Times*, 8 November. http://www.timesonline.co.uk/tol/news/environment/article5682887.ece (accessed 3 August 2010).

Acknowledgements

It is not uncommon for academics to first write a scientific book, and then develop a popularised version in order to stimulate a debate in society. We proceeded in a different order. At the end of 2012, our book *De mythe van de groene economie* appeared in Dutch, sparking a lot of interest and triggering a surprisingly vibrant debate, including many articles in newspapers and magazines, interviews on public television and radio and a large number of lectures and debates. The book was to a large extent based on our academic work, even though it was oriented to a larger, non-academic audience. It provided us with a great opportunity to discuss many of our ideas with a variety of audiences: from activists to academics, from trade unionists to civil servants, from students to politicians. The current book has enormously profited from the chance we had to talk with hundreds, maybe thousands of people about our ideas.

The Limits of the Green Economy is not simply a translation of our Dutch book. Although some passages and a number of ideas have been integrated in the current book, they all have been profoundly rewritten, refined and updated. A large number of paragraphs are completely new and are directly related to our research. Writing this academic version of our argument has allowed us to be much more conceptually precise, go more in-depth, and situate our ideas better in the existing literature.

Since we started working on the green economy, an interesting body of (critical) scholarship emerged on the topic. It is evident that we owe much to the debates and insights this scholarship has produced over the last few years, both about the green economy in particular and about the broader trend of the rise of economic or market approaches to environmental questions. The list of people who inspired or helped us is long, but should certainly include Erik Swyngedouw, who is a pioneer in introducing theories of post-politics in the ecological debate; Derek Wall, who wrote fascinating things about commons and ecological politics; Gareth Dale, for the inspiring talks we had in Leuven and Ghent; Tadzio Mueller, who was one of the first to make us aware of the newly emerging faultline between the green economy and the climate justice perspective; Daniel Tanuro, who contributed many interesting analyses on green capitalism; Michael Löwy, who first brought us into contact with ecosocialist perspectives; Chantal Mouffe, who is one of our main sources of inspiration in political theory; Ulrich Melle, whose open-minded but radical approach to environmental philosophy is more than refreshing. Other important sources of inspiraton include John Bellamy Foster, Paul Burkett and André Gorz.

One practical lesson is often more valuable than a hundred theoretical arguments. Therefore we want to express our gratefulness, above all, to the many politically engaged activists we have encountered over the last years. We also would like to thank very warmly Nicola Freeman and David Heller, who did a great work translating a number of texts from Dutch into English. Moreover, as experienced environmental campaigners, they gave valuable feedback on a couple of issues. Last but not least, we want to thank Maarten Loopmans, without whose encouragement this book would not have been realised in the first place. It goes without saying that all remaining errors in this book are wholly our responsibility.

The aim of this book is modest: it is to contribute to an already ongoing debate about the merits or demerits of the green economy project, from a specific perspective, namely the question of post-politics and 'the political'. We hope it will inspire fellow scholars, concerned citizens or activists to think anew about what the struggle for a different social-ecological future could mean, and about where we can find leverage in the present to realise it.

1 The green economy
The meaning of a new narrative

Introduction

On 20 June 2012, more than 50,000 people took to the streets in Rio de Janeiro, Brazil. It was the apotheosis of a nine-day event, the 'People's Summit' for 'Social and Economic Justice', set up by hundreds of civil society organisations and grassroots movements. At the same time, the Rio+20 United Nations Conference on Sustainable Development took place right outside the city centre, entirely dedicated to the 'green economy'. Targeting the lack of effective policies to tackle the ecological crisis, the protests especially attracted peasant and environmental movements, women groups, indigenous people and trade unionists.

But more was at stake than the demand to take effective action and halt oil extraction in ecologically vulnerable areas or stop tar sands exploitation. 'A água não tem dono' ('No one owns water'), sounded one of the slogans on the street. 'Nature is not for sale' was to be read on placards, next to the demand for 'buen vivir' ('the good life'). 'We reject the green/d economy' was probably the most straightforward slogan conveyed by demonstrators. The protestors did not come merely to give support to pro-environmental politicians negotiating in the official conference. Their aim was more confrontational. 'Green economy, the new enemy', sounded the headline of a special edition of Terra Viva, edited by Inter Press Service (IPS 2012).

This struck more than one observer as odd. How can one be against a 'green economy'? Was this not a moment to unite forces, especially after the dramatic failure of the important Copenhagen summit on climate change in 2009? Is calling the green economy an 'enemy' not completely misguided, given the challenges we are confronted with, and the urgent action that is needed? Is it really necessary to be so critical of this project in the early stage of its development? Does this not boil down to throwing away the baby with the bathwater?

For the time being, this critical attitude remains limited to a minority. At least so it seems if we consider how many government leaders, politicians from all sides of the political spectrum, high-level civil servants and CEOs are picking up on the newly developing discourse of the green economy. From Goldman Sachs, which right before the Rio+20 summit announced billions of dollars in investments in green economy projects which it considers amongst 'the greatest opportunities for profits' at the moment (SustainableBusiness.com 2012), via Al Gore, famously claiming that 'the transition to a green economy is good for our economy and for all of us' and that he has therefore invested in it (Allen 2009), to the director of the International Monetary Fund (IMF) Christine Lagarde, praising the green economy's capacity to create jobs (Singleton 2013): enthusiasm on the newly emerging paradigm abounds.

The emergence of the green economy discourse has changed the terms of the ecological debate. The force field of environmental actors and movements is in full transformation. Bring some of the pioneers of the 1972 UN Conference on the Human Environment in Stockholm fast-forward to Rio in 2012 and they would probably have been stunned to see large business actors defending environmental causes and protest movements attacking environmental policies.

How to understand what is happening? How to make sense of this shift on the environmental terrain? In his 1886 novel *A Dream of John Ball*, William Morris wrote a phrase which sheds an interesting light on a number of contemporary phenomena, including the emergence of green economy discourse: 'Men fight and lose the battle, and the thing that they fought for comes about in spite of their defeat, and then it turns out not to be what they meant, and other men have to fight for what they meant under another name' (Morris 1886, quoted in Negri and Hardt 2000). This statement trenchantly uncovers part of the historical significance of the green economy discourse. One of the guiding ideas of this book is that green economy thinking, as it is currently becoming hegemonic in the environmental field, appropriates, translates and integrates (or recuperates?) critical green thinking, somehow realising green visions, but in a completely different fashion than ecological protagonists had intended during many years of protest and resistance.

Such shifts are not new. Negri and Hardt have used this quote by Morris to make sense of the emergence of what they call 'empire', a new type of global sovereignty that was developed as an answer to forms of conflict which threatened to overflow and subvert previous mechanisms of political control based on national sovereignty (Negri and Hardt 2000). In a similar vein, we will argue, the green economy ought to be understood as a fascinating attempt by existing political and economic institutions to reinvent themselves in response to forms of environmental conflict and contestation and to the major financial and economic crisis which erupted in 2008.[1] The result is a profound transformation of the terrain of ecological struggle, affecting the identities of the camps involved, and often turning conflictual into consensual discourses aimed at integrating environmental, economic and social concerns. The conditions under which the ecological movement was built during many decades are changing, as a result of which the very means of contestation have to be reinvented.

The emergence of a discourse

After the failure of the 2009 UN climate summit in Copenhagen, international environmental talks were in tatters, so it seemed. Yet, about a week later, on

24 December 2009, the UN General Assembly adopted a resolution which launched the preparations for the Rio+20 summit. This international meeting would consecrate an ideological development that was already making headway during and before the Copenhagen summit: the rise of so-called green economy thinking. Since then, this notion has gained centre stage in the international conversation on environmental policies, rapidly filling the gap left by the failure of Copenhagen. The green economy, so the messages goes, would be good for the economy, for jobs, for the environment, and for us all. Importantly, it opens a sphere of activity and initiative for private actors such as companies, banks and non-governmental organizations (NGOs). Solving global environmental problems ought not only, or even not in the first place, to depend on negotiations between states, so it is suggested: other actors, such as companies, can already start experimenting with new business models, new green products and investment strategies under the banner of the 'green economy'. The emerging green economy discourse thus epitomises a kind of bottom-up and even emancipatory promise. One no longer has to wait until the next climate summit to undertake some action and hope government leaders will arrive at an agreement. Other actors, in particular economic actors, can start 'greening the economy' right away.

Admittedly, the term 'green economy' had been used before, primarily by academics (e.g. Jacobs 1991, Pearce, Markandya and Barbier 2000) but also by some political parties and NGOs. However, until the beginning of the first decade of the twenty-first century, it was far from central in the international debate on environmental policies, and it did not yet have the specific meaning which it in the meantime has obtained. Especially from the end of that decade onwards, the term has become the linchpin of an emerging, although for the time being incomplete consensus amongst international policymakers.

Its core proposition is rather straightforward: the 'green economy' refers to the possibility to reconcile environmental protection with economic growth. Often framed as 'green growth' instead of 'green economy', this simple idea underpins a stream of publications of international institutions since 2009. A milestone was the United Nations Environment Programme's voluminous report *Towards a Green Economy: Pathways to Sustainable Development and Poverty Eradication* (2011), which defines a green economy as 'one that results in improved human well-being and social equity, while significantly reducing environmental risks and ecological scarcities' (UNEP 2011, 16). The report addresses issues which have become key to the green economy debate, including the valuation of natural capital, investment in renewable energy and resource efficiency. It also outlines green investment scenarios which are supposed to create new jobs and tackle poverty.

Other influential publications include the Organisation for Economic Co-operation and Development's *Interim Report of the Green Growth Strategy* (OECD 2010), the World Bank report on *Inclusive Green Growth* (World Bank 2012), the World Economic Forum report *More with Less: Scaling Sustainable Consumption and Resource Efficiency* (WEF 2012) and the EU's *Roadmap for Moving to a Competitive Low Carbon Economy in 2050* (European Commission 2011). In

2010, a Global Green Growth Institute was launched, 'founded on the belief that economic growth and environmental sustainability are not merely compatible objectives; their integration is essential for the future of humankind'.[2] It was established by a series of states such as the United Kingdom, Australia and Mexico, and includes the World Bank and the Davos World Economic Forum, multinational corporations such as Vestas and research institutes such as the Brookings Institution amongst its partners. NGOs such as World Wildlife Fund, lobby groups, think tanks and a number of green parties have also jumped upon the bandwagon, advocating a green economy.

The context in which these reports appeared is significant: in 2008, the biggest financial and economic crisis in more than half a century erupted, challenging international institutions to rethink their paradigms and policy recipes and to develop strategies to overcome the economic downturn. These international institutions, moreover, had been confronted with a legitimacy crisis, which was a result of both protest movements against corporate globalisation and geopolitical shifts. The latter urged institutions such as the IMF and the World Bank to redefine their role, as emerging countries became ever more reluctant to use the institutions' financial assistance. The search for an economic recovery in the slipstream of the crisis provided an opportunity for these international institutions both to upgrade their environmental credentials and to point to new fields of economic activity, which could relaunch the global market.

The United Nations Conference on Sustainable Development in 2012 aimed to be a catalysing moment for the newly emerging policy paradigm. Twenty years after the UN Conference on Environment and Development, and 40 years after the UN Conference on the Human Environment, in Stockholm, the so-called Rio+20 conference was entirely dedicated to the green economy. Entitled 'The Future We Want', the outcome document adopted at the conference confirms a commitment to the development of 'a green economy in the context of sustainable development and poverty eradication' (UN 2012).

A consensus thus seems to be emerging amongst certain international institutions, governments (the British government being one of the most active), lobby groups and think tanks around the notion of the green economy. Some have called it a new Washington Consensus, a statement which, given the obstacles the project faces in really becoming hegemonic and, especially, in being put into actual practice, is perhaps too far-fetched (Working Group on Green Economy (WSF) 2012). However, it has rapidly become a nodal point in the global discourse on environmental politics, around which a large set of actors is gathering.

Green economy, the patchwork

Although the rapid emergence of the term 'green economy' occurred only recently, the ideas underpinning it can be traced back to crucial debates on environmental policy over the last decades (e.g. Bernier 2012). The 1972 UN

Conference on the Human Environment at Stockholm, often hailed as a break-through in international environmental cooperation, already attempted to strike a balance between economic development and the recognition of the limits of the planet (UN 1972). However, it still recognised the importance of economic planning, thus refraining from advocating the downright market orientation currently *en vogue*.

Since then, a creeping economisation of the language used in the outcome documents of international summits can be observed. A turning point was the Earth Summit in 1992 in Rio de Janeiro, where 'sustainable development' became the nodal point of international environmental discourse. This notion had gained centre stage after the launch of the 1986 Brundtland report, which advocates a reconciliation of economic development, social equity and respect for the environment. As has been pointed out in much of the academic literature, the notion of sustainable development stands on two legs: sustainability and economic development. Considering it far from evident to balance both, a number of scholars have referred to this notion as an 'oxymoron' (Redclift 2005, Robinson 2004, Sachs 1999).

The green economy can be seen as a further development of the debate on sustainable development, whereby economic (market) mechanisms and approaches have become increasingly predominant. Yet, the green economy comes with many varieties. This should not be surprising, as the conversation on the green economy has only recently gained real momentum. Scholars have made different attempts to distinguish between varieties of the green economy. On the basis of a qualitative analysis, Olivia Bina subdivides different variants of green economy or green growth discourses into three categories: business as usual (e.g. stimulus packages including green investments during the economic crisis), proposals to 'green' the economy (e.g. UNEP's Green New Deal) and proposals for more far-reaching social and economic transformation (e.g. Degrowth) (Bina 2013). She argues that each of these categories is characterised by a specific aim, a socio-economic paradigm and a conception of progress. Mueller and Bullard rather situate the different variants of the green economy on a political left/right axis, ranging from 'nationalist-mercantilist' variants (such as the Green Revolution advocated by Thomas Friedman) to a more leftist variant epitomised by the British Green New Deal Group (Mueller and Bullard 2011). Ferguson, in contrast, opposes different variants of the project in terms of the economic theoretical frame it is based upon (Ferguson 2014). He thus distinguishes green Keynesianism, with its focus on green fiscal stimuli in the wake of the economic crisis, from green growth theory, which attempts to arrive at a correct valuation of natural capital, and from a green industrial revolution, which stresses the importance of innovation for competitiveness. Undoubtedly, other categorisations and subdivisions could also be developed.

Overlooking the field, it sometimes looks as if the notion of green economy can mean anything. Throughout the different approaches, however, a common core is emerging. We can provisionally delineate four key ingredients to the emerging green economy discourse, all of which will be discussed in more detail in the remainder of this book (see also Kenis and Lievens forthcoming). The first is the most important, namely the idea that sustainability need not be incompatible with the market economy. Even stronger, not only can a sustainable transition take place via market mechanisms, but the crisis of the market could even be overcome through a new focus on sustainability (more on this later). Evidently, markets can be corrected via taxes or subsidies. But one can also create new markets, such as markets for innovative 'green' products (e.g. electric cars, solar panels) or markets where new, artificial products, such as emission rights, are traded. This is what sparks most enthusiasm amongst the economic actors who have discovered the environmental theme over the last few years: new markets mean new investment opportunities.

The second ingredient is the stress on technology and technological innovation. 'If you are in the technology business today and you have not been invited to a green-tech conference somewhere, you must not be breathing, or everybody has lost your e-mail address,' Thomas Friedman writes in his bestseller *Hot, Flat, and Crowded*, suggesting a green technology revolution is not only strongly needed, but is also under way (Friedman 2008, 204). Innovation becomes the key word: 'We need many more people, companies, and universities trying many more things and a market that will quickly scale the most promising new ideas,' the well-known *New York Times* columnist states (Friedman 2008, 188).

A third recurring ingredient is sustainable entrepreneurship and the development of new business models by companies. 'Business has long been a leader,' Achim Steiner, UNEP executive director, writes in a report on *The Business Case for the Green Economy* (UNEP 2012, 1). 'Its ability to embrace ideas, to innovate, to conceptualise and develop solutions in the form of new products and services is something that we will need to emulate at all levels of society if we are to achieve a Green Economy transformation.' Over the last decade, a remarkable growth in corporate social responsibility (CSR) initiatives, sustainable investment and new business practices could be observed, many of which are now synthesised and promoted within the emerging green economy discourse.

Finally, individuals also have a role to play, via sustainable consumption. 'Every one of us may contribute to stopping or, at least, limiting the climate change,' it could be read on the official website of the nineteenth session of the Conference of the Parties (COP 19), the 2013 climate summit in Warsaw sponsored by the UN Framework Convention for Climate Change, which strongly involved a number of corporate actors in its preparatory process.[3] The summit hosts summed up a series of things everyone can do: 'Reduce the use of electric energy – at home and at workplace'; 'Save water – by remembering to close the tap'; 'Save paper – by printing on both sides of a sheet of paper'; but especially: 'Become a conscious consumer.'

While the market is primordial, this does not mean that governments or public authorities do not have a role to play. On the contrary, regulation and intervention by states and international organisations are seen as crucial for making possible the forms of competition and innovation needed to 'green' the economy, and for steering companies' and individuals' behaviour in a sustainable direction.

In this sense, if we stress the 'market' aspect of the green economy, we do not operate with a naive distinction between the state and the market. As Michel Foucault has argued, market competition is not a 'natural' state of affairs, which can be 'suppressed' by the state. On the contrary, it comes into being through a complex set of power mechanisms which actually produce market competition and the subjectivities this requires (Foucault 2004a, 2004b). Similarly, profound government interventions and regulations are required to put in place complex cap and trade systems, or to create competitive markets in environmental goods. We could even argue that never before have so many complex rules been needed to create markets in fields where that was far from evident.

Overlooking the green economy arena, it is not only worthwhile to pinpoint some of the core elements that recur in different green economy discourses. It is also interesting to take a look at those elements that are *lacking* in most authoritative versions of the green economy. First and foremost, the idea that the limits of the planet should be respected by putting a limit on economic growth is explicitly rejected. As we will argue, however, this is the Achilles' heel of each sustainability project. Second, no attempt is made at reducing forms of (international) competition which stand in the way of the forms of global cooperation needed for tackling climate change or other global ecological crises such as biodiversity loss. The fact that this competitive context plays a crucial role in explaining the successive failures of international climate summits, where negotiators often defend their country's competitiveness and market share rather than pursue global solutions, is seldom acknowledged. Third, with the exception of some critical variants of the green economy (such as the original version of the Green New Deal), the complex techniques used on financial markets are not rejected. On the contrary, similar mechanisms as those which led to the financial crisis in 2007 are being experimented with on carbon trading markets, as we will show. Finally, the other sacred cow of market globalisation, namely free trade, also remains unaffected. 'The best way to accelerate [green] technology diffusion is to reduce trade barriers,' writes the World Bank, leaving the enormous ecological footprint of the global trade system largely unaddressed (World Bank 2012, 20). In *The Future We Want*, the outcome document of the Rio+20 conference, 'arbitrary' trade barriers are explicitly rejected: 'green economy policies in the context of sustainable development and poverty eradication should [. . .] [n]ot constitute a means of arbitrary or unjustifiable discrimination or a disguised restriction on international trade' (UN 2012).

As already suggested, at first sight, the green economy might appear as a mere continuation of the sustainable development discourse. Indeed, many of its elements are not so new at all: resource efficiency, green investments, recycling, technological innovation, etcetera. As the notion of sustainable development has been considered an oxymoron by a number of scholars, a similar argument has been made concerning the green economy (Brand 2012). However, in our view, the emergence of the green economy discourse is a significant event, as it qualitatively reinforces a number of developments which were already at play. Three elements typically characterise the green economy as an innovative approach. First, the green economy discourse openly attempts to appeal to economically significant actors such as banks, investors and large companies. More than ever, it is suggested 'becoming green' has to be seen as an economic opportunity, which it would be stupid to miss. Underlying this is a strategic estimation of who can be a protagonist in the struggle against environmental crises, and which type of alliances this requires. Typically, a 2014 campaign launched by the World Bank to put a price on carbon reaches out not only to countries, but especially to 'companies and other stakeholders' (World Bank 2014).

Second, and more importantly, the green economy stands for a new relation to nature, and new types of intervention in nature. Nature is increasingly considered as a specific type of capital, which needs to be measured, conserved, produced and even accumulated. The concept of 'natural capital' has a longer history (e.g. Schumacher 1977), but it is only in recent years that it has started to underpin relatively large-scale policy experiments. Indeed, the measurement of 'natural capital' is not a merely academic exercise anymore, but provides the basis for the development of new financial products, new types of property, and new commodities. It has led to the establishment of policy frameworks based on principles such as cap and trade and payment for ecosystem services. As we will argue, this has profound effects on how society relates to nature: the latter for the first time becomes an integral part of the capital cycle, which is a social, ecological, economic and even philosophical event of the highest significance. Third, the notion of (sustainable) 'development', which admittedly very often already connoted 'growth', has been significantly replaced by the explicit use of the term of '(green) growth'. Each of these elements pinpoint an increasing 'economisation' of environmental discourse.

Dissecting green economy discourse

As already stated, green economy discourse comes with many variants. Yet, with the help of political discourse theory, a common red thread can be discerned in many versions of it (Howarth, Norval and Stavrakakis 2000, Laclau 1996, Laclau and Mouffe 2001). The notion of the 'green economy' is a typical example of what Ernesto Laclau and Chantal Mouffe have called a tendentially empty signifier which functions as a nodal point holding a discourse together (Laclau 1996, 2005, Laclau and Mouffe 2001). According to these authors, a discourse with hegemonic pretensions operates by equivalentially grouping a series of elements or demands which are held together and are represented by a specific signifier, which, precisely because it stands for the whole chain of equivalences, becomes tendentially empty. A typical example is the Polish trade union 'Solidarity' in the eighties: the signifier 'solidarity' was a specific demand which came to stand for a whole series of demands directed against the bureaucratic state, such as democracy, equality, justice, etcetera. As a result of this equivalential logic, a more or less coherent discourse developed which was able to unify the multiple demands emerging against the bureaucratic state and which had counterhegemonic potential.

In the case of the green economy discourse, the attempt to establish relations of equivalence between discursive elements is quite explicit: the very aim of this discourse is to suggest that 'economy' and 'ecology' are reconcilable. In certain versions of the green economy discourse, this relation of equivalence is even broadened so as to include social concerns. The Rio+20 summit in 2012, for example, was dedicated to the 'green economy in the context of sustainable development and poverty eradication'. Similarly, during the COP 19 summit in Warsaw, the Minister of the Environment of Poland and President-Designate of the summit Marcin Korolec stated: 'By being creative, the world can reduce greenhouse gas emissions while creating jobs, promoting economic growth and ensuring better living standards. Where there is a will, there is a way!'[4] What happens in such discourse, which could be analysed more in detail, is that discursive elements (or demands) are enumerated in such a way that they appear as equivalential (i.e. relating in a similar way to existing discourses and states of affairs) and are integrated into one coherent discourse.

Many scholars state that 'green economy' is a very vague or indefinable term (Brand 2012). From the point of view of discourse theory, however, it is inevitable that the nodal point of a discourse becomes tendentially empty, because it represents a whole chain of equivalence. In other words, if 'green economy' stands for a whole series of elements which are equivalentially brought together, including, for instance, green growth, economic recovery, market-based solutions, sustainability, transition, green technology, etcetera (sometimes even including elements such as poverty reduction, social equity and improved human well-being), this notion must by necessity be emptied in order for it to be able to represent this wide variety of demands or concerns. The significance of 'green economy' discourse should therefore not be sought in the intrinsic meaning of the concept itself, but resides in the very fact that it establishes relations of equivalence between different elements, most importantly, between economy and ecology. This is indeed the big statement of green economy discourse, which is perhaps not spectacular in itself, but has far-reaching implications: economy and ecology can be reconciled, or, to use the technical language of political discourse theory, they can be brought together in a 'relation of equivalence'.

Importantly, this is the essence of a hegemonic operation. Such an operation tries to appropriate core elements of existing political discourses in order to integrate them into a new discourse which appears as all-inclusive, universal and oriented to the general interest. Stating that the notion of the 'green economy' is an oxymoron can only be done from a rationalistic point of view. But political discourses do not follow the ideal typical logic of academic or scientific, rationalistic discourse. They have their own mode of operation. According to political discourse theory, each political discourse basically functions as just described, and therefore it inevitably has to deal with tensions between the elements that are part of its chain of equivalence.

The equivalence or reconciliation between economy and ecology can mean different things, though. Moderate versions of the green economy discourse (including many academic versions) especially claim that there is no necessary trade-off between both, and that economic and ecological values or objectives can be realised concomitantly. In its landmark report on the green economy, UNEP claims, for example, that there should not be a trade-off between economic growth or profit on the one hand and environmental concerns on the other. 'Perhaps the most prevalent myth is that there is an inescapable trade-off between environmental sustainability and economic progress,' the report states (UNEP 2011, 16). 'There is now substantial evidence that the greening of economies neither inhibits wealth creation nor employment opportunities. To the contrary, many green sectors provide significant opportunities for investment, growth and jobs.' Although a number of advocates admit such trade-offs do exist (e.g. Barbier 2012), they stress the need to design good policies in order to avoid them as much as possible. The World Bank acknowledges, for example, that '[w]e cannot presume that green growth is inherently inclusive. Green growth policies must be carefully designed to maximise benefits for, and minimise costs to, the poor and most vulnerable, and policies and actions with irreversible negative impacts must be avoided' (World Bank 2012, xi).

However, there is also a stronger version of the green economy discourse, which does not merely affirm that economy and ecology are reconcilable, but argues that effectively addressing ecological problems can become the motor for a new wave of dynamic economic growth, through the creation of new markets and business models. This appears to be the most attractive and challenging part of the green economy argument. At stake is more than a technical or economic issue: its underlying promise is that the green economy can usher in a new type of development, based on a new relation to nature, novel types of markets and products and a new consumer and corporate morality. In order to really assess the green economy project, it is crucial to pay heed to this broader historical promise of the green economy.

The historical significance of a shift in environmental thinking

In his book *Hot, Flat, and Crowded: Why We Need a Green Revolution – and How It Can Renew America*, Thomas Friedman quotes Lois Quam, managing director of alternative investments at Piper Jaffray, who states the following: 'The green economy is poised to be the mother of all markets, the economic investment opportunity of a lifetime, because it has become so fundamental.' Moreover, '[t]he challenge of global warming presents us all with the greatest opportunity for return on investment and growth that any of us will ever see. To find any equivalent economic transformation, you have to go back to the Industrial Revolution' (Friedman 2008, 172). Similar statements abound in many publications on the green economy. 'The Green Economy provides a clear opportunity to boost economic development at a time of low GDP growth and recession,' it is argued in a

UNEP report on *The Business Case for the Green Economy* (UNEP 2012, 6). The report estimates that

> the annual financing demand required to create the Green Economy is in the US$ 1–2.5 trillion range. This level of investment represents an enormous opportunity for the private sector to provide the infrastructure, equipment, goods and services that will drive the transition.
>
> (UNEP 2012, 4)

As already suggested above, what is at stake in the emergence of green economy discourse is a complex process through which powerful agencies respond to challenges that emerge from a situation of economic and ecological crisis and, to a lesser extent, from contestation by antagonistic actors, including social movements and other oppositional forces (but also critical scholars who start asking thorny questions). As Antonio Negri and Michael Hardt have shown, the most intelligent way capitalist power can deal with opposition is not through repression but by feeding itself from the creative capacities of the forces of opposition and resistance (Negri 1988, Negri and Hardt 2000, 2003). In other words, capitalist power most vigorously reproduces itself by appropriating and translating the ideas or practices of its opponents and by thus transforming its own mode of operation. The classical example is Negri's analysis of Keynesianism, whereby the state responds to workers' protest by becoming a planner state in which labour is fully acknowledged as a key independent variable in the process of capitalist development while it is at the same time controlled through macro-economic policies focused on managing incomes in view of mass consumption (Negri and Hardt 2003). Keynesianism aimed at reintegrating workers' subjectivities within the process of capital accumulation, while the latter at the same time gained in strength to the extent that mass production increasingly faced mass purchasing power. In other words, intelligently reacting to workers' resistance was key to creating the conditions for the long wave of dynamic economic growth during the 1950s and '60s. Other examples include how capital later responded to demands for more freedom and autonomy in the sphere of work by shifting the hegemonic economic paradigm from material to immaterial production and its related mode of exercising power from discipline to control in the latter decades of the twentieth century (Negri and Hardt 2000).

It needs to be stressed that this complex mechanism is more than a compromise between opponent forces, as if the latter would consciously negotiate such an outcome. What is at play is rather the outcome of a broad field of struggles in which capitalist power strategically attempts to respond to and reintegrate forms of resistance, while at the same time transforming the latter. Moreover, the process cannot be dismissed as mere 'recuperation' of resistance either. Capitalist power has to restructure and reinvent itself, and the partial integration of transformed ideas and demands from oppositional forces might create new opportunities for autonomous resistance. In a way, power is 'pushed' by resistance to reorganise itself.

Importantly, capitalist power restructures itself in such a way as to also modify the conditions under which its opponent manifests itself. Using Negri's language, it 'decomposes' the working class and creates the conditions for a new composition of labour, characterised by new and potentially more forceful forms of resistance. The shift from material to immaterial production, for instance, implied the disintegration of huge industrial complexes and the industrial proletariat, but at the same time created new productive relations in which autonomy, freedom, cooperation and communication became crucial productive factors. These bring forth a new figure of the working class which can experiment with new forms of resistance.

Although Negri almost never refers to that other great Italian thinker (an exception is Negri 1989, 75), the foregoing analysis strongly parallels Antonio Gramsci's theory of passive revolution or 'revolution-restoration' (Gramsci 1998). Such a process of passive revolution can be set in motion when an oppositional movement (in Gramsci's case the factory councils movement after the First World War) has not succeeded in realising its objectives, but the crisis or problems which this movement was a response to remain in existence. The forces who hold (state) power then have to restructure their power apparatus politically, ideologically and economically to regain full control. Again, appropriating ideas or forces from the opponent is key. Gramsci analysed, for example, how the idea of economic planning was translated from a workers' demand into a tool for the rationalisation of industrial capitalist society. Similarly, in a passive revolution, the power bloc attempts to reinforce itself by integrating sections of the opposite camp, a process which Gramsci called 'transformism'. Concretely, social democratic leaders increasingly became a part of the state apparatus and were made co-responsible for managing capitalism. Together with the economic and political restructuring of society (e.g. the massification of industrial production, the enlargement of the state apparatus and increasing state intervention in the economy), this modified the terrain on which the workers' movement could manifest and build itself.

In other words, through passive revolution, or through the process of de- and recomposition as described by Negri, a process of the creative reinvention of capitalism takes place. Although he acknowledges the revolutionary, and thus transformative, aspect of passive revolution, Gramsci also stresses the fact that this transformation remains within the fundamental parameters of capitalist civilisation, including the crucial separation between the 'leaders' and the 'led'. Moreover, Gramsci (and Negri) points to the fact that the success of such a process of restructuration is far from guaranteed. It is a story of trial and error, whose result can adopt very different shapes. For example, capitalist restructuration from above after the First World War took the form of Americanism and Fordism in the US, including new management techniques and modes of organisation on the level of production, higher wages, and the moral disciplining of workers' ways of life. In Italy, in contrast, revolution-restoration took shape under Fascism, which developed its own tools for the rationalisation of the industrial economy, e.g. through forms of corporatism.

Both Gramsci's and Negri's analyses focus on the dynamic of class conflict and composition. While this conflict is less central to our topic, the green economy, core features of this analysis can illuminate what is at stake in this new discourse. As we will try to show in this book, green economy discourse is a similar attempt, through trial and error, to respond to a conflict matter by translating it into a new motor for capitalist growth and development. As can be expected, this attempt results in different variants of the same project, as we already hinted at above. Typical for such a restructuration is the attempt to translate ecological concerns and demands into a framework that allows for the (ecological) 'modernisation' of the existing paradigm. In other words, management techniques, notions of growth and development, accounting techniques and business models have to be redefined, without, however, moving beyond the confines of the capitalist economy. Fundamentally, such a passive revolution attempts to turn one of the most fundamental challenges to the market paradigm, namely the ecological critique, into a new motor for accumulation. A matter of conflict thus becomes a topic for cooperation and development.

Importantly, this analysis is not something we project onto the green economy discourse, but can almost be literally found in major green economy documents. As we hinted at above, the latter contain many statements and slogans stressing that 'greening' is an economic opportunity, that it can generate new forms of growth, that it can provide states and international institutions with new legitimacy, and that it creates the terrain for new forms of collaboration. We will come back to those issues in later chapters.

Interestingly, to the extent that the green economy project is put into practice, similar phenomena like Negri's decomposition and Gramsci's transformism manifest themselves: actors who previously adopted a critical and oppositional stance on industrial or market society are tempted to become part of the project and exchange conflict for cooperation, contestation for consensual governance. What previously was a matter of conflict (as in the title of one of John Bellamy Foster's books, *Ecology against Capitalism* [Foster 2002]), is turned into an area of consensus-seeking.

As we will argue in the second chapter, post-politics is the result: green economy discourse often conceals the fundamentally political and contested nature of the ecological crisis and its solutions. This critique of 'post-politics', grounded in post-foundational political theory, is a key red thread throughout this book (e.g. Marchart 2007, Mouffe 2006, Rancière 1999, Žižek 2000). We hope this focus adds an interesting and novel perspective to the emerging scholarly discussion on the green economy. The relevance of this focus on how the green economy produces post-political or depoliticised representations of reality is twofold. On the one hand, as we will argue, it might be the case not only that the policies currently promoted by green economy discourses will be insufficient to ward off catastrophic climate change but that some of them even risk to deepen social and ecological crises on other terrains (e.g. agrofuels leading to higher food prices, biodiversity loss on large plantations or increasing concentration in landed property, while actually contributing very little to climate mitigation). In order to deal with current ecological challenges, much farther-reaching forms of transformation will thus be needed, and this will require a profound repoliticisation of the present. In other words, given the profound nature of the current crisis (see Chapter 3), it will be entirely insufficient (and maybe even counterproductive) to approach the 'greening' of our societies as a matter of technology, sound market policies or good governance. A project aiming at deeper forms of social-ecological change will need to profoundly challenge the basic parameters of current society and therefore move beyond a post-political economic and managerial discourse.

On the other hand, the critique of post-politics is a crucial precondition for envisaging a democratic form of social-ecological change. Post-political representations conceal those things which are of essence for democracy: power, conflict, decision. Democracy is about making these things visible, giving them a place. If power is concealed behind a technological or economic discourse, we will argue, it cannot become the object of democratic debate or contestation.

In the second chapter, we will introduce this red thread, both conceptually and empirically. As we will argue, repoliticising the environmental field happens first and foremost through a debate on the root causes of climate change and other forms of ecological destruction. In Chapter 3, we will therefore develop a number of anchor points for a critical analysis of the root causes of the current crisis. We will argue that grasping the peculiar dynamic of capitalism is key to understanding our present predicament. Ecological destruction is rooted in capital's intrinsic urge to grow and in the specific way it represents the world, based on forms of calculation which remain blind to qualitative, political and holistic dimensions. Although the green economy discourse usually addresses a wider set of ecological problems, for reasons of space and because of its political importance, we will mainly focus on climate change. This is not only one of the major global environmental crises which we are confronted with today, but it is also the ecological crisis around which – rightly or wrongly – much of the current environmental debate is centred (MacGregor 2014).

Chapter 4 will then address some of the core themes of the green economy discourse, including the establishment of new property rights in nature, the need to correct market prices by internalising externalities, and the experiments with cap and trade systems. Although many technical issues are at stake in this discussion, our main focus is on the overall political dynamic behind the green economy both as a passive revolution and as an example of post-politics.

Chapter 5 discusses the limits of the transformational potential of the green economy discourse by focusing on the latter's stress on technology, corporate self-regulation, sustainable consumption and, to a lesser extent, population control. While core features of the capitalist economy remain unaffected by the green economy discourse, other aspects, including the behaviour of individual economic actors, have to be changed, through sometimes subtle steering mechanisms which, again, fail to fully account for their political purport.

In Chapter 6, finally, we argue that the emergence of the green economy discourse also triggers a recomposition of the field of environmentalism. If environmental movements see their concerns being mainstreamed, they face the choice of either joining the green economy project or reinventing ('recomposing') themselves in a critical way. In this context, we develop an analysis of what the repoliticisation of the environmental field can mean, drawing on the example of the emerging climate justice movement, and illustrating this analysis with a discussion on the commons.

Notes

1 A similar analysis is made by Mueller and Passadakis (2010).
2 See the website of the Global Green Growth Institute: http://gggi.org
3 See the official COP 19 website: http://www.cop19.gov.pl/about-climate-change
4 See the UNFCCC website on the Warsaw Climate Change Conference: http://unfccc. int/meetings/warsaw_nov_2013/meeting/7649txt.php

References

Allen, Nick. 2009. "Al Gore 'Profiting' from Climate Change Agenda." *The Telegraph*, 3 November.

Barbier, Edward B. 2012. "The Green Economy Post Rio+20." *Science* 338:887–888.

Bernier, Aurélien. 2012. *Comment la mondialisation a tué l'écologie. Les politiques environmentales piégées par le libre échange*. Paris: Mille et Une Nuits.

Bina, Olivia. 2013. "The Green Economy and Sustainable Development: An Uneasy Balance?" *Environment & Planning C: Government and Policy* 31:1023–1047.

Brand, Ulrich. 2012. "Green Economy – the Next Oxymoron? No Lessons Learned from Failures of Implementing Sustainable Development." *GAIA* 21(1):28–32.

European Commission. 2011. *A Roadmap for Moving to a Competitive Low Carbon Economy in 2050*. http://ec.europa.eu/clima/policies/roadmap/index_en.htm (accessed 22 September 2014).

Ferguson, Peter. 2015. "The Green Economy Agenda: Business as Usual or Transformational Discourse?" *Environmental Politics*, 24(1):17–37.

Foster, John Bellamy. 2002. *Ecology against Capitalism*. New York: Monthly Review Press.

Foucault, Michel. 2004a. *Naissance de la biopolitique*. Paris: Gallimard/Seuil.

Foucault, Michel. 2004b. *Sécurité, territoire, population. Cours au Collège de France, 1977–1987*. Paris: Gallimard/Seuil.

Friedman, Thomas. 2008. *Hot, Flat, and Crowded: Why We Need a Green Revolution – and How It Can Renew America*. New York: Farrar, Straus and Giroux.

Gramsci, Antonio. 1998. *Selections from the Prison Notebooks*. London: Lawrence & Wishart.

Howarth, David, Aletta J. Norval, and Yannis Stavrakakis. 2000. *Discourse Theory and Political Analysis. Identities, Hegemonies and Social Change*. Manchester: University Press.

IPS. 2012. "Green Economy, the New Enemy." *Terra Viva*, June.

Jacobs, Michael. 1991. *The Green Economy: Environment, Sustainable Development and the Politics of the Future*. London: Pluto Press.

Kenis, Anneleen, and Matthias Lievens. Forthcoming. "Greening the Economy or Economizing the Green Project? When Environmental Concerns Are Turned into a Means to Save the Market." *Review of Radical Political Economics*.

Laclau, Ernesto. 1996. *Emancipation(s)*. London: Verso.

Laclau, Ernesto. 2005. *On Populist Reason*. London: Verso.

Laclau, Ernesto, and Chantal Mouffe. 2001. *Hegemony and Socialist Strategy: Towards a Radical Democratic Politics*. London: Verso.

MacGregor, Sherilyn. 2014. "Only Resist: Feminist Ecological Citizenship and the Post-politics of Climate Change." *Hypatia* 29(3):617–633.

Marchart, Oliver. 2007. *Post-Foundational Political Thought: Political Difference in Nancy, Lefort, Badiou and Laclau*. Edinburgh: Edinburgh University Press.

Morris, William. 1886. *A Dream of John Ball*. https://www.marxists.org/archive/morris/works/1886/johnball/johnball.htm (accessed 22 September 2014).

Mouffe, Chantal. 2006. *On the Political*. London: Routledge.

Mueller, Tadzio, and Nicola Bullard. 2011. "Beyond the 'Green Economy': System Change, Not Climate Change? Global Movements for Climate Justice in a Fracturing World." UN Research Institute for Social Development conference, Geneva, 10–11 October.

Mueller, Tadzio, and Alexis Passadakis. 2010. "Another Capitalism Is Possible? From World Economic Crisis to Green Capitalism." In *Sparking a Worldwide Energy Revolution. Social Struggles in the Transition to a Post-Petrol World*, edited by Kolya Abramsky, 554–563. Oakland, CA: AK Press.

Negri, Antonio. 1988. *Revolution Retrieved. Writings on Marx, Keynes and Capitalist Crises and New Social Subjects (1967–1983)*. London: Red Notes.

Negri, Antonio. 1989. *The Politics of Subversion*. Cambridge: Polity Press.

Negri, Antonio, and Michael Hardt. 2000. *Empire*. Cambridge, MA: Harvard University Press.

Negri, Antonio, and Michael Hardt. 2003. *Labor of Dionysus. A Critique of the State-form*. Minneapolis: University of Minnesota Press.

OECD. 2010. *Interim Report of the Green Growth Strategy. Implementing our Commitment for a Sustainable Future*. http://www.oecd.org/greengrowth/45312720.pdf (accessed 22 September 2014).

Pearce, David, Anil Markandya, and Edward Barbier. 2000. *Blueprint for a Green Economy*. London: Earthscan Publications.

Rancière, Jacques. 1999. *Disagreement: Politics and Philosophy*. Minneapolis: University of Minnesota Press.

Redclift, Michael. 2005. "Sustainable Development (1987–2005): An Oxymoron Comes of Age." *Sustainable Development* 13(4):212–227.

Robinson, John. 2004. "Squaring the Circle? Some Thoughts on the Idea of Sustainable Development." *Ecological Economics* 48(4):369–384.

Sachs, Wolfgang. 1999. *Planet Dialectics: Explorations in Environment and Development*. London: Zed Books.

Schumacher, Ernst Friedrich. 1977. *Small Is Beautiful. A Study of Economics as if People Mattered*. London: Sphere Books.

Singleton, Malik. 2013. "IMF Director Says Green Economies That Respond to Climate Change Will Create Jobs." *International Business Times*, 27 June.

SustainableBusiness.com. 2012. *Goldman Sachs Commits to $40 Billion in Green Economy Investments*. http://www.sustainablebusiness.com/index.cfm/go/news.display/id/23728 (accessed 22 September 2014).

UN. 1972. *Declaration of the United Nations Conference on the Human Environment*. http://www.unep.org/Documents.Multilingual/Default.asp?documentid=97&articleid=1503 (accessed 22 September 2014).

UN. 2012. *The Future We Want*. Rio+20 Outcome Document. Rio de Janeiro, Brazil.

UNEP. 2011. *Towards a Green Economy: Pathways to Sustainable Development and Poverty Eradication.* http://sustainabledevelopment.un.org/index.php?page=view&type=400&nr=126&menu=35 (accessed 15 November 2014).

UNEP. 2012. *The Business Case for the Green Economy. Sustainable Return on Investment.* http://www.unep.org/greeneconomy/Portals/88/documents/partnerships/UNEP%20 BCGE%20A4.pdf (accessed 22 September 2014).

WEF. 2012. *More with Less: Scaling Sustainable Consumption and Resource Efficiency.* http://www.weforum.org/reports/more-less-scaling-sustainable-consumption-and-resource-efficiency (accessed 22 September 2014).

Working Group on Green Economy (WSF). 2012. *Is the 'Green Economy' a New Washington Consensus?* GlobalResearch. Centre for Research on Globalization. http://www.globalresearch.ca/is-the-green-economy-a-new-washington-consensus/29462 (accessed 17 September 2014).

World Bank. 2012. *Inclusive Green Growth. The Pathway to Sustainable Development.* Washington: International Bank for Reconstruction and Development/International Development Association or the World Bank. http://siteresources.worldbank. org/EXTSDNET/Resources/Inclusive_Green_Growth_May_2012.pdf (accessed 22 September 2014).

World Bank. 2014. *Statement: Putting a Price on Carbon.* World Bank Group. http://www. worldbank.org/en/programs/pricing-carbon (accessed 17 September 2014).

Žižek, Slavoj. 2000. *The Ticklish Subject. The Absent Centre of Political Ontology.* London: Verso.

2 A post-political climate

Time is short

'Time is short. We therefore have to think bigger. A few years ago, you would not have heard me saying this, but I think we have to recruit enlightened spirits amongst the entrepreneurs.' Thus argued Susan George during an intervention in a conference in Tilburg (Netherlands) in January 2008.[1] Alluding to Al Gore's famous film, the theme of the conference was 'A comfortable truth – Towards a sustainable and solidary economy'. In view of the coming climate catastrophe, George argued, it is time to opt for a broad alliance based on a 'minimum consensus' aiming at 'saving the planet'.

This statement surprised quite a few people who had been following her, as George is a radical and very engaged voice in the debate. As a co-founder of Attac and president of the Transnational Institute, she is one of the well-known faces of the global justice movement and a sharp critic of the current economic system. She admits it herself: it feels strange for people like her to reach out to 'enlightened entrepreneurs'. In a later piece in *NewScientist*, she advocates an 'ecological keynesianism', quite a radical programme including the compulsory provision of funds to environmentally friendly production by bailed-out banks, and 10% rates for lending to 'big greenhouse polluters' (George 2008, 51). At the same time, she presents the programme as a 'win-win scenario that could provide something for everyone'.

George is not the only figure who, confronted with a threatening climate catastrophe, advocates an approach which is supposed to reconcile seemingly opposite forces, generate 'win-win' situations and spark forms of cooperation beyond previously existing fault lines. Even a number of grassroots environmental organisations, which in several regards are quite radical, embrace the new mantra for all-round collaboration. For instance, Rob Hopkins, co-founder of the Transition movement, states we can no longer afford to lose time engaging in strategies which divide people. The climate crisis is much too urgent for that. As he argues, 'a successful transition through peak oil and climate change will by necessity be about a bringing together of individuals and organisations, rather than a continued fracturing and antagonising' (Hopkins 2008a). In order to adequately deal with 'the scale of the challenge', he pleads for 'a degree of dialogue and inclusion that has rarely been achieved before' (Hopkins 2008b, 141).[2]

Hopkins not only argues in favour of far-going collaboration, but also criticises other, more oppositional approaches. As he firmly states, '[o]ne fundamental mis-understanding [. . .] is the belief that change is something that we have to fight for, that those in positions of power will cling to business as usual for as long as possible, that globalisation will only wobble if we shake it hard enough' (Hopkins 2008a). According to Hopkins, business will soon enough realise that they have something to win by joining the Transition movement (Hopkins, 2008b).

Hopkins appears to have a point: within the world of business, similar calls for new forms of collaboration can indeed be heard. For instance, Richard Branson, CEO of Virgin, states that 'NGOs, governments and businesses will have to work together' if we want to appropriately tackle current ecological challenges (*The Economist* 2010). Interestingly, the alliances that are thus promoted often give a central place to entrepreneurs or business leaders. '[O]ur success and survival as a species are largely and directly tied to the new eco-entrepreneurs – and the success and survival of their enterprises,' Van Jones writes in his book *The Green Collar Economy* (Jones 2008, 86). Therefore, 'civic leaders and voters should do all that can be done to help green business leaders succeed. (. . .) We cannot realistically proceed without a strong alliance between the best of the business world – and everyone else.'

As such, cooperation is an important value that needs to be cherished. But the repeated invocation of the need to work together is significant in itself. An idea which has fast gained centre stage in the environmental debate is that we can no longer afford to withdraw into our own camp and lose our time by engaging in partial struggles, as we should all work together against the common univer-sal threat. A number of recurring arguments are invoked to support this call for cooperation. First and foremost, there is the time constraint. We are approaching critical tipping points, beyond which climate change threatens to become uncon-trollable. 'In order to stay below 2°C, global emissions must peak and decline in the next 10 to 15 years,' reads the text of the 2007 Bali Climate Declaration by Scientists.[3] '[S]o there is no time to lose,' they continue. The problem is 'too seri-ous for the world any longer to ignore its danger or split into opposing factions on it', Tony Blair argued in a speech in 2005. A second argument is that we are 'all in the same boat', as Kofi Annan stressed in an opinion piece in *The Guardian* (Annan 2009). We are 'all in this together', as we all belong to our single planet Earth.[4] The argument is that the environmental crisis affects us all, so we would all have a similar interest in tackling it.

These statements convince a number of environmentalists, but also leave many puzzled. Does this mean existing political divisions should be transcended and left behind, in the name of pragmatic solutions on the short term? What do these pragmatic solutions then consist of? Should environmental organisations stop contesting polluting practices of companies or environmentally unfriendly measures taken by politicians, sit around the table with them and try to realise change 'from within'? Can corporations and politicians from all sides of the polit-ical spectrum become sustainability partners, and under what conditions? What kind of dialogue can be engaged in with which actors?

The occurrence of such a shift in environmental discourse towards consensus-seeking, cooperation and dialogue partly reflects changes that have taken place on the side of corporations and economic policy circles. An increasing awareness of the dangers of climate change has challenged them to come up with their own solutions and answers. They have been urged to do so by economists who calculate the price of inaction towards climate change (e.g. Gordon 2014, Stern 2006). This new awareness at the side of the world of business has modified the terms of the conversation and the strategic field of the ecological question. Environmentalists' previous opponents appear to have become potential partners in a dialogue. From big banks to multinationals, from marketing companies to media corporations: an increasing number of them seem to have discovered the environmental crisis, develop specific projects to address it and profile themselves as protagonists in the fight against, amongst others, climate change. Referring to the old slogan 'People Planet Profit', UNEP Executive Director Achim Steiner summarises in a report on *The Business Case for the Green Economy*: 'as we switch to a more resource efficient and Green Economy – one in which economic growth, social equity and human development go hand-in-hand with environmental security – business and industry will be a key driving force' (UNEP 2012, 1).

The evidence that the business world is embracing the environmental cause seems to be overwhelming. There is no big bank or multinational which does not sponsor some environmental project. Sustainable entrepreneurship has become a must. International climate summits are exquisite venues for companies to display their environmental commitments. During the (in)famous climate summit in Copenhagen in 2009, which marked a turning point for international climate negotiations and for the emergence of green economy discourse, the city of Copenhagen launched a big city marketing campaign around the slogan 'Hopenhagen – when people lead, leaders follow', supported by companies such as BMW, Siemens and Coca-Cola.[5] Siemens advertisements used as a baseline 'Proud citizen of Hopenhagen'. Coca-Cola's famous bottles were renamed 'bottles of hope'. Cyclists received seat protectors from the Dutch airline KLM with the message: 'Good, you are cycling! Going further? Then fly green, fly with KLM – the greenest airline five years in a row.' Windmill producer Vestas brought its own message to the negotiators: 'The time is now. For a price on CO_2.' This trend was pursued at later climate summits. Large corporations, many of which we would hardly consider as close allies in the struggle against climate change, such as ArcelorMittal, BMW, Opel and Alstom, even became official partners of COP 19, the nineteenth session of the Conference of the Parties summit sponsored by the UN Framework Convention on Climate Change in Warsaw in 2013.

A number of non-governmental organizations (NGOs) respond by engaging in new forms of collaboration with actors which many critical environmentalists would rather consider as opponents. The World Wildlife Fund (WWF), for example, is sponsored by companies such as Nokia, HP, Volvo, IKEA and Sony. It even receives money from Monsanto, obviously one of the main enemies of many environmentalists (Langenau 2011). The result is defended as a win-win situation. NGOs receive sometimes large amounts of funding, and companies acquire environmental know-how and can present themselves as environmentally responsible.

An important question is, of course, whether this really changes something. How 'green' is the result? Is this about more than greenwashing or serving a small but interesting market niche? Several companies produce green products or support environmental organisations, but at the same time, they often continue to also serve their traditional markets and invest money for less noble ends. HSBC, one of the biggest banks in the world, engaged in an HSBC Climate Partnership with the Climate Group, Earthwatch Institute, the Smithsonian Tropical Research Institute and the WWF between 2007 and 2011.[6] At the same time, the bank was involved in investments in ecologically destructive tar sands exploitation (Gass 2011). There are many similar stories. Unsurprisingly, many critical environmentalists wonder how genuine are the environmental commitments of banks and corporations. Critical NGOs uncovered that so-called sustainable climate funds launched by banks such as BNP Paribas Fortis and Delta Lloyd invested in companies involved in nuclear energy, biofuels and even arms industries (Claeys et al. 2008). Of course, there are also companies whose commitment is genuine, trying to realise profound changes in their technology, management techniques and production processes. No easy or rapid conclusions can be drawn from all this.

But whether such initiatives are really genuine or effective from an environmental point of view is not the main question that interests us. The point of the matter is: the strategic field of environmentalism has changed and become more complex. At least in certain parts of the world, such as Western Europe, few would still dismiss the seriousness of the ecological crisis. This mainstreaming of environmental concerns has not only been key to the emergence of the green economy discourse, which has quickly succeeded in occupying the discursive terrain. It has also profoundly changed the terms of the conversation: if everyone subscribes to the green cause, the political dynamics of the environmental field are modified, opening the door for new forms of cooperation, but also for forms of consensual governance and multiple stakeholdership which are embedded in profoundly post-political representations of society.

Post-politics

The tendency to leave behind 'old' oppositions and antitheses and develop new forms of cooperation beyond previously existing fault lines has historical roots. Within green movements and parties, there has been a recurring attempt to adopt a position 'beyond left and right'. This slogan originated with Herbert Gruhl, a former Christian Democrat in Germany who at the end of the seventies became a member of the Green party, leaving it again a few years later in order to found his own, conservative ecological party, the Ökologisch-Demokratischen Partei (Wall 2010, 16). In the recent climate debate, the idea behind it has received renewed impetus from people such as Anthony Giddens. Giddens is a member of the Green Growth Council, which advises Green Growth Leaders, a global alliance of cities, regions, countries and corporations aimed at promoting the green economy. In his book *The Politics of Climate Change*, he typically writes: 'Climate change should be lifted out of a right-left context, where it has no place [. . .] there has to be agreement that the issue is so important and all-encompassing that the usual party conflicts should be suspended or muted' (Giddens 2009, 114).

This focus on dialogue and consensus is typical for what an important stream of critical literature calls 'post-politics' or 'post-democracy' (Marchart 2007, Mouffe 2006, Rancière 1999, 2006, Žižek 2000). As the concept of post-politics is being increasingly questioned over the last few years, including by critical scholars, (Chatterton, Featherstone and Routledge 2013, Featherstone 2013, Larner 2014, McCarthy 2013, North 2010, Urry 2011), it is important to delineate it very precisely. First and foremost, the notion of post-politics or depoliticisation evidently does not mean there is no more politics in the conventional sense of the term. There are still governments, states, parliaments and parties: social realities which are usually referred to as 'politics'. The notion of post-politics or depoliticisation[7] does not regard conventional 'politics', but 'the political'. This distinction between politics and the political, which has become the hallmark of so-called post-foundational political theory, has been defined slightly differently by various authors (Marchart 2007). In the context of this discussion, we need not enter into the vicissitudes of this debate (see Kenis and Lievens 2014). What matters in this framework is that 'the political' refers to an order of discourse or representation (a 'symbolic order', as the French political theorist Claude Lefort [1986, 1988] would say), through which power, conflict, inequality and decisions can be made visible or not.

A second element which needs to be stressed, therefore, is that only *discourses* can be called post-political or depoliticised. It does not make much sense to state that a practice, such as buying organic food, is post-political in itself. It is the *meaning* that is given to this act, through specific discourses or representations, which can be post-political. Post-politics is thus about a way to represent or interpret social reality. More precisely, post-political discourses portray social reality as if it were devoid of what is of the essence of politics, namely power, conflict and decision.

The authors who coined the notion of post-politics all somehow suggest that society is deeply political, in the sense that it has no *ultimate* foundation, but is the provisional and contingent result of political decisions and power struggles. However, this political foundation of society (which, given its instability and contingency, is not really a foundation in the strict sense of the term) can be rendered invisible by depoliticised discourses. Society is then represented as if it had an ultimate foundation, for example in 'human nature' (its competitive character, or its survival instinct and related short-termism). Such representation of society closes off the possibility to contest and change its order. It takes away the symbolic conditions of possibility of conflict and contestation, which, as a result, are neutralised. Therefore, post-political or depoliticised representations of society are far from innocent, post-foundational theorists argue. Indeed, they render invisible that society is a contingent construction, that it could have been different, and that there should therefore be scope for questioning currently existing social arrangements. This is fundamentally what democracy is about: maintaining an openness for society to be put into question, which can happen through forms of conflict, debate or resistance.

A third aspect which is important to underline in order to fully bring out the theoretical sophistication of the concept of post-politics is that post-political discourses not only portray social reality in neutralising terms, but also neutralise or depoliticise their own relation to social reality. The point is that representation does more than portray social reality: it co-produces this reality by providing it with an image of itself. Representation is therefore far from an innocent affair: without discourses and representations, society could not possibly exist. As the French political theorist Claude Lefort stressed, representation, interpretation or what he called the 'symbolic order' is constitutive of society (Lefort 1986, 1988, Lievens 2012). In this sense, post-political discourses have performative effects on society, on how it interprets itself, or how social actors understand their own place within it. Post-political discourses not only conceal the political nature of society, but also remain blind to the inevitably political nature of their own relation to society, namely to the fact that they co-produce or 'institute' it, to use Lefortian terminology.

The critique of post-politics is therefore a critique of discourses, or a kind of ideology critique: it aims to reveal what a discourse conceals, namely the contingent and therefore changeable political nature of society and of a discourse's relation to it. Looking from this perspective to consensual discourses, it is important to stress that there is no intrinsic problem with consensus-seeking as such, unless such discourses conceal and thereby repress really existing oppositions and disagreements, or when they misrecognise that they are only one contingent way to conceive of society, or in this context, of climate politics.

Nature

One could argue that there is a difference between discourse about society and discourse about nature. While society is co-produced by discourse, nature would be ontologically independent from social discourses and representations. This makes sense in a specific way: when an individual speaks about a tree, nothing changes in the tree whatsoever. However, that does not mean that discourse or representation is a free-standing activity with regard to nature. Discourse is always embedded in concrete practices and interventions, affecting society and nature. In this sense, the shift in how nature is represented in the green economy discourse (which we will further analyse below) is significant. Representing nature as a complex, overarching ecosystem of which humans and societies form part results in completely different practices than representing nature as, for instance, 'natural capital'. In other words, even representations of nature are political, in the sense that they co-constitute the type of nature that will be socially produced (through productive practices, policies, etc.), even if a representation does not affect nature 'directly'. Moreover, the type of nature produced will also have an impact upon society.

In this context, scholars prefer to speak about socioecological assemblages (Swyngedouw and Heynen 2003, 912), socio-natural entanglements, or social ecological configurations (Heynen, Kaika and Swyngedouw 2006, 7, 2), notions which do more justice to the inevitably social character of even the most remote 'natural' phenomenon. Indeed, as even Marx argued already in the 19th century, there is no 'pure' nature anymore (Marx and Engels 1998). The choice we are confronted with is thus not one between influencing or not influencing nature, but between different socio-environmental projects (Swyngedouw, 2007). By pointing this out, scholars such as Swyngedouw repoliticise our relation to nature.

This is obviously of great democratic importance. As already suggested, one of the reasons why the critique of post-politics is relevant is its connection with democracy. As several political theorists argue, politicisation is a precondition for democratisation: it is only by making disagreement and conflict visible that one can deal with them in a democratic way (Lefort 1988, Mouffe 2006). Moreover, as Lefort and Mouffe have shown, it is of the essence of a democratic society that it acknowledges the legitimacy of disagreement and conflict. Democratic institutions such as parliaments and a vibrant civil society are structurally configured in such a way that conflict has a central place in them. For instance, the way the parliament functions provides society with an image of itself: the conflict between majority and opposition shows society that it is divided, and that this should not be a problem (Lefort 1988). On the contrary, recognising division is a precondition for freedom, as it enables the free choice between different projects for society. In the context of environmental issues, we similarly need to create a plural and democratic space in which it becomes possible to make visible the existence of 'conflicting and alternative trajectories of future socio-environmental possibilities and of human–human and human–nature articulations and assemblages' (Swyngedouw 2010a, 228).

Green economy and the political

At first sight, it might appear as if certain green economy discourses do refer to an alternative societal project, and thus a political opponent, termed the 'brown economy', and thereby acknowledge their insertion in a plural and divided political space (e.g. UN 2011, UNEP 2011, 17). But that would constitute a rather superficial reading of the documents concerned. The brown economy is mostly considered as a factual situation rather than as an alternative political project endorsed by specific social and political forces. The point is that it is only by acknowledging the latter that 'the political' as a space of plurality is fully made visible, and a truly political, including strategic, reflection becomes possible. As one critical NGO argues, UNEP's green economy report

> does not fault brown economies for riding on economic and social inequities to create wealth, such as by exploiting labor and by taking advantage of asymmetric market, trade and financial mechanisms. The green versus brown

distinction boils down to a choice of investment and technology: those that enhance natural capital as against those that deplete it.

(IBON 2011, 4)

As a result, '[s]hifting from brown to green is [. . .] not so much a fundamental paradigm shift as an emphasis shift' (IBON 2011, 5). It becomes less a confrontation of different projects for society than a change in management and investment decisions.

Although the green economy discourse could potentially have been much more political, in actual fact it is often centred around a number of ideas that lead it into a post-political direction. The suggestion that the reconciliation of divergent values is possible through win-win-win situations is often the hallmark of a post-political discourse. '[E]nhancing economic growth, social progress and environmental stewardship can be complementary strategic objectives [. . .] the need for possible trade-offs among them *en route* to their realisation can be overcome,' a UN report on technological transformation typically argues (UN 2011, v). As such, pursuing win-win strategies is laudable. The question is, of course, between *what* one exactly wants to realise a win-win, whether this is possible and especially why one *represents* something as a win-win when in reality difficult trade-offs (will) have to be made. Indeed, many policies which are defended in these terms turn out to inflict losses to certain actors and spark new conflicts (e.g. Montefrio 2013). Referring to the pitfalls of carbon trading, which we will discuss in Chapter 4, Naomi Klein aptly states: 'there are a lot of losers in the win-win strategy. A lot of people are sacrificed in the name of win-win' (Mark 2013). Green economy projects are indeed confronted with trade-offs, as even its proponents acknowledge (Barbier 2012, World Bank 2012, xi). The discourse about win-win situations often aims at foreclosing opposition by taking 'everyone on board'. However, it also conceals that what is a 'win' is always framed in a particular, contestable way and that exclusion is always present – even if everyone is *considered* to be on board (MacGregor 2010). From a democratic point of view, the fact that there are losses for certain actors is much less bad (as this is unavoidable) than the fact that potential losses and trade-offs are misrecognised. If it is inevitable that some lose, it is important to create conditions that allow the losers to contest their predicament. This also makes it possible to deepen the debate about social justice, assessing who wins and who loses (and what precisely is won or lost).

To repeat, seeking agreements and pursuing a consensus through negotiations in order to collectively tackle climate change is not a problem in itself. It becomes a problem, though, if the stress on the need to find consensus conceals the fact that a particular policy package to tackle climate change (say, the green economy) is only one possible option. There is no 'neutral' way to tackle climate change: even when there is agreement about the need to act, many strategies and policies remain available. Misrecognising conflict threatens only to displace and aggravate the problem: adversity does not thereby disappear, but, as Mouffe and Schmitt have forcefully argued, conflict threatens to intensify when misrecognised, repressed or hidden (Lievens 2010, 2013, Mouffe 2006, Schmitt 1996).

In a context of disagreement and potential conflict, it is of course tempting to choose for technical or economic solutions, which give the impression to be neutral and could therefore help to avoid potential adversity and find common ground. But even if it is represented as beyond politics, the choice for technical or economic solutions is actually far from innocent, but implies a very specific way to relate to climate change and society at large (Lohmann and Hildyard 2013, Machin 2013). As we will see further in this book (Chapter 5), technological choices have social and political ramifications, which means technological choices are about more than the question of whether a new technology is effective or not. The point is that a focus on technology often remains blind to the political stakes underpinning specific technologies and it tends to lead to strategies which remain within the fundamental parameters of what currently exists. Indeed, if changing technology would suffice, we might no longer need to question private property, economic growth or social inequality. In other words, the fundamental institutions of our current form of society would be preserved. This radically narrows down the debate about what a sustainability transition means.

As Carl Schmitt, one of the pioneers of contemporary theories of the (post) political, has argued, presenting oneself as taking a 'scientific' or 'technical' view does not amount to transcending conflict, but to engaging in conflict in a very particular way.[8] Indeed, such a self-representation entails a specific type of polemic, whereby the opponent is delegitimised from the very start, as she is ideological, merely political or non-scientific. Such a delegitimisation of the other potentially occurs if one represents and disqualifies the opponent 'as political in order to portray oneself as non-political (in the sense of purely scientific, purely moral, purely juristic, purely aesthetic, purely economic, or on the basis of similar purities) and thereby superior' (Schmitt 1996, 32). The claim that one's policy agenda evades politics but is based on science, economics or technology is thus a form of politics in disguise, Schmitt would argue. It engages in a subtle conflict while depoliticising it at the same time: making it invisible as a political conflict.

The point is that when an apparent consensus is represented in scientific or technical terms, it becomes very difficult to disagree. Disagreements which occur are then easily portrayed as 'ideological', and the scope of the debate is unduly narrowed. As we just explained, this threatens to intensify conflict, as the latter does not find a legitimate and orderly way to express itself. Slavoj Žižek considers this the masterstroke of ideology: to portray itself as non-ideological. The dominant ideology is the one that succeeds in presenting itself as the opposite of ideology: as natural, logical, evident or as so-called neutral science or technique (Žižek 1994).

For example, in a text delivered at a lecture in Rome in 2012, UNEP Executive Director Achim Steiner stated that the green economy project was contested by some people who argued that it relied too much on commodification. Yet, he vindicated the fact that 'the debate is generally maturing beyond ideology into managing legitimate concerns and ensuring that social outcomes, including poverty eradication, are maximised' (Steiner 2012). While it is evidently legitimate for Steiner to defend the green economy, portraying the debate, as it is conducted within UNEP, as moving 'beyond ideology' is not an innocent thing to do.

Contesting such a discourse can be difficult. It implies engaging in a conflict which is inevitably asymmetrical and unequal. Because an advocate of technical solutions presents her own proposals as neutral (and everything else as ideological), the person who disagrees on non-technical, but social, moral or political grounds will have to undertake extra efforts to create a space where her point can become visible or hearable as such. She thus not only has to engage in a struggle to convince others of her opinion, but also has to make sure others first and foremost recognise this opinion as a legitimate point of view.

As Jacques Rancière states, this is actually what political action is ultimately always about: the attempt to make something visible or hearable which it is not, undermining an existing order of what is visible and hearable (Rancière 1999). Our current 'consensual times', he suggests, make this ever more difficult (Rancière 2005). In a post-political setting, whether reinforced by consensus thinking or technical discourses, the scope for genuine conflict and contradictory debate can become very narrow. To put it more precisely, the fundamental type of equality or reciprocity which is required for a conflict to be a *political* conflict, whereby the opponents fight each other but recognise each other as legitimate political opponents rather than as criminals, is then under pressure (Lievens 2010, 2013).

The peculiar place of 'the political' in environmental politics

Authors such as Mouffe and Rancière suggest we have entered a post-democratic era, precisely because conflict or resistance is increasingly considered as illegitimate or obsolete, and technocratic and market logics have gained almost uncontested hegemony (Mouffe 2006, Rancière 1999). This context certainly also affects the debate on the ecological crisis: no wonder that market models and technical solutions are central features of the emerging hegemony of the green economy within the environmental field.

But is post-politics in ecological affairs merely the result of the particular ideological context as described by Mouffe and Rancière? In this section, we argue that there is something peculiar about the ecological question, which makes it particularly liable for depoliticisation (see also Swyngedouw 2007, 2010a). Three elements are central to this: the fact that ecological questions lack an evident subject of change (as becomes manifest in the idea that 'we are all in this together' (MacGregor 2006, 101)), the fact that its object potentially includes everything, and the specific role that 'nature' plays as a supposedly external factor, whose scientific study would yield objective results from which unequivocal policy conclusions could be drawn.[9]

Let us first address the issue of the subject of change. Carl Schmitt has argued that subjectivity is crucially important in political matters (Schmitt 1996, 27). According to him, subjectivity is one of the crucial elements that demarcate the political from morality or science (we will come back to the relation between science and politics later in this chapter). At least in the way the fields of science and morality describe themselves, they make abstraction from the speaking or acting subject. Moral thinking very often starts from the idea that it is possible to solve a conflict on the basis of ethical principles that are somehow standing above the conflicting parties or subjects, and are even universal. In the scientific field's dominant self-description, subjectivity is also radically excluded (according to Schmitt): scientists represent their own activity as guided by purely objective standards, as they try to filter out all subjective elements. This does not mean that science is purely objective in actual facts. The focus is here on how a social field understands itself or gives meaning to itself. The fact that the scientific field thinks of itself as being exclusively focused on objectivity entails, for example, that it is very difficult to politicise this field, for instance by representing it in terms of we/them distinctions. In contrast, political discourse starts with acknowledging subjectivity. It implies the recognition that one does not take a 'view from nowhere', but that one is concretely inserted in a force field characterised by conflicts and power relations. Political affairs are the realm of subjectivity *par excellence*: one cannot understand politics in abstract terms without referring to concrete subjects or actors who decide, take sides, struggle and exercise power.

As Erik Swyngedouw has shown, however, there is no privileged subject of ecological struggle (Swyngedouw 2007). For many of the problems taken up by social movements, such as feminism, the civil rights movement or the LGBTQ movement, the question of who is the subject of this struggle is easily answered. For example, even though men can support the women's movement and can even become involved in it, women are the evident subjects of feminist struggles: they have most legitimacy to speak up about what is exactly the problem and what has to change. Genuinely emancipatory struggles always require a kind of self-emancipation: oppressed groups can only bring liberation by liberating themselves. Therefore, a crucial contribution of the feminist movement has been to construct a new subject in the political arena, and the same is valid for many other social movements.

The ecological struggle, however, lacks such a clear subject. Who is best positioned to take up this struggle? The victims of ecological destruction? This suggests it is possible to separate those who are affected by the consequences of, for instance, climate change from those who are not. Admittedly, the burden of ecological disasters is very unevenly distributed, but it is also true that even the wealthiest cannot completely shield themselves from climate change or other ecological problems such as chemical pollution.

It makes no sense to suggest that 'nature' itself is the subject. Nature always has to be represented to become politically relevant, and this constitutes a core difficulty in the ecological debate. Nature only gets a political voice when people speak in its name. Climate change has been taking place for decades, but a myriad of reports by climate scientists and many environmental actions and campaigns were needed to make the issue visible and put it on the agenda. The ecological crisis only exists *socially* when people speak about it, or when there are socially perceivable consequences. This also explains the dramatic invisibility of, for instance, the biodiversity crisis, which remains socially intangible to a much larger extent than climate change, while its potential consequences are at least as ominous.

The opposite is also true: a myriad of conflicts have ecological causes, which are not recognised as such. Think about many wars which are fundamentally about access to soil, water, oil, gas, etcetera. Only seldom are these framed as eco-logical conflicts. Mostly, they are described in nationalist, ethnic, economic or geopolitical terms. Again, it is human beings who make the ecological dimension of social affairs visible or not. As a result, they will be the subject of ecological change (or not).

To sum up, in contrast to many other political struggles, the fight against cli-mate change and other forms of ecological destruction is not evidently an eman-cipatory struggle based on a conflict of one social group against an other. As climate change (or air pollution, for instance) does not stop at borders, nor at the front door of a bourgeois house, we are without any doubt all victims of ecological destruction, and we could all claim to raise our voices on that basis. Because we are all part of one overarching ecosystem, the conclusion is easily drawn that we are all sitting in the same boat, and thus all have a stake in changing our ecologi-cal predicament. Furthermore, since human life inevitably has some ecological impact, it could be claimed that we all bear some responsibility, which, although this claim misrecognises huge differentials in ecological impact between different social groups (Spitzner 2009), is correct *in principle*.

We do not want to downplay social-ecological inequalities, neither with regard to who is first and foremost affected nor with regard to who bears the main responsibilities. As Sherilyn MacGregor states,

> [t]here is widespread agreement among climate change analysts and policy-makers that the more socially and economically marginalised people are, the more vulnerable they are to the effects of global warming. The poor will be hurt the most. However, few [. . .] put the *global feminisation of poverty* into the frame.
>
> (MacGregor 2010, 130)

In other words, it is essential to make an intersectional analysis of who is affected by climate change, taking gender, class, race and age into account.

The point of our argument is thus *not* that these intersecting inequalities would not exist, or would not be important; what we aim to do is to understand through what discursive strategies the idea is constructed that 'we are all in this together,' as the slogan sounds of the 2010 biodiversity campaign by the European Com-mission. The fact that, despite huge inequalities, we are all part of the same atmosphere and we all have an ecological impact can be invoked to buttress this conclusion. If there is a subject of ecological struggles, in other words, it appears as if it can only be humanity as a whole, an idea which underpins typical forms of depoliticisation in environmental discussions (Swyngedouw 2007, 2010a). The evident conclusion is that cooperation and consensus-seeking are needed, and that conflict should be overcome in the pursuit of partnerships. Division and dis-agreement are then covered up. Significantly, if green economy discourses differ-entiate at all between people, they make an implicit division between those who steer and manage the transition and those whose behaviour has to be steered, as we will further argue in Chapter 5. The inclusion of all under the guidance of 'transition managers' is evidently not a political, let alone democratic, representation of what a sustainability transition can mean.

A second specific characteristic of ecological issues is that there is not only no specific subject, but neither is there a clear object that needs to be addressed in order to tackle them (Kenis and Lievens 2014). Indeed, every single social relation, practice or event has an ecological impact, and therefore, everything (and everyone) can – in principle – be the focus of environmental concern: eating, moving, building, etcetera. This could lead one to conclude that nothing less than revolutionary change is needed, whereby each and every aspect of human society is transformed. Most often, however, another conclusion is drawn. The target is then no longer specific practices that are particularly harmful, or specific actors who engage in strongly polluting activities, but CO_2 as such, whose emission is the side effect of a myriad of human practices (Swyngedouw 2007, 2010a).

The representations underpinning green economy policies which aim at putting a price on CO_2 are a good example of this tendency. Take the carbon trading system, about which we will be speaking at length in Chapter 4: it equalises a whole range of practices, all of which emit greenhouse gases. From a technical point of view, a tonne of CO_2 is a tonne of CO_2. But from a social and political perspective, a tonne emitted when building a new road does not equal a tonne emitted during the construction of windmills. A tonne emitted for heating school buildings is socially and politically not equivalent to a tonne emitted when flying tourists to their destination. Underlying these technically equal emissions of CO_2 lurk difficult social and political realities and choices. Moreover, if all CO_2 emitted is considered equal, it becomes impossible to think in terms of strategic priorities and their social and political implications. Cap and trade systems and similar policy mechanisms which are central to the green economy paradigm therefore tend to render invisible the deeper social and political stakes of the ecological crisis and its solutions.

A third element underpinning the tenacity of post-politics with regard to ecological issues is the peculiar place of 'nature' in environmental discourses. More in particular, to the extent that nature is seen as external to society, it can start to function as its foundation, which is precisely what underpins depoliticisation, as we argued above. Under modern conditions, nature is often considered to be something outside us, something 'out there' (Castree 2005, Smith 2006, Swyngedouw 2007, 2010b). The use of the word 'environment' is very typical in this regard, as if nature is what surrounds us. This externalisation of nature allows one to conceive of nature as an external standpoint or place from where one can also speak about social or human practices, and even judge them. This can have depoliticising consequences, especially when nature is turned into a norm in terms of which social practices can be evaluated: from the (un)naturalness of homosexuality, via the foundation of economic competition or cooperation in the evolution of the 'human species', to the justification of the position of women in society by referring to their so-called natural or biological constitution. Alternatively, the externalisation of nature creates the conditions for turning nature into an object of scientific knowledge from which one can allegedly unilinearly deduce precepts for political or moral action.

The depoliticising effect of discourses on nature crucially depends on the extent to which one makes abstraction from the fact that the way we conceive of nature is fundamentally socially and politically determined. Moreover, the way we represent nature informs the way nature is shaped through social practices, as we argued above, resulting in different types of social-ecological assemblages (Swyngedouw 2010b). The implication of this argument is that the concept of nature has no stable meaning, but is at least to a certain extent the object of forms of social and political construction and contestation. Depoliticisation sets in when this is misrecognised. As Swyngedouw states, '[e]very attempt to suture, to fill in exhaustively and to colonise the meaning of Nature is part of hegemonising drives that are inherently political, but are not recognised as such' (Swyngedouw 2010b, 301).

To put it differently, the attempt to ground the social in a specific image of nature implies society understands itself in a non-political way. It then loses out of sight that society is politically instituted, that it is contingent and indeterminate, and that it therefore can be changed (Lefort 1988). More in general, if one claims that one's social and political conceptions are grounded in nature, these are rendered immune for critique and contestation. Invoking nature as a foundation for a vision of society shifts the discussion from the political to the scientific plane. This threatens to undermine the terrain for the genuinely political encounter of a plurality of positions. Moreover, it leads to a misrecognition of the indeterminacy and contingency of society, as a result of which society's democratic quality is damaged.

The political in and beyond science

The relation between scientific knowledge and (de)politicisation is tremendously complex. Many theorists of science have shown that what we conceive as 'objective' scientific insight is inevitably conditioned by social and cultural factors (Robbins 2012). The latter influence what is considered relevant or worthy to be studied, how a problem field is delineated, an object of research is carved out, scientific questions and methods are framed. In other words, there inevitably are 'social biases that enter into scientific exploration' (Robbins, p. 128; see also Demeritt 1998). Furthermore, it has been argued that even the most basic scientific practice entails making choices, as a result of which particular elements are included and others excluded (Demeritt 2001, Wynne 2010, Goeminne 2012). On the basis of these observations, a number of scholars have tried to provide a politicised representation of science (Goeminne 2012, Machin 2013).

Even if one accepts science's self-description and the rules that govern its exercise and radically exclude subjectivity and politicisation, discourses that claim to be scientific are present in the public realm and have particular political effects there. We already referred to Schmitt's analysis of the polemic effect of invocations of science in the public realm above. The claim of scientificity can be a claim to a superior position, which gives one party in a conflict more legitimacy and credibility than the other, and therefore gives it the right to settle the conflict. It is a claim that appears as non-political, but has subtle political effects nonetheless. It is a claim which makes invisible that it is only a claim, by suggesting it is neutral and objective.

This is not to suggest that there is no role for science in environmental politics, on the contrary. Still, scientists have to be conscious of the inevitably social character of their endeavour, which manifests itself both during the process of producing scientific knowledge and at the moment when scientific insights are introduced into the political arena. In particular, they have to be cautious not to straightforwardly 'deduce' social or political conclusions from scientific insights, as this means they would circumvent the complex debate about societal root causes of ecological destruction, socio-ecological alternatives and strategies of change. If the IPCC, for example, goes beyond studying the facts of climate change in order to suggest that technologies such as nuclear energy can help bring about a reduction in fossil fuel consumption, as it did in its 2007 report, it provokes quite some controversy (IPCC 2007). A similar thing happens when a co-chairman of the IPCC suggests shale gas could be used as a temporary substitute for coal, as a 'bridging fuel' (Kirby 2014). Even if social and political constructions are to a limited extent already at play in the production of natural science, there is still a difference between what can be stated from the point of view of science, and what is the proper terrain of the political. Upholding a claim to scientificity on the latter terrain can easily lead to forms of technocracy that are fundamentally post-political.

Climate denialism

Some scholars who also make a critical diagnosis of post-politics in ecological affairs have claimed that climate denialism or scepticism should be diagnosed as an attempt to repoliticise the climate debate, or at least as a 'return of the political' (Goeminne 2012, Machin 2013). But does this diagnosis make sense? Does the discourse of climate sceptics indeed bring the political back into the climate debate? This is a challenging thesis, but we would reject it. What climate denialists do is exactly the opposite of what we just argued: they blur the different types of knowledge that are involved in the environmental debate, and instrumentalise their version of 'climate science' for political goals. Paradoxically, they also neutralise the political, as we will show, by grounding their own policy viewpoints on (alternative) scientific foundations (about whose quality a lot of critical questions can be asked).

In order to address climate change, we need different types of 'knowledge': not only natural scientific knowledge about the state of the planet, but also knowledge about the social-historical root causes of ecological destruction, visions on alternatives, and strategies to realise these (Jensen 2002).[10] The crux of the matter is that natural scientific knowledge about the state of the planet should be clearly distinguished from those other relevant domains of knowledge. When we move from natural science to these other domains, the terrain becomes increasingly ideological and political (Kenis and Mathijs 2012). This is not to suggest that natural science is completely neutral. But it is evident that there is more space for 'political' disagreement in the discussion on the root causes of climate change, and even more in the debate on alternatives and strategies. A critique of post-politics in the climate change debate should therefore primarily focus on these latter domains.

If we look at the climate debate of the last decade from this vantage point, we come to remarkable observations. That which is most difficult to turn into the object of a struggle, namely the scientifically established fact of climate change, is being contested particularly fiercely. In comparison, debates on root causes, alternatives and strategies, are rather tame. Climate denialists have played a crucial role in this.

In their book *Merchants of Doubt: How a Handful of Scientists Obscured the Truth on Issues from Tobacco Smoke to Global Warming*, Naomi Oreskes and Erik M. Conway show that climate denialists' strategy is to sow doubt by suggesting the scientific debate on climate change has not ended, and much uncertainty remains (Oreskes and Conway 2010). The denialists appeal to a certain democratic sensitivity: they suggest there are different sides to the debate, and these all have the right to be heard. In this way, they attempt to keep the discussion alive, to postpone or forestall government intervention or regulation.

Using the argument that there is no certainty, they claim it is unwise to prematurely take measures to avert polluting practices. Using the argument of uncertainty, they turn the essence of science on its head. In science, there is by definition never complete certainty, although this does not mean that there cannot be an overwhelming consensus on issues such as climate change. What is really at stake for the denialists, however, is something else. By calling for the recognition of multiple voices in the debate on climate change, they might give the impression to break a consensus logic and to repoliticise the debate. But what they are especially aiming at is to stop action from being taken on climate change, and especially to ward off a tendency towards government regulation, which they deem undesirable. In this way, they evade the real political debate. Or better, they try to win the debate without having to engage in it, namely by replacing it with a scientific non-debate. The denialists do not openly oppose regulation as such (which would be a legitimate thing to do), but they conceal their political preferences behind seemingly scientific viewpoints, as a result of which these preferences can no longer be recognised as such.

What climate denialists do is therefore quite ingenious. In a certain way, they use the critique of post-political consensus thinking in order to spread doubt concerning climate science itself, and thus to postpone the taking of action. They suggest climate scientists do nothing else but defend political positions and interests, while instrumentalising climate 'science' in view of political values is exactly what the denialists do themselves: they focus on advancing alternative 'scientific' arguments rather than on the actual policy debate. They attempt to rupture the scientific consensus because they fear the latter will undermine the consensus on free market thinking. They thus also do not contribute to creating a democratic conflict and debate about that which should really be the central topic of debate, namely the question of how to (re)organise society.

Hegemony

The idea that 'we are all in this together', which we referred to above, is typical for the type of passive revolution the green economy discourse attempts to operate, whereby a conflict is turned into a matter of all-round cooperation in an attempt to relaunch economic growth. Our critique of such forms of depoliticisation is not only important from a democratic point of view. As we will argue, the green economy project is likely to remain insufficient to ward off catastrophic climate change, and for this reason as well, seeking ways to repoliticise the contours of the debate is of crucial importance. In other words, there should be space for alternative voices which ask more probing questions than green economy advocates do, and urge a more fundamental transformation of the parameters of the current form of society (e.g. the role of competition, private property, economic growth).

As we showed in the previous chapter, such voices are already trying to rupture the green economy discourse (Mueller and Bullard 2011). This should not surprise scholars who are familiar with the logic of the political. As several political theorists have argued, one cannot simply get rid of 'the political'. In the words of Chantal Mouffe: 'The political in its antagonistic dimension cannot be made to disappear simply by denying it, by wishing it away [. . .] ' (Mouffe 2002). One can conceal certain tensions or oppositions through specific discourses, but these oppositions threaten to return in a different guise. It is no coincidence that many environmental NGOs, such as the WWF, are increasingly contested by more radical ecologists, who stress the need for social justice and advocate the end of the economic growth machine (Kenis and Mathijs 2014a). A number of NGOs have tried to mainstream their concerns by engaging with the green economy project, but this move beyond an oppositional strategy has led to the return of oppositions and conflicts within the environmental movement itself.

If green concerns move from the margins of the political spectrum to the mainstream, a confrontation can be expected between different ways to frame these concerns and translate them politically. A crucial question in this regard is which actor should take a leading role in a sustainability transition. Which social group or actor can become the protagonist of a way out of the crisis? Is it socially responsible entrepreneurs, trade unions, women's movements, indigenous peoples, sustainable consumers, green or other political parties, international institutions? As we stated, there is no evident subject of the ecological question, and this has led to the post-political conclusion that humanity as such is this subject. However, an alternative conclusion is also possible: the fact that we are all part of the ecosystem means we can all speak in its name, but we should therefore not speak with one voice. There can be different views on the ecological crisis and its solution, put forward by different subjects. The political conflict is then about which subjects or actors have the most credible strategy or project. Moreover, at stake is how these actors should relate to each other: do they clash or can they work together? With whom should they enter into conflict and with whom can they cooperate? This is the object of a hegemonic struggle whose terrain the project for a green economy is currently occupying to a large extent. The term 'hegemony' was coined by the Italian philosopher Antonio Gramsci, who used it to analyse how groups in society exercise power not merely through force, but especially through ideas (Gramsci 1998). A group can become hegemonic when it succeeds in making large parts of the population think in terms of its own concepts and frameworks. In other words: when its way of thinking has become 'common sense'. In order to realise this, a group has to be seen as legitimate, as the bearer of a general or even universal interest. The passive revolution is an attempt to repair capitalism's weakened hegemony by forms of social, political and economic restructuration which on the one hand incorporate elements of opposite forces, and on the other hand reproduce fundamental parameters of the existing model.

Although they most certainly have not read Gramsci, many defenders of the green economy appear to have understood this very well. For instance, they defend the right to development for the global South, possibly in an attempt to win the support of both people from the global South and many progressive people from the global North against radical ecologists who argue growth should be limited. Moreover, they claim the new markets and business models made possible by the green economy can offer a credible way out of the economic crisis, hoping this can help enlist working people in green economy projects. One of the aims of this book is to disclose this terrain of hegemonic struggle in order to assess what is at stake in the emergence of green economy discourse, to make the struggles it is engaged in visible and to repoliticise the terrain. This inevitably presupposes that we take a standpoint ourselves: one cannot criticise post-politics while claiming to remain neutral.

Notes

1 For a report of this event in Dutch, including quotes from the presentations, see http://platformdse.org/samenvattend-verslag-tilburg-2008/

2 See Kenis and Mathijs (2014b) for an analysis of the Transition movement from the perspective of theories of the (post-)political.

3 The text of this declaration can be found on the following website: http://www.climate.unsw.edu.au/news/2007/Bali.html

4 See, for example, the website of the Clinton Foundation: https://www.clintonfoundation.org/get-involved/take-action/action/were-all-together

5 On the website www.hopenhagen.org the following was stated: 'Our sincerest thanks go to our Founding Partners, whose support from the very beginning has made Hopenhagen possible: Coca-Cola, SAP, Siemens. Thanks also to our Supporting Partners who have lent their strong voices to the movement: BMW, The Climate Group, Dupont, Gap Inc., Hubculture, Method, Recyclebank.'

6 See the website of WWF UK: http://www.wwf.org.uk/about_wwf/working_with_business/companies_we_partner/hsbc_climate_partnership.cfm

7 We will use the terms 'post-politics' and 'depoliticisation' interchangeably, both terms indicating discourses which misrecognise 'the political' and deny their own political nature.

8 Carl Schmitt is a controversial figure, because of his authoritarian visions and his involvement with the Nazis between 1933 and 1936. Yet, over the last 25 years, many contemporary political theorists have profited from his insightful texts in order to reconceptualise sovereignty, the political and democracy. As Chantal Mouffe states, '[n]o doubt Schmitt is an adversary, but an adversary of remarkable intellectual quality, and one from commerce with whom we could benefit' (Mouffe 1999, 1). We can learn most from Schmitt, Andreas Kalyvas argues, when we read him not in an apologetic or

dismissive, but in a reconstructive and selective way (Kalyvas 1999, 89). Importantly, Schmitt was the first to use the concept of 'the political' as distinguished from the concept of 'politics'.
9   A number of the ideas discussed in this paragraph have been elaborated at length in Kenis and Lievens (2014).
10 Jensen (2002) uses this fourfold distinction in particular in the domain of environmental education, but it can be easily generalised to the discussion on environmental action.

References

Annan, Kofi. 2009. "Climate Change Puts Us All in the Same Boat. One Hole Will Sink Us All." *The Guardian*, 10 December.

Barbier, Edward B. 2012. "The Green Economy Post Rio+20." *Science* 338:887–888.

Castree, Noel. 2005. *Nature*. New York: Routledge.

Chatterton, Paul, David Featherstone, and Paul Routledge. 2013. "Articulating Climate Justice in Copenhagen: Antagonism, the Commons, and Solidarity." *Antipode* 45 (3):602–620.

Claeys, Bram, Anton Gerits, David Heller, Inez Louwagie, and Sam Van den Plas. 2008. *Een kritische doorlichting van de klimaatfondsen op de Belgische markt*. Brussels: Netwerk Vlaanderen, Bond Beter Leefmilieu, Friends of the Earth, Greenpeace, WWF.

Demeritt, David. 1998. "Science, social constructivism and nature," in *Remaking Reality: Nature and the Millennium*. eds. Bruce Braun and Noel Castree, 173–193. New York: Routledge.

Demeritt, David. 2001. "The Construction of Global Warming and the Politics of Science." *Annals of the Association of American Geographers* 91 (2):307–337.

Featherstone, David. 2013. "The Contested Politics of Climate Change and the Crisis of Neo-liberalism." *ACME. An International E-Journal for Critical Geographies* 12 (1):44–64.

Gass, Henry. 2011. "Barclays, HSBC and RBS Linked to 'Dirty Financing' for Fossil Fuels." *The Ecologist*, 14 June.

George, Susan. 2008. "We Must Think Big." *NewScientist* 2678:50–51.

Giddens, Anthony. 2009. *The Politics of Climate Change*. London: Polity.

Goeminne, Gert. 2012. "Lost in Translation: Climate Denial and the Return of the Political." *Global Environmental Politics* 12 (2):1–8.

Gordon, Kate. 2014. *Risky Business: The Economic Risks of Climate Change in the United States Risky Business Project*. http://riskybusiness.org/uploads/files/RiskyBusiness_Report_WEB_09_08_14.pdf (accessed 22 September 2014).

Gramsci, Antonio. 1998. *Selections from the Prison Notebooks*. London: Lawrence & Wishart.

Heynen, Nik and Swyngedouw, Erik (2003) Urban Political Ecology, Justice and the Politics of Scale. *Antipode* 35 (5):898–918.

Heynen, Nik, Kaika, Maria and Swyngedouw, Erik (2006) Urban political ecology. Politicizing the production of urban natures. In: Heynen, Nik, Kaika, Maria and Swyngedouw, Erik, *In the Nature of Cities. Urban political ecology and the politics of urban metabolism*. London: Routledge, 1–19.

Hopkins, Rob. 2008a. *The Rocky Road to a Real Transition: A Review*. http://transitionculture.org/2008/05/15/the-rocky-road-to-a-real-transition-by-paul-chatterton-and-alice-cutler-a-review/ (accessed 22 September 2014).

Hopkins, Rob. 2008b. *The Transition Handbook: From Oil Dependency to Local Resilience*. White River Junction, VT: Chelsea Green Publishing.

IBON. 2011. "Green Economy: Gain or Pain for the Earth's Poor?" *Policy Brief.*

IPCC. 2007. Bert Metz, Ogunlade Davidson, Peter Bosch, Rutu Dave, and Leo Meyer, eds. *Contribution of Working Group III to the Fourth Assessment Report of the Intergovernmental Panel on Climate Change, 2007.* Cambridge: Cambridge University Press.

Jensen, Bjarne Bruun. 2002. "Knowledge, Action and Pro-environmental Behaviour." *Environmental Education Research* 8 (3):325–334.

Jones, Van. 2008. *The Green Collar Economy: How One Solution Can Fix Our Two Biggest Problems.* New York: HarperOne.

Kalyvas, Andreas. 1999. "Review Essay: Who's Afraid of Carl Schmitt?" *Philosophy & Social Criticism* 25 (5):87–125.

Kenis, Anneleen, and Matthias Lievens. 2014. "Searching for 'The Political' in Environmental Politics." *Environmental Politics* 23 (4):531–548.

Kenis, Anneleen, and Erik Mathijs. 2012. "Beyond Individual Behaviour Change: The Role of Power, Knowlegde and Strategy in tackling Climate Change." *Environmental Education Research* 18 (1):45–65.

Kenis, Anneleen, and Erik Mathijs. 2014a. "Climate Change and Post-politics: Repoliticizing the Present by Imagining the Future?" *Geoforum* 52:148–156.

Kenis, Anneleen, and Erik Mathijs. 2014b. "(De)politicising the Local: The Case of the Transition Towns Movement in Flanders (Belgium)." *Journal of Rural Studies* 34:172–183.

Kirby, Axel. 2014. "IPCC's Shale Gas Error." *The Ecologist*, 14 April.

Langenau, Lars. 2011. "WWF und die Industrie – der Pakt mit dem Panda." *Süddeutsche Zeitung*, 22 June.

Larner, Wendy. 2014. "The Limits of Post-Politics: Rethinking Radical Social Enterprise." In *The Post-Political and Its Discontents: Spaces of Depoliticisation, Spectres of Radical Politics*, edited by Japhy Wilson and Eric Swyngedouw, 189–243. Edinburgh: Edinburgh University Press.

Lefort, Claude. 1986. *The Political Forms of Modern Society.* Cambridge, MA: MIT Press.

Lefort, Claude. 1988. *Democracy and Political Theory.* Cambridge: Polity Press.

Lievens, Matthias. 2010. "Carl Schmitt's Two Concepts of Humanity." *Philosophy & Social Criticism* 36 (8):917–934.

Lievens, Matthias. 2012. "Ideology Critique and the Political. Towards a Schmittian Perspective on Ideology." *Contemporary Political Theory* 11 (4):381–396.

Lievens, Matthias. 2013. "Carl Schmitt's Metapolitics." *Constellations* 20 (1):121–137.

Lohmann, Larry, and Nicholas Hildyard. 2013. *Energy Alternatives. Surveying the Territory.* Manchester: The Corner House.

MacGregor, Sherilyn. 2006. "No Sustainability Without Justice: A Feminist Critique of Environmental Citizenship." In *Environmental Citizenship*, Andrew Dobson and Derek Bell, eds. 101–126. Cambridge, MA: MIT Press.

MacGregor, Sherilyn. 2010. "A Stranger Silence Still: The Need for Feminist Social Research on Climate Change." *Sociological Review* 57:124–140.

Machin, Amanda. 2013. *Negotiating Climate Change. Radical Democracy and the Illusion of Consensus.* London: Zed Books.

Marchart, Oliver. 2007. *Post-Foundational Political Thought: Political Difference in Nancy, Lefort, Badiou and Laclau.* Edinburgh: Edinburgh University Press.

Mark, Jason. 2013. "Conversation: Naomi Klein." *Earth Island Journal* 28 (3). http://www.earthisland.org/journal/index.php/eij/article/naomi_klein (accessed 23 September 2014).

Marx, Karl and Engels, Friedrich (1998) *The German Ideology.* New York: Prometheus Books.

McCarthy, James. 2013. "We Have Never Been 'Postpolitical.'" *Capitalism Nature Socialism* 24 (1):19–25.

Montefrio, Marvin Joseph F. 2013. "The Green Economy and Land Conflict." *Peace Review: A Journal of Social Justice* 25 (4):502–509.

Mouffe, Chantal, ed. 1999. *The Challenge of Carl Schmitt*. London: Verso.

Mouffe, Chantal. 2002. *Politics and Passions. The Stakes of Democracy*. London: CSD Perspectives.

Mouffe, Chantal. 2006. *On the Political*. London: Routledge.

Mueller, Tadzio, and Nicola Bullard. 2011. "Beyond the 'Green Economy': System Change, Not Climate Change? Global Movements for Climate Justice in a Fracturing World." UN Research Institute for Social Development conference, Geneva, 10–11 October.

North, Peter. 2010. "Eco-Localisation as a Progressive Response to Peak Oil and Climate Change – a Sympathetic Critique." *Geoforum* 41 (4):585–594.

Oreskes, Naomi, and Erik M. Conway. 2010. *Merchants of Doubt: How a Handful of Scientists Obscured the Truth on Issues from Tobacco Smoke to Global Warming*. New York: Bloomsbury Press.

Rancière, Jacques. 1999. *Disagreement: Politics and Philosophy*. Minneapolis: University of Minnesota Press.

Rancière, Jacques. 2005. *Chroniques des temps consensuels*. Paris: Seuil.

Rancière, Jacques. 2006. *Hatred of Democracy*. London: Verso.

Robbins, Paul. 2012. *Political Ecology: A Critical Introduction*. Sussex: Wiley-Blackwell.

Schmitt, Carl. 1996. *The Concept of the Political*. Chicago: University of Chicago Press.

Smith, Neil. 2006. "Foreword." In *In the Nature of Cities: Urban Political Ecology and the Politics of Urban Metabolism*, edited by Nik Heynen, Maria Kaika, and Erik Swyngedouw, xii–xv. London: Routledge.

Spitzner, Meike. 2009. "How Global Warming Is Gendered." In *Eco-Sufficiency and Global Justice: Women Write Political Ecology*, edited by Ariel Salleh, 218–229. London: Pluto Press.

Steiner, Achim. 2012. *The Sustainable Transition. Overcoming the Crises from Rio to Rio and Beyond*. http://www.climatescienceandpolicy.eu/2012/03/the-sustainable-transition-overcoming-the-crises-from-rio-to-rio-and-beyond/ (accessed 4 September 2014).

Stern, Nicholas. 2006. *Stern Review on the Economics of Climate Change*. London: HM Treasury.

Swyngedouw, Erik. 2007. "Impossible 'Sustainability' and the Postpolitical Condition." In *The Sustainable Development Paradox*, edited by Rob Krueger and David Gibbs, 13–40. London: The Guilford Press.

Swyngedouw, Erik. 2010a. "Apocalypse Forever?" *Theory, Culture & Society* 27 (2–3):213–232.

Swyngedouw, Erik. 2010b. "Trouble with Nature – Ecology as the New Opium for the People." In *The Ashgate Research Companion to Planning Theory. Conceptual Challenges for Spatial Planning*, edited by Jean Hillier and Patsy Healey, 299–320. Farnham: Ashgate.

The Economist. 2010. "Sir Richard Branson Makes a Call for Enlightened Leadership." 26 November.

UN. 2011. *The Great Green Technological Transformation*. New York: United Nations Economic and Social Affairs.

UNEP. 2011. *Towards a Green Economy: Pathways to Sustainable Development and Poverty Eradication*. www.unep.org/greeneconomy (accessed 23 September 2014).

UNEP. 2012. *The Business Case for the Green Economy. Sustainable Return on Investment*. http://www.unep.org/greeneconomy/Portals/88/documents/partnerships/UNEP%20BCGE%20A4.pdf (accessed 22 September 2014).

Urry, John. 2011. *Climate Change and Society*. Cambridge: Polity Press.

Wall, Derek. 2010. *Green Politics*. Oxford: New Internationalist Publications.

World Bank. 2012. *Inclusive Green Growth. The Pathway to Sustainable Development*. Washington: International Bank for Reconstruction and Development/International Development Association or the World Bank. http://siteresources.worldbank.org/EXTSDNET/Resources/Inclusive_Green_Growth_May_2012.pdf (accessed 22 September 2014).

Wynne, Brian. 2010. "Strange Weather, Again: Climate Science as Political Art." *Theory, Culture & Society* 27:289–305.

Žižek, Slavoj. 1994. *Mapping Ideology*. London: Verso.

Žižek, Slavoj. 2000. *The Ticklish Subject. The Absent Centre of Political Ontology*. London: Verso.

3   The roots of the crisis

'Climate change worries me,' Bill Clinton stated in a remarkable speech at the World Economic Forum in Davos in 2006. 'It's the only thing I think has the power to fundamentally end the state of civilisation as we know it' (ENS 2006). Those are powerful words. Is that what we are currently facing? An ecological disaster that threatens to overwhelm the whole of 'civilisation'? Such fears are no longer only to be found with prophets of doom. James Hansen, former director of NASA's Goddard Institute for Space Studies in New York, puts it bluntly:

> If we burn all available fossil fuels, we will destroy the planet as we know it. The amount of carbon dioxide in the atmosphere would then be increased to 500 ppm [parts per million] or more. The planet is then on course to become ice-free, with sea levels 75 meters higher than today. Climate disasters would occur continually.
>
> (Hansen 2009)

Many documentaries, movies and books provide us with images of what such a civilisational collapse could look like. They are often made with the intention to critically question naively optimistic beliefs that in the end, everything will be just fine, and to stir more decisive action on climate change. From the enormous floods and extremely low temperatures in a dystopian, future New York depicted in the film *The Day After Tomorrow*, to the ravages wrought by catastrophic climate change in the year 2055 in *The Age of Stupid*: they leave no one undisturbed.

Parallels are often drawn with major ecological crises of the past, which indeed swept away whole civilisations. Jared Diamond talks about 'ecocides', referring to civilisations from Easter Island to the Mayan Empire, from the Sumerians to the Norse settlements in Greenland, all of which undermined their own ecological life conditions (Diamond 2005).[1] It seems that ecological crises are not new after all. In fact, since the development of agriculture, some 10,000 years ago, all forms of society and economic systems have, to a certain extent, contributed to ecological destruction (Jones and Jacobs 2007).

But what should we conclude from this? That 'humanity' is doomed to destroy the ecosystems on which it fundamentally depends? That basic traits of the 'human species' inevitably lead it to environmentally unfriendly behaviour? That it is people's short-term thinking, egocentrism or sheer stupidity which makes ecological catastrophes almost unavoidable?

The key question, however, is how relevant comparisons with ecological crises of the past actually are. Do they tell us something about our current predicament? Or are completely different causal mechanisms involved? To find an answer to these questions, it is crucial to analyse the root causes of contemporary global ecological crises, such as climate change. This is not a merely academic exercise. It has fundamental implications for how these crises and potential ways out are framed. If we analyse climate change as the result of basic traits of the 'human species', the psychological immaturity of human beings or the simple fact that there are too many of us (overpopulation), we arrive at completely different political conclusions than if we analyse its root causes in economic, cultural or political terms.

The debate on root causes is thus crucial. Yet, this appears to be one of the difficult issues many green economy discourses circumvent. In their focus on 'positive' stories of win-win solutions around which a manifold of actors can gather, the possibly contentious conversation on root causes is all too often avoided.

The contrast between the penetrating diagnoses of a civilisation crisis mentioned above and the extremely limited analysis of the root causes of the problem in green economy reports is striking. Most often, the latter leap from a short description of the state of the planet to actual solutions. In so far as an analysis of root causes is included, it is mostly implicitly under the heading of 'obstacles' on the road to a green economy. The World Bank's *Inclusive Green Growth* report, for example, states that 'a mix of governance and market failures, complex political economy, entrenched interests and behaviors, and financing constraints are significant obstacles' (World Bank 2012, 12). More profound analyses of the fundamental motive forces behind the current ecological crises are sorely lacking.

More than a few indications of root causes cannot be found in the major green economy and green growth reports. The United Nations Environment Programme (UNEP) is perhaps an exception to this, as it explicitly but only very shortly addresses the issue. Its landmark report *Towards a Green Economy* argues:

> The causes of these crises vary, but at a fundamental level they all share a common feature: the gross misallocation of capital. During the last two decades, much capital was poured into property, fossil fuels and structured financial assets with embedded derivatives. However, relatively little in comparison was invested in renewable energy, energy efficiency, public transportation, sustainable agriculture, ecosystem and biodiversity protection, and land and water conservation.
>
> (UNEP 2011, 14)

According to UNEP, this misallocation of capital was rooted in 'development and growth strategies [which] encouraged rapid accumulation of physical, financial and human capital, but at the expense of excessive depletion and degradation of natural capital' (UNEP 2011, 14).

Other relevant documents refer in passing to similar topics, including market failure or governance failure, without, however, developing this analysis in detail (e.g. OECD 2011, 11). 'Climate change is the greatest market failure the world has ever seen, and it interacts with other market imperfections,' Nicolas Stern wrote in his famous 2006 report *The Economics of Climate Change* (Stern 2006, viii). Unsurprisingly, the solutions proposed are already contained in the diagnosis of the problem. In many documents it is, for instance, stated that to overcome market failure, market prices should be corrected and the incentive structure should be modified. As the UNEP report argues, '[t]he use of market-based instruments, the creation of markets, and where appropriate, regulatory measures [. . .] [are] important in correcting the market and policy failures that distort the economic incentives for improved environmental and ecosystems management' (UNEP 2011, 19).

It is precisely because a problem analysis already anticipates solutions and strategies to realise these that this analysis can be a highly contentious and politically charged issue, which merits a central place in public debates on how to address climate change. Remarkably, for example, in the passage addressing the mentioned problem of capital misallocation, the UNEP report includes a text box about what it calls 'the population challenge' (UNEP 2011, 15). UNEP thus seems to suggest that population growth should be considered an additional cause of the current ecological crises, without, however, discussing this topic more systematically. Still, such suggestions implicitly bring in a specific frame of analysis, including certain strategies or solutions to tackling climate change (see also Chapter 5).

This chapter will elaborate more profoundly on how we can understand the root causes of our current predicament. Repoliticising the environmental debate implies bringing the often implicit assumptions about root causes to the centre of the public debate. Surprisingly perhaps, we agree to a certain extent with the problem diagnoses included in the aforementioned green economy reports. Rather than to attribute ecological destruction to human nature or civilisation as such, we also think that the current ecological crises should be understood from the point of view of how our economic system (mal)functions today. Contrary to the green economy discourse, however, we think 'market failure' is too superficial a diagnosis. Interestingly, Environmental Justice Organisations Liabilities and Trade (EJOLT), a research project funded by the European Commission, made a similar analysis in its statement on the occasion of the Rio+20 summit, which argued that 'unsustainable development is not a market failure to be fixed but a market system failure: expecting results from the market it cannot deliver, like long-term thinking, environmental consciousness and social responsibility' (EJOLT 2012). This strong statement puts the finger on the wound. The ecological crisis results from the failure of our current economic system, but this failure is much more profound than advocates of the green economy project seem to acknowledge.

In this chapter, we will provide a review of some of the main arguments underpinning the idea that we are dealing with a fundamental market system failure. More precisely, we will look at a number of social and political arguments which provide us with a point of view external to the market in order to understand the latter (and its failure) more profoundly, which is precisely what most green economy advocates refrain from, as their reflections remain within a market paradigm. This also allows us to introduce a number of ideas or concepts which will be important for the remainder of the book.

Planetary boundaries

Can our current predicament be compared to previous forms of civilisation collapse, or should we rather stress its specific, social and historical dimensions? If we only observe the depth and scope of the current crisis, it is already clear the latter cannot easily be compared to any previous crisis. The ecological destruction that we are witnessing today is unprecedented. In a study by the Stockholm Resilience Centre, a group of researchers (including James Hansen) analyse nine 'planetary boundaries' that are crucial to maintaining the planet in a state in which 'humanity can operate safely' (Rockström 2009, Rockström et al. 2009). Each of these limits is currently threatened by ecological crises. Climate change is one of them, in addition to biodiversity loss, ocean acidification, the hole in the ozone layer, the disruption of the nitrogen and phosphorus cycles, the decreasing global supply of fresh water, land use change, chemical pollution and the concentration of aerosol particles in the atmosphere. The researchers show that all these processes were set in motion over two centuries ago, and have been moving radically in the wrong direction since then. They point to the Industrial Revolution as the starting point of these ecological crises, a revolution which was associated with the onset of the capitalist mode of production.

Three of these processes have already reached a critical threshold. In the case of climate change, the pre-industrial atmospheric carbon dioxide concentration was 280 ppm, the critical threshold is 350 ppm and at the moment the study was published, levels were at around 390 ppm. Biodiversity loss is measured on the basis of the rate of extinction of species. Since the Industrial Revolution, this process is happening 100 to 1,000 times faster than the 'historical norm'. This is unprecedented since the extinction of the dinosaurs. The third major issue is the disruption of the nitrogen cycle. On that level as well, the critical threshold has been largely exceeded. There is only one bit of good news in the whole story: the enlargement of the hole in the ozone layer was sent into reverse after governments banned all ozone-depleting substances, although this has recently again become the object of controversy due to the discovery of new ozone-depleting substances (Laube et al. 2014). All other processes, however, are evolving in a highly problematic direction and are nearing or have moved beyond planetary boundaries. In each case, we are facing ecological crises of global proportions, which have not only profound social-economic causes, but also widespread social effects.

As becomes clear in the study by the Stockholm Resilience Centre (but also in many other studies), the ecological crises we are witnessing today are the product of the past two centuries. The roots of the current environmental crises thus coincide with the emergence of capitalist production, which ushered in a period of enormous economic growth, booming consumer cultures and market globalisation. The term 'capitalism' is conspicuously absent from many green economy discourses, as it is from many other hegemonic policy discourses. In a critical vein, the political philosopher Slavoj Žižek asks: 'What better proof of the total triumph of capitalism than the virtual disappearance of the very term in the last two or three decades?' (Žižek 2007).

Yet, there is overwhelming evidence to suggest that there is something fundamentally anti-ecological about the specifically capitalist way of organising society. Jason Moore has therefore spoken of our current era, which he thinks began 500 years ago, as the 'Capitalocene', a notion which he puts forward as an alternative for the often used term 'Anthropocene', which refers to the era in which the human impact on the Earth's atmosphere has become so profound as to constitute a new geological epoch (Moore 2014). The term 'Capitalocene' has the merit of referring to socially and historically specific determinants of ecological destruction, in contrast to the very general notion of 'Anthropocene', which implicitly suggests 'human activity' as such is to blame. In a genuinely *political* discussion on how to tackle climate change and other ecological crises, it is of crucial importance to be socially, historically and politically precise.

In what follows, we will argue that specific modes of social and economic organisation underpin the tremendous changes we are witnessing today. Crucial in this regard is an impressive historical trend destroying various forms of 'commons' and replacing them with privately owned commodities.

The privatisation of the commons

There are some facts and figures whose repercussions sometimes do not fully sink in. The following is one of them: for some years, more than half of the world's population has lived in cities (UNFPA 2007). According to UN estimates, the global rural population has already reached a peak and will start to decline from 2020 (UN 2008). Future population growth will be almost entirely within cities, primarily due to the constant influx of migrants from the countryside (Davis 2007, 2). Mega-cities such as Mexico City, Seoul, Sao Paulo, Mumbai and Delhi, each with around 20 million inhabitants, are growing rapidly.

No less staggering is the following fact: a billion people currently live in slums, townships, barracks, shanty towns or favelas (Kempf 2007, 48). That is a third of the global urban population. Slums are growing even faster than the cities themselves. In countries such as Ethiopia and Chad, 99% of the urban population live in slums. In Afghanistan this figure is 98.5%, and in Nepal 92%. Cities like Mumbai, Mexico City and Dhaka are each home to 10 million slum dwellers (Davis 2007, 23).

Slums are almost always social and ecological catastrophes, located on landfills, on steep slopes, on the banks of dangerous rivers, near chemical dumps or on the edge of major motorways or railways. They are pockets of extreme pollution, epidemics, violence (especially against women), bitter poverty, extortion, exploitation, state repression and a chaotic and highly polluting motorisation, although they are also places where an enormous amount of creativity is deployed to organise everyday life, and a lot of social protest takes place. Breathing the air of Mumbai is equivalent to smoking 2.5 packs of cigarettes a day (Davis 2007, 134). In Mexico City, ozone concentrations exceed recommended levels 300 days a year. In Cairo, the gridlock is so extensive that the average speed of cars and buses is 10 km per hour.

Yet people continue to move away from the countryside in large numbers, hoping to find a better life in the city, or simply because there is no choice: they are driven away from the countryside by the expropriation or privatisation of lands that they were dependent on for their livelihood.

This is not a new phenomenon. The fifteenth and sixteenth centuries already saw widespread enclosures of common land in England, not coincidentally the country where capitalist production first started to develop. Commons, used by peasants to graze cattle or collect wood, were enclosed and appropriated by landowners. The percentage of agricultural land that was privatised in this way increased from 47% in 1600 to 71% in 1700. The process of land privatisation and concentration continued unabated, and by the end of the eighteenth century almost half of the cultivated land in England was owned by 5,000 families, and 25% was owned by just 400 families (Foster 1999, 51). This concentration of landownership robbed large numbers of farmers of their livelihoods, and forced them to leave the countryside to look for paid work in the city (Marx 1982, 876).

The enclosures not only made it possible for large-scale landownership to thrive, but they also had an interesting 'side effect' for budding industrialists in the city, providing them with an influx of cheap labour that was not linked to the established guilds. This was one of the factors that allowed for the rapid growth of an emergent industry. But this obviously did not happen without resistance and opposition. Jean-Jacques Rousseau famously criticised the enclosures in his *Discourse on Equality*: 'The first man who, having enclosed a piece of ground, to whom it occurred to say *this is mine*, and found people sufficiently simple to believe him, was the true founder of civil society' (Rousseau 1997, 164). Many farming communities were keenly aware of the importance of the commons. There is a long and interesting history of resistance against the privatisation of the commons: from the Diggers during the mid-seventeenth-century English Revolution, to the landless peasant movement in Brazil today (e.g. Frederici 2009, Linebaugh 2008).

Moreover, there was mass resistance in the cities too. The former peasants who had left the English countryside were often reluctant to earn a living in stinking factories, in which iron discipline was the norm. Many chose a life as vagabonds or beggars above this new form of slavery. The English state reacted by enacting a series of laws against vagrancy in an attempt to transform these new citizens into a disciplined mass that was suited to the new industrial working conditions (Marx 1982, 896 ff). Technology was deployed as a disciplining instrument (Cleaver 1979, 85). Instead of being free producers, workers increasingly became appendages of machines.

The privatisation of the commons, the transformation of small farmers into wage labourers and urbanisation all played a key role in facilitating the emergence of capitalism. But these phenomena also formed the basis of one of the biggest ecological crises of the nineteenth century. In his reconstruction of Marx's ecological thought, John Bellamy Foster has shown how the newly formed social relations played a crucial role in explaining new types of ecological crisis (Foster 2000, 2002, 2009, Foster, Clark and York 2010). The concentration of land property led to increasing urbanisation, and thereby also to the disruption of the metabolic cycle: essential nutrients did not return to the soil after the consumption of food products by masses of city dwellers, but were drained to sewers in the city and then polluted rivers. Significantly, the solutions that were found for this crisis of soil depletion would generate new social and ecological problems. In the first instance, fertile soil was imported from abroad, mainly in the form of guano. The guano trade is a story of globalisation *avant la lettre*. Coolies, workers imported from China, harvested the bird droppings in Latin America, often in very harsh conditions (Foster, Clark and York 2010, 405). At the end of the nineteenth century, the USA also sent ships looking for guano, and occupied 94 islands and rocks where it could be found. Nine of these are still in American hands (Foster 2009, 49). In other words, England and the US engaged in new forms of ecological imperialism, with all the social and ecological consequences that resulted from this.

Eventually the crisis appeared to be really solved at the beginning of the twentieth century when two German scholars developed what would be called the Haber-Bosch process. However, one hundred years later, the negative consequences of the massive use of chemical fertilisers which this process made possible are well documented (Rockström et al. 2009).

The importance of this example is not only that it shows that *social relations* (the privatisation of the natural commons, and the increasing separation of city and countryside) are at the basis of ecological crises. It also draws attention to a fascinating mechanism characterising capitalism. More than any previous form of society, the capitalist system is capable of finding sometimes incredibly creative solutions to the crises with which it is confronted. At the same time, these solutions often lead to new social and ecological problems. The crisis is not really solved, but rather displaced, only to come back later in a different guise, and often on a larger scale. In other words, the solution for the first crisis sows the seeds of the next. We will provide other examples of this in the remainder of this book. The agricultural crisis of the nineteenth century sets the tone: importing fertiliser from the global South solved the problem of the 'metabolic rift' between city and countryside in England, but recreated problems on a global scale.

Representing the world

Many social problems that we face today have deep roots in the way society relates to and appropriates ecosystems. That is why social and ecological problems are often very closely connected. The private appropriation of the commons was not only a major driver of the concentration of agricultural land, but also of urbanisation, the emergence of wage labour, the sharpening of the differences between the urban and the rural (and then between the global North and the global South), the emergence of the modern classes of the bourgeoisie and proletariat, the logic of accumulation and growth and the commodification of almost everything. To a certain extent, the private appropriation of natural commons lay thus at the basis of a whole new way of organising society: capitalism.

Capitalism is the first economic order in history which has a 'systemic' character, and which functions as if it need not take natural or other social processes into account. This semi-autonomous mode of operation makes it possible for economic actors to uniquely focus on prices and profits, whereby natural or other social processes appear to be only of secondary importance. As Karl Polanyi argued, the economy becomes tendentially 'disembedded' from society at large (Polanyi 2001). The 'fictitious commodification' of land (nature), money and labour plays a crucial role in this process. Even though this tendency to become disembedded is intrinsic to the market economy, Polanyi points to the utopian nature of the liberal project to complete this movement and create a fully self-regulating market: 'the idea of a self-adjusting market implied a stark utopia. Such an institution could not exist for any length of time without annihilating the human and natural substance of society' (Polanyi 2001, 3). In other words, the market economy tends to make abstraction from wider social and ecological conditions, but remains fundamentally dependent on them, and threatens to spark major crises when its movement towards disembeddedness goes too far.

From an ecological point of view, it is evident that the economy is and remains dependent on the ecosystems which encompass it (Daly and Farley 2004). Indeed, capitalism cannot exist without extracting matter and energy from the ecosystems, and emitting these back into the ecosystems in a less valuable form (as pollution). Every production process inevitably has a material dimension. Yet, ecosystems and the capitalist system have their own modes of operation, which increasingly conflict with each other: on the one side, ecosystems are characterised by specific natural cycles and processes; on the other side, there is the economic system in which money and commodities circulate, and which seems to have its own logic. From an ecological point of view, the flows of matter and energy are crucial, while for capitalism it is the flows of money and capital that matter.

One thing is to argue that capitalism necessarily remains dependent on its natural conditions. Another is to analyse how capitalism's logic implies a specific way to represent the world, and especially to make abstraction from its natural conditions, and the effect this has on those conditions. Interestingly, the representations underpinning capitalism's mode of operation imply subtle forms of depoliticisation, as we will show. Capitalism operates as if it is a world unto itself, which can abstract itself from the ecosystems. This implies a unique way of looking at and representing the world, characterised by a kind of system blindness: it continues to produce and pollute, regardless of the actual state of the ecosystems.

'The hard truth,' Al Gore admits, 'is that our economic system is partially blind. It "sees" some things and not others' (Gore 2007, 182–183). He evidently refers to the blindness of the economic system for its ecological conditions and effects.

For the normal functioning of capitalism, such 'blind' spots are not so much problems, but rather conditions of possibility: it is precisely by making underlying social and ecological processes invisible that the market economy can function in a systemic way. In essence, capitalism operates according to a kind of mathematical and mechanical logic that holds the gaze fixed on economic data. Social or environmental problems are only visible in as far as they affect prices and profits, in other words, as far as they are represented within a logic the system spontaneously understands. This is why, for instance, the destruction of biodiversity continues unhindered: the loss of species does not immediately show up in the system's economic indicators. Like many other proponents of the green economy, Al Gore believes that this short-sightedness can be corrected by giving nature a price. This would make nature visible again within the system's indicators, but as we will see later in this book, this is not as easy as it might seem.

Whether the market is corrected or not, economic actors focus on a limited number of figures (e.g. prices and profits), and make abstraction from a whole series of ecological, social or political conditions which cannot always (easily) be represented in economic terms. Each time a concrete material or social good is turned into an economic good, abstraction is made from certain of its qualitative characteristics, and a new type of representation of the good emerges which makes these characteristics invisible. Importantly, this 'abstraction' is both a 'real abstraction', actually operational in the exchange of commodities, which are rendered equivalent purely in quantitative terms, and a way to represent the world in consciousness (Sohn-Rethel 1978). In other words, both the actual economic process and the way people think about it are based on abstractions.

Capital is thus based on a specific logic of calculation which inevitably generates blind spots that cannot be overcome unless one gives up the project to turn an increasingly large domain of society into commodities that can be rendered equivalent on the market through exchange. Mainstream economic science reinforces this blindness by accepting the market abstractions (commodities, prices and other economic figures) at face value, and by thus refusing to pierce the veil which hides underlying social, political and ecological conditions. Importantly, the green economy project tends to even reinforce such forms of abstraction, precisely by inventing market solutions for ecological problems. Carbon trading is a case in point. When it renders all types of CO_2 emissions equivalent, it also operates a form of abstraction. Through this operation of abstraction, the concrete, material and social characteristics of processes whereby CO_2 is emitted are rendered invisible. And this also impedes their politicisation: making social and ecological processes invisible is paramount to their depoliticisation.

It is obviously not just managers and bankers who become 'alienated' from nature as a result of this abstraction process. In a capitalist society, the vast majority of people depend entirely on the market to provide for their basic needs. Access to nature is almost always mediated by money and the economic laws of the market, reproducing the blind spots characterising it. This process is deepening as commodification reaches deeper into daily life-worlds (Kovel 2007). Until a few decades ago, key elements of daily life (growing vegetables, repairing clothes or tools, reusing stuff in creative ways) still took place largely outside the market. Today, almost everything is purchased, and if something is broken, it is thrown away and replaced. Our dependence on the market has never been greater. This is not to idealise a romantic past, or suggest we should go back to it, far from it: the aim is to pinpoint a process of commodification and marketisation, and the way in which this makes material flows and processes partly invisible. This invisibilisation also fundamentally affects people's life-worlds.

Calculating nature

Many products of nature are valuable (and often vital) for humans, even if we do not put a price on them. But in a capitalist economy, only the price counts at the end of the day. On closer inspection, it does not really matter from the point of view of capital how profit is realised. Whether this is done through the exploitation of labour, the exploitation of the soil or simply through speculation, what counts is the bottom line. All commodities are equal in that respect: this is exactly what the above-mentioned process of 'abstraction' boils down to. The money gained by illegal deforestation is worth just as much as that from the production of wind turbines.

Capital is interested in the products of nature, but not in 'nature' as such. It does not look at a forest as an ecosystem, but as the sum of so many thousands of marketable pieces of wood. It has a unique way of looking at things: forests are seen as a wood pile, land as real estate and oceans as fish stocks.

We again encounter the selective blindness of capital at this point: capital not only is blind to certain things or qualitative dimensions of things, but it also splits up the integrity of the ecosystems, which can actually only be understood as a whole (Kovel 2007, 113). From capital's perspective, nature becomes a set of objects that can be disassembled and separated from each other. Money functions as a crowbar for this fragmentation, and as an instrument of representation, which demarcates what is visible and what is not. It is capable of representing the (exchange) value of the fish, for example, but not of the ocean they are swimming in. As we will argue, even if market prices are ecologically corrected, money might be capable of representing *an* exchange value of the ocean, but not its (intrinsic) ecological value.

Indeed, capitalism can surely be corrected and reformed, and this is undoubtedly what the green economy attempts to do. However, it appears to be structurally incapable of the kind of holistic thinking that is necessary to understand ecology as such. For capital's spontaneous mode of representing the world, the value of an ecosystem is at most the sum of the (financial) values of its parts. As we will argue, capital's blindness is fundamentally not remedied in the green economy project, but it is reproduced on new levels. For example, the endeavour to economically account for ecosystem services (e.g. the fact that ecosystems purify air or water) yields ambiguous results. On the one hand, it is an attempt to remedy capital's blindness for the importance of ecosystems, by putting an economic value on the services ecosystems deliver. On the other hand, however, such systems reproduce capital's blindness to the whole of the ecosystem by disintegrating nature and reducing it to 'services' which are useful for human beings, and especially for the economy.

Over the last two decades, Robert Costanza and his team have undertaken large-scale research in order to determine the 'value' of the world's ecosystems (Costanza et al. 2014). They define ecosystem services in terms of the benefits people derive from ecosystems, and subsequently try to put a price on these benefits. Coastal wetlands, for example, contribute to protecting against storms. In 1997, the total value of the global ecosystems was estimated at about $46 trillion per year, which was far more than global GDP at that time. In 2011, due to 'a better understanding of just how valuable some of these ecological services are', their recalculations led to a sum of $145 trillion per year. 'Our estimates,' the researchers write, 'show that global land use changes between 1997 and 2011 have resulted in a loss of ecosystem services of between 4.3 and 20.2 trillion dollars/year, and we believe that these estimates are conservative' (Costanza et al. 2014, 157).

Responding to criticisms that were levelled against their approach, Costanza and his colleagues argue that 'expressing the value of ecosystem services in monetary units does not mean that they should be treated as private commodities that can be traded in private markets' (p. 157). As they state, their avowed aim is to raise awareness of the importance of ecosystems services, and the magnitude of the loss we are currently incurring by destroying ecosystems. Moreover, so they stress, valuation is unavoidable in decision-making procedures. The question, however, is whether *monetary* valuation is the most adequate way to express value, and whether, despite the aims of the researchers, such calculations do not contribute to (mentally) prepare people for policy measures which actually monetise and marketise ecosystems. As Castree has argued, Constanza et al. engage in a kind of 'proxy commodification' which 'can pave the way for real commodification' (Castree 2003).

Indeed, a similar project aimed at calculating the value of 'natural capital' has helped to provide the ideological backbone for the emergence of green economy thinking. *The Economics of Ecosystems and Biodiversity (TEEB)* study, undertaken under the auspices of UNEP, was initiated at the 2007 G8 summit, and has been fundamental for the green economy debate. The study claims to recognise the plurality of values at stake. For instance, it draws a distinction between 'intangible values, which may be reflected in society's willingness to pay to conserve particular species or landscapes' and 'more tangible values like food or timber' (TEEB 2010, 3). In the end, however, economic value turns out to be the alpha and omega of the report. Coral reefs, for example, are considered one of the most precious ecosystems on Earth, valued at about $1.2 million per hectare per year. This value is especially determined in terms of the tourism income the coral reefs yield. But would that mean that this value would be lower when watching coral reefs would get out of fashion amongst tourists?

Strikingly, the value of ecosystems is determined from the point of view of how they contribute to the reproduction of the capitalist economy. Indeed, TEEB defines ecosystem services as the 'flows of value to human societies as a result of the state and quantity of natural capital' (TEEB 2010, 7). This means capital, and its specific modes of calculation and valuation, becomes a decisive criterion. Even though TEEB argues that 'such valuation does not imply that *all* ecosystem services must *necessarily* be privatised and traded in the market' (TEEB 2010, 12), it opens the door for such policies. The point is that the use of a capitalist mode of valuation and measuring is the precondition for making commodification possible. Systems for the payment for ecosystems services (PES), such as paying landowners for keeping trees standing or for using sustainable agricultural techniques, are examples of the policies which such calculation enables, as are markets for ecosystems services (MES), including emission trading schemes.

It is striking, indeed, that also in the work of Costanza and his colleagues, 'natural capital' is represented as part of a broader system of capital. As a response to critics who state that the value of ecosystems should be infinite, as without them, human life would end, the researchers argue:

> Our estimate is [. . .] analogous to estimating the total value of agriculture in national income accounting. Whatever the fraction of GDP that agriculture contributes now, it is clear that if all agriculture were to stop, economies would collapse to near zero. What the estimates are referring to, in both cases, is the relative contribution, expressed in monetary units, of the assets or activities at the current point in time.
>
> (Costanza et al. 2014, 157)

Ecosystems services, in other words, are portrayed as a component part of the capitalist economy, just like any economic sector is.

As we explained in Chapter 2, representation is not an innocent affair. It can make people aware (as Costanza's avowed aim is), but it can also blind them to certain things. As TEEB argues, the aim of natural capital accounting, which is a very specific way to represent nature, is 'making nature's values visible'.[2] 'The invisibility of biodiversity values has often encouraged inefficient use or even destruction of the natural capital that is the foundation of our economies,' it is stated in the TEEB report (TEEB 2010, 3).

Within a capitalist logic, this argument surely makes sense: it helps to take those things into account which are otherwise completely neglected. It is supposed to lead to other calculations, underpinning other economic decisions. At the same time, however, the specific type of visibilisation pursued here generates new forms of invisibility. The blind spots of a capitalist mode of valuation, the latter's socially and historically relative nature, the fact that the construction of 'natural capital' and the determination of its value are contingent and contestable, that specific values rather than others are taken into account, that establishing relations of equivalence (e.g. between several forms of nature) entails the exercise of a specific type of power: all these facets remain invisible in such a seemingly technical and scientific exercise.

The use of the notion of 'natural capital' has profound consequences, including on the political level. This notion operates according to a quantitative logic of equivalence, as if one can express the value of very divergent ecosystems in one single measure. To put it bluntly, X quantities of forest equals Y quantities of ocean. This results in forms of abstraction and blindness for qualitative differences that are typical of capital's way to represent the world, and return in a number of green economy policies.

It appears that the emergence of the green economy discourse has thus led to novel representations of nature, or at least to a qualitative deepening and reinforcement of specifically capitalist ways to represent nature. In the green economy, nature is no longer a mere object that can be instrumentalised in economic production, but is considered as a living process, a process of production. It is an economy in itself.

A strange process of translation and resignification has thus been taking place. Interestingly, notions such as 'natural capital' and the 'natural economy' have not always been given the meaning they currently acquire in the green economy discourse. Vandana Shiva, for instance, speaks in several of her books about 'nature's economy', explaining how nature operates on the basis of principles which are entirely different from those of the market economy (Shiva 1991, 2006). Proponents of the green economy, however, have given these notions other meanings. 'Nature is the largest company on Earth,' states the International Union for the Conservation of Nature (IUCN 2009). Similarly, Bond Beter Leefmilieu [Federation for a Better Environment], the platform of environmental non-governmental organizations (NGOs) in Flanders (Belgium), representing tens of thousands of people, waged a campaign in 2014 around the slogan 'Everyone is a shareholder of the environment, the biggest multinational ever. It works 24/24 for us.'

Considering nature as an economy, based on specific forms of capital, implies that like all economies, its component parts can be measured, calculated, compared, rendered commensurable, normalised. Such an approach to nature ultimately serves to integrate nature and its cycles and processes within the economic cycle. Referring to Michel Foucault, we could argue that such operations can be understood as forms of power, as they enable acts of classification, control or discipline (Foucault 1997). It is precisely by making that visible that the green economy's representations of nature can be contested and politicised.

Fundamentally, concepts like natural capital, its measurement and accumulation are the result of a process of social construction which is inevitably contentious and contestable. Even the concept of ecosystem services is such a contestable social construction, Barnaud and Antona argue:

> This social construction process looks like a mix of battles of intimate representations of the human–nature relationships and conflicts of economic and political interests, not only between different scientific communities with different backgrounds and perceptions, but also among them and various

stakeholders, from local farmers to national decision makers and international agencies.

(Barnaud and Antona 2014, 120)

Barnaud and Antona therefore call for 'questioning the values underlying the concept of ecosystem services'.

The risk, indeed, is that economic or monetary values or forms of valuation prevail in how the concept of ecosystems services is constructed and assessed. As Engelen and Neuteleers have argued, monetary valuation is not an innocent affair (Neuteleers and Engelen 2014). It not only misrecognises other modes of valuation, but also threatens to fundamentally transform people's attitudes to nature and its protection. The authors argue it might generate a 'crowding out' effect, as a result of which intrinsic motivation to protect nature (e.g. for moral, aesthetic or other reasons) is replaced by extrinsic motivation (to protect nature in view of a potential financial gain). They argue that commodification *discourses*, rather than commodification per se, can already generate this effect. Monetary valuation, in other words, is not only incapable of grasping intrinsic ecological value (Kovel 2007), as it expresses everything in monetary terms, but it is also incapable of providing an intrinsic, ecological motivation to protect nature. If the only motivation to protect ecosystems is extrinsic and based on financial gain, moreover, permanent trade-offs will be made as to what is the most beneficial outcome. As the British journalist George Monbiot argues:

As soon as something is measurable it becomes negotiable. Subject the natural world to cost-benefit analysis and accountants and statisticians will decide which parts of it we can do without. All that now needs to be done to demonstrate that an ecosystem can be junked is to show that the money to be made from trashing it exceeds the money to be made from preserving it.

(Monbiot 2010)

Capitalism is remarkably dynamic and responsive to challenges from outside. As several scholars have shown from different perspectives, it is capable of restructuring and reforming itself as an answer to forms of resistance (Boltanski and Chiapello 2007, Negri and Hardt 2000), but also as an answer to ecological destruction (Kovel 2007, Mueller and Passadakis 2010). However, it is not capable of grasping these challenges in their own terms, which are radically heterogeneous to the logic of the calculation of capital. It only acknowledges these challenges to the extent these impact upon relevant financial data (the price of resources, taxes, wages, etc.) and to the extent they can be measured in monetary terms. Policies can thus play an important role in *correcting* the system, trying to take ecological concerns into account, but only by operating a complex and finally impossible exercise of translation, in which a number of important things are unavoidably lost.

The attempt to express the 'value' of an ecosystem (let alone something as complex as the climate) in financial terms is, as we will argue, a questionable project. Furthermore, one can try to calculate the contribution ecosystems make to the economy, but one cannot express the value of their very *existence* in monetary terms. What is a condition of possibility of the economic systems cannot become part of its mode of functioning and calculation. To put it more precisely, the social and ecological conditions of capitalism by definition exceed capital's very mode of representation and calculation. In this sense, as Joel Kovel has argued, a distinction should be drawn between 'exchange' value and 'intrinsic' ecological value (Kovel 2007). This latter, critical notion serves to demarcate the limits of economic calculation and valuation.

This is not to suggest that attempts, for example, to express the cost of climate change in monetary terms are completely useless. A number of influential reports have undertaken such an endeavour in order to show that inaction on climate change is more costly than taking appropriate measures (Gordon 2014, Stern 2006). With this message, they attempt to convince companies and policymakers to take action, often with some success. The point is that one should be wary of the idea that such calculations can be conclusively made. They can play a limited role: to expose the blindness of the capitalist system. Such calculations can reveal that something is concealed, not taken into account, hidden in the very way the system operates. However, as we just argued, we should not have the illusion that novel economic calculations and valuations can correct this and fully reveal, let alone monetarily grasp, what is thus covered up. Quite the contrary, this way of bringing nature in risks leading to new forms of blindness.

Furthermore, calculations of the cost of climate change often make a number of assumptions which can be put into question. Can one put a price tag on (future) social and ecological crises, on losses of human lives, on extinct species? Is the price of climate change equal to the addition of various costs, such as building higher dikes, cleaning up debris after natural disasters, reduced agricultural yields and a whole range of other unpredictable events? How can we grasp the unpredictable consequences of global warming of 6°C or more? The bigger picture threatens to remain invisible. Amongst other things, the fact that ecological processes do not follow a linear path is often not taken seriously. There are critical thresholds or tipping points: as soon as a certain temperature is reached, ecosystems can make a qualitative leap, with consequences that are very difficult to predict, let alone to put a price on.[3] Likewise, it is impossible to divide the ecological crisis into seemingly independent problems: climate change, biodiversity loss, desertification, etcetera. The connections between them are often not recognised. 'Solutions' for one ecological problem sometimes risk making other problems worse. For instance, agrofuels are presented as a solution to climate change (although we may question whether they actually emit less greenhouse gases than fossil fuels), but also often lead to deforestation and undermine biodiversity (Shiva 2008).

Efficiency through competition?

One of the red threads of UNEP's green economy report is resource efficiency. The latter is one of the royal roads to realising 'win-win' situations, as it simultaneously allows cutting costs and reducing ecological impact. As this and other reports convincingly argue, there is still quite some scope for enhancing resource efficiency, and a number of policy measures can help to realise this potential. At the same time, however, it should be observed that resource efficiency is already part of the DNA of capitalism, and is therefore nothing new. In stark contrast to bureaucratic command economies such as the Soviet Union, capitalism is characterised by in-built incentives to reduce resource use: competition urges each company to cut costs, e.g. by reducing the input of energy, materials or labour. In a similar vein, reusing waste or by-products could be logical from a capitalist point of view, in so far as it helps save costs, or possibly even generates additional income.

At least, this is the theory. In practice, the picture is less rosy. The ecological cost of production is usually passed on to society and the ecosystems (or in more technical terms, the environmental costs are 'externalised' – more about this in Chapter 4). Furthermore, companies can also cut costs (or generate new incomes) by engaging in wasteful practices: using disposable rather than reusable instruments (e.g. plastic cutlery or plates in restaurants) or producing and selling goods whose lifespan is limited and which cannot easily be repaired (e.g. mobile phones). The environmental and social costs of these choices do not rest on their shoulders, but on those of society as a whole. The additional profit from making these choices will, however, accrue to the companies involved.

Yet, there are also other mechanisms at play which mean that competition and increased efficiency do not necessarily benefit the environment. Labour productivity increased dramatically over the past two centuries. In principle, this creates the conditions for people to work fewer hours and have more free time: we would then be producing as much as before, but in a shorter amount of time. Labour time reduction has been a historical demand of the labour movement. In Belgium, for example, the 8-hour working day was introduced in 1921 after years of intense struggle. In 1964, the 45-hour week became the norm, and by 1974 it had declined in most sectors to 40 hours (Lievens 2005). Since then, labour productivity has further increased, but without leading to reduced working hours or to proportionately higher wages. Increased production rather underpinned higher profits. This sums up capitalism in a nutshell: it seems to have an ingrained prejudice against free time. 'Time is money!' as Benjamin Franklin famously stated. Every hour without production is seen as a potential loss. The ecological consequences are obvious: the higher the productivity, the greater the environmental impact of each hour of production. The consumption of raw materials and energy and the emission of waste products (the material flow) then increases rapidly.

Jevons' paradox

In his book *Hot, Flat, and Crowded*, Thomas Friedman, the well-known columnist for the *New York Times*, describes in technicolour detail his visit to a 'green'
Wal-Mart store in McKinney, Texas, near Dallas (Friedman 2008, 71). During
the trip, his enthusiasm wanes. On his way back from the store, he sees with
dismay a fifty-mile-long ribbon of construction projects, from restaurants to shop-
ping malls, petrol stations and even a new non-green Wal-Mart. In Friedman's
own words:

> I spent the whole trip just staring out the window at the sprawl and thinking
> to myself: "We're on a fool's errand. Whatever energy this green Wal-Mart
> store might save, or even a thousand green Wal-Marts might save, will be
> swamped by this tidal wave of development," which looked like it was des-
> tined to rumble all the way to the border of Oklahoma.
>
> (Friedman 2008, 72)

In other words, one can try to be as resource efficient as possible, but economic
growth threatens to make these efforts effectless. Friedman refuses to draw this
conclusion and to question economic growth. The evidence is, however, centuries old. In the nineteenth century, William Stanley Jevons (1835–1882) made
a peculiar observation: the machines and factories were becoming more efficient
in their use of coal, but this was not leading to a decrease in the total consumption of coal. 'It is wholly a confusion of ideas to suppose that the economical use
of fuel is equivalent to a diminished consumption,' he argued in his book *The
Coal Question*. 'The very contrary is the truth' (quoted in Foster, Clark and York
2010, 171). The answer to the riddle is that individual machines become more
efficient, but precisely for this reason it becomes economically possible to install
more machines, so that the total consumption continues to increase rapidly. The
reason for this is obviously the growth logic of capital: more efficiency means
more profits, and thus more capital accumulation, more machines and a scaling
up of the economy. As Magdoff and Foster argue, '[t]he Jevons Paradox is now
widely recognised by environmentalists as a key reason why technology alone –
outside the transformation of social relations – cannot solve the ecological con-
tradictions of capitalism' (Magdoff and Foster 2011, 111). Jevons' observation is
extremely important: an increase in production efficiency can be perfectly well
combined with an increase in the total consumption of raw materials. In fact, it
is often the cause of it!

Many proponents of the market economy attempt to refute the ecologist critique of economic growth by saying that the capitalist economy is becoming more
efficient, and is slowly 'dematerialising'. Some even go so far as to claim that in
the long term this trend could lead to economic growth being completely decoupled from resource use. Following this logic, economic growth could continue
unimpeded by the problem of finite supplies of energy and raw materials.

In many areas, however, we see how Jevons' paradox catches up with this optimism. It is true that the amount of raw material and energy required per unit of output is declining in many production processes. But this relative decline is often accompanied by an absolute increase in raw material consumption at the level of the economy as a whole (Foster 2002, 23). In fact, as already suggested, some dematerialisation is part of the DNA of capitalism. Competition forces all industries to look for more efficient means of production, so that less labour, raw materials and energy are required for each product. But this dynamic ensures simultaneously that the *total* input of matter and energy and the *total* production of waste have increased massively since the emergence of capitalism.

The same phenomenon applies to CO_2 emissions: the carbon intensity of the global economy fell from 0.35 kilograms of carbon per dollar of product in 1970 to 0.24 kilograms in 2000. But the total CO_2 emissions still continued to grow: from over 4 gigatonnes in 1970 to almost 7 gigatonnes in 2000 (Canadell et al. 2007, IPCC 2007). Remarkably, from 2000 onwards, the carbon intensity even began to rise again by 0.3% per year. This means more CO_2 is emitted per unit of production. One of the reasons for this is the increased use of coal during the first decade of the twenty-first century.

Efficiency is both economically and ecologically interesting, but in a capitalist context it often has disastrous ecological consequences. It is no coincidence that the countries with the most efficient technologies are often the biggest polluters and the main consumers of raw materials. There are numerous examples which illustrate how greater efficiency can at the same time mean more pollution.

Similar phenomena also occur on the consumption side. Consider the so-called environmentally friendly car, which is sometimes advocated by proponents of the green economy (Lööf and Goldmann 2011). While car engine efficiency is increasing, the total emissions from road transport continue to rise. This is because the number of cars on the road continues to increase, as does the number of kilometres each car drives. For instance, the number of kilometres driven on the road is steadily increasing in Belgium and the Netherlands. Records are broken almost every year. In 2010, Belgian cars drove a total of 82.6 billion kilometres, and Dutch cars 113.2 billion kilometres (Thys 2012).[4] The mandatory standards imposed by the EU on car manufacturers brought more energy-efficient cars onto the market (MIRA 2012). The total emissions from Belgian cars therefore fell a bit in the period 2000–2010. But the number of kilometres driven by new cars is higher than is the case with old cars. For example, a new diesel car drives more than twice as many kilometres as a five-year-old one. As a result, the total decline in emissions remains less than what could be expected on the basis of the increased efficiency that was enforced by public authorities. In this case, Jevons' paradox was mitigated by the strength of the EU standards, resulting in a more limited 'rebound effect'. In the freight transport sector, however, the Jevons' paradox was fully at work: the total emissions from freight increased in the same period by about 16%, despite the fact that trucks were also becoming more energy efficient (MIRA 2012, 48).

Although overall efficiency is still increasing rapidly, economic growth is rising faster. Even the Organisation for Economic Co-operation and Development (OECD) admits in its *Environmental Outlook 2010*: 'the use of natural resources, water and energy has to some extent been decoupled from continuing economic growth (i.e. become more efficient per unit of GDP). [. . .] However, in most cases, the increasing pressures on the environment from population and economic growth have out-paced the benefits of any efficiency gains' (OECD 2008, 6).

Although such phenomena have in the meantime been well documented and studied, many green economy discourses claim it will be possible to circumvent Jevons' paradox by a mix of policies. UNEP, for instance, acknowledges Jevons' paradox, but argues it will be reduced by 'significant energy price increases', which can be expected 'once the costs of CO_2 abatement have been set at levels sufficiently high to stabilise atmospheric CO_2 and have been fully internalised to users' (UNEP 2011, 269). It concludes that 'greater take-up of more efficient technologies will help to abate the otherwise negative impacts on economic growth resulting from higher energy prices.' Similarly, the World Bank report on *Inclusive Green Growth* argues that the rebound effect which might be generated by fuel efficiency standards for cars can be limited by also increasing prices through taxes or carbon trading (World Bank 2012, 59).

In contrast, in a survey article on Jevons' paradox, Alcott argues that 'if Jevons is right, then efficiency policies are simply counter-productive. Even taxes on fuel or CO_2 will be compensated by efficiency increases, and moreover they [i.e. policies focused on enhancing efficiency] face the problem that tax revenue also gets spent on material and energy' (Alcott 2005, 19). As an alternative, Alcott proposes to reconsider resource rationing as a serious option, referring to the Kyoto protocol as an example. As we will argue in the next chapter, however, emissions trading, one of the capstones of Kyoto, has very problematic ecological and social side effects, which might only leave us with the option of rationing without compensatory market mechanisms.

Infinite growth on a finite planet?

The dominant, neoclassical economic theory emphasises balance – for instance, between supply and demand. But we do not see much balance in reality. Capitalism is constantly changing: it is an exceptionally dynamic system, based on continuous growth and accumulation (Foster, Clark and York 2010, 29). This is one of the main reasons why capitalism leads to such ecological destruction. Even if economic growth remains relatively modest, the ecological impact increases rapidly. According to the OECD, average global economic growth from 2000 until 2009 was 3.3% (OECD 2013, 12). If such growth rates continue, global output (expressed in monetary terms) doubles every 22 years. It increases more than 25 times in a century, and more than 660 times in two centuries (see also Foster 2002, 45). As we just explained, if some degree of dematerialisation takes place, the physical size of the economy will rise less rapidly. But there is no doubt that it will greatly increase nevertheless. The idea that by the year 2200, the world economy will be hundreds of times its current size is dazzling from an ecological point of view.

It is sometimes argued that in the future, we will witness not only a far-going dematerialisation, but growth would also shift towards the service sector and various forms of 'immaterial' production (Coutrot and Gadrey 2012). This would have a beneficial impact on CO_2 emissions (Stern 2006, 180). Could it therefore make continuous economic growth possible? Admittedly, teaching has a smaller environmental impact than running a steel mill. But we have to add a few caveats. It is true that in many countries of the global North the service sector is growing in size compared with industry. But that does not mean that industry cannot continue to grow in absolute terms. Moreover, industry has not disappeared, but largely moved to a number of emerging economies such as China, which are producing on a massive scale for Western consumption. The pollution this causes may be out of sight, but that does not mean that it has magically disappeared.

Furthermore, it is also sometimes overlooked that the so-called virtual economy is built on a base of very real material and energy use. Take the Internet, for example. According to a 2009 report by the environmental consultancy ICF International, commissioned by McAfee, the volume of spam that was sent over the Internet in 2008 requires as much energy as one and a half million American households, or 3.1 million cars (*The Economist* 2009). If this energy were produced by coal-fired power plants, this would have resulted in 17 million tonnes of CO_2 emissions per year, equal to 0.2% of total CO_2 emissions. According to Alex Wissner-Gross, a physicist who works at Harvard and carries out research into the energy consumption of the Internet, it takes an average of 20 milligrams of CO_2 per second to visit a website. With hundreds of millions of Internet users, this quickly mounts up. In 2011 it was calculated that Google accounted for 1.5 million tonnes of CO_2 emissions per year, which is equivalent to the emissions of the United Nations organisations (Clark 2011). In total, the global information technology sector has been estimated to represent 2% to 4% of global greenhouse gas emissions (Combiner 2011). Moreover, the Internet is in full expansion. The energy consumption of the web is increasing every year by more than 10% (Johnson 2009). However 'dematerialised' or even virtual, all economic activity has an ecological impact.

Such observations obviously present a huge challenge to discourses on 'green growth' and scenarios aimed at greening the economy. For example, UNEP projects two green investment scenarios in its green economy report: G1 and G2, which respectively entail 1% and 2% of global GDP yearly investment in greening the economy, especially targeting energy production, manufacturing, transport, buildings, waste, agriculture, fishing, water and forestry. These scenarios focus on a wider range of environmental problems, but if we look specifically to climate change, the result is disappointing. G2, which is the most ambitious scenario UNEP outlines, reduces CO_2 emissions by only a third in 2050 compared with 2011. This amounts to a reduction of 4%–7% compared with 1990 (IBON 2011, 7, UNEP 2011). As UNEP admits, '[t]he green investment scenario G2 does not fully achieve the emissions reductions [. . .] necessary for limiting atmospheric concentrations to 450 ppm. Part of this difference is due to the positive effect of various green investments on overall economic growth (GDP) that, in turn, results in increased energy demand, a form of the rebound effect' (UNEP 2011, 224–225).[5]

Similar conclusions have been reached by a number of other authors and reports. According to Minqi Li, there remains almost no scope for economic growth if we want to stabilise greenhouse gas concentrations in the atmosphere on a level of 445 ppm CO_2eq, unless (unrealistically?) high reductions of the energy and carbon intensities of the economy are realised (Li 2008). He calculates that the average reduction of emissions intensity (the amount of emissions per unit of energy consumed) of the global economy was 0.3% per year in the period from 1973 to 2005. The average reduction of energy intensity (the amount of energy needed per unit of GDP) was 0.9% per year. At the same time, average growth amounted to 3%. Even in very ambitious scenarios, where emissions intensities diminish by 2.7% per year and energy intensities by 2% (much more than what is currently realised), the economy would still have to contract by 0.7% in order to reach the stated climate objective, he argues.

PricewaterhouseCoopers (PWC) is not an organisation which one would expect to be an advocate of a degrowth perspective. Yet, the company made similar calculations. In a 2012 report, it estimates that the average rate of decarbonisation in the first decade of the twenty-first century was 0.8%. PWC argues that 'the required improvement in global carbon intensity to meet a 2°C warming target has risen to 5.1% a year, from now to 2050,' which appears an impossible task (PWC 2012, 1). The firm concludes that 'businesses, governments and communities across the world need to plan for a warming world – not just 2°C, but 4°C, or even 6°C.' Unsurprisingly, PWC does not question economic growth as such, although this conclusion imposes itself. As Peter Victor argues:

> To reduce greenhouse-gas emissions (GHG) by 80% over 50 years, an economy that increases its real gross domestic product (GDP) by 3% a year must reduce its emissions intensity – tonnes of GHG per unit of GDP – by an astonishing 6% a year. For an economy that does not grow, the annual cut would be a still very challenging 3.2%.
>
> (Victor 2010, 370)

If that is correct, different and more radical measures will be needed. A report by the UN Department of Economic and Social Affairs goes so far as to state that if technological progress in energy efficiency and renewable energy production does not suffice, 'it may be necessary to impose caps on energy consumption itself in order to meet climate change mitigation targets in a timely manner' (UN 2011, 19). 'The need to consider placing certain limits on the total volume of world output and consumption was also recognised by the Brundtland Commission in its report,' it is stated. In the end, the report does not fully endorse such a radical approach imposing limits to growth, but especially stresses how difficult this would be: 'Acceptance and implementation of prosperity without growth will therefore require major structural transformations of economies and societies' (UN 2011, 20).

A steady-state economy

A growing number of ecologists criticise the logic of economic growth and call for degrowth, or for a steady-state economy, which is an economy in which the flow of matter and energy is limited to what the ecosystems can support (e.g. Daly 1996, Jackson 2009, Victor 2010). But is this possible in a capitalist context?

From an ecological point of view, a steady-state economy is both logical and rational. From a capitalist point of view, it is anything but (Foster 2011). The only time there is no growth or negative growth in capitalism is during periods of crisis and recession. It is no coincidence that the environmental pressure sometimes decreases in such periods. In recent decades, there have been only two brief periods in which greenhouse gas emissions substantially decreased: after the collapse of the Soviet Union, and during the global economic crisis of 2008–2009. The Russian economy shrank by about 40% between 1989 and 1992. During the 90s, Russian greenhouse gas emissions also fell at a certain point to about 40% under its level of 1990 (Smith 2007, 22). At the height of the economic crisis, CO_2 emissions from European factories and power plants decreased noticeably: by 6% in 2008 and 11% in 2009 (Chaffin 2010). This is telling: emissions decrease only when the economy is in crisis.

If emissions decrease for other reasons, then the reduction is always rather limited. As Nicolas Stern explains, the British 'Dash for Gas', which entailed a shift from coal to gas as an energy resource, resulted in an average decrease of emissions by 1% during the 1990s (Stern 2006, 204). Similarly, as a result of reforestation programs in China, land use emissions decreased by 29% per year in the 1990s, but total emissions kept rising by 2.2%.

The question is whether it is actually possible to reduce emissions significantly without bringing the economy to the brink. Capitalism without growth means not only economic crisis, but also social misery. A recession inevitably means mass layoffs, unemployment and increasing poverty. Capitalism without growth does not seem to be a stable model. The choice seems to be: capitalism or a steady-state economy.

The notion of growth plays an important ideological role (Dale 2012). It is the alpha and omega of the dominant economic ideology: economic growth is presented as the solution to every social problem, from poverty to power shortages and even ecological destruction. More growth, so the argument goes, will generate more income, and those with higher incomes will have the purchasing power to choose the more expensive environmentally friendly products or energy sources. Governments adopt this mantra and stimulate growth, often in the name of employment and international competiveness. In the end, the ideological legitimation of capitalism is grounded on two principles: technological progress and economic growth. The ecological crisis is shaking both principles to their foundations (see also Chapter 5).

The problem can be summed up thus: ecosystems are limited, while capital knows no limits. However, capitalism has a very ambiguous relationship with boundaries. On the one hand, it seems unable to respect those boundaries. It represents the world as unlimited: 'the sky is the limit.' On the other hand, however, without these boundaries, capitalism could not possibly exist. As we have explained above, the private appropriation of nature (primarily land) was a crucial factor in the development of capitalism. This set in motion a whole series of processes, such as agricultural concentration, urbanisation and the emergence of a proletariat. But privatisation ('enclosure') would not have been possible if the Earth was unlimited. If there was an abundance of natural resources, there would be no money to be had from selling them. If land (or raw materials) were infinite, then it could not be appropriated in such a way that the majority of the population would be excluded from it. Colonial looting and conflicts in areas abundant in natural resources would simply make no sense. As Daniel Tanuro aptly states: 'without natural limits, capitalism is impossible' (Tanuro 2010, 269).

It is only when something is limited that it can be privatised and monopolised, and thus reap profits. The massive profits yielded by the fossil fuel industry are a case in point: if it would not be possible to privately appropriate oil and gas reserves, the latter could not be so lucrative. As we will see, this is also the principle behind carbon trading and so-called cap and trade systems: governments put artificial limits on the amount of CO_2 that can be emitted. This makes private appropriation of available CO_2 quota, monopolisation and trade possible.

Obstacles and barriers

When overlooking the ecological catastrophes while global capital markets continue to grow, we are faced with a peculiar paradox. Capitalism is causing ecological havoc, and yet this hardly seems to affect the system itself. A number of reports forecast future heavy costs in business-as-usual scenarios (e.g. Gordon 2014, Stern 2006). Yet, the current high levels of pollution and biodiversity loss do not directly affect its mode of operation. There is, of course, the continuing economic crisis, and rising prices of oil and other commodities are a challenge. Yet, all in all, the machine continues to run relatively smoothly. The climate is changing, we are experiencing a biodiversity crisis of enormous proportions. Earlier civilisations perished in the face of far more limited ecological crises. How is it that capitalism remains intact, and seems to be much more resilient than other civilisations?

A beginning of an answer has already been given above: capitalism operates in such a way that it repeatedly manages to transcend the limits of local ecosystems, and hence local ecological crises. The above-mentioned example of nineteenth-century agriculture in England is very enlightening in this regard. The solution to the problem of soil depletion was simple: to import soil or fertilisers from elsewhere. Through money and trade (and exploitation and plunder) the limits of local ecological conditions could be transcended or compensated for.

If local natural resources are depleted, one can simply buy replacements on the market. If there is no market for these yet, it can be created, if necessary by force. In the example of nineteenth-century England, guano replaced natural soil nutrients, later followed by artificial fertilisers. Similarly, on the moment almost all trees had been cut down, the exploitation and import of fossil fuels began. At the end of the production process, something similar happens: if waste becomes a problem, new industries almost spontaneously emerge which export, burn, or bury it underground. Every time again, the dynamic of the market brings forth new companies that (partly) tackle, but often rather shift, the problem.

Indeed, the emergence of new industries does not mean that ecological destruction is thereby reversed. But because capitalism has created a global system of production and trade relationships, it is capable of using quite ingenious means to circumvent the problems it faces. Compared with earlier, more locally based forms of society, capitalism is not dependent on local ecosystems, but only on the planet as a whole (Burkett 1999, 66). It is therefore able to continue plundering ecosystems without immediately undermining itself.

In a remarkable passage in the *Grundrisse*, Marx writes the following, which further illuminates the above analysis:

> [A]s representative of the general form of wealth – money –, capital is the endless and limitless drive to go beyond its limiting barrier. Every boundary is and has to be a barrier for it. Else it would cease to be capital – money as self-reproductive.
>
> (Marx 1973, 334, quoted in Lebowitz 2003).

As Marx suggests, capitalism's dynamism leads it to transform every boundary into a barrier that opens the door for new opportunities. In other words, there are no hard or strict limits for the development of capital: through innovation and marketisation, capital displaces and transforms the limits it is confronted with. This is not to suggest that this complex operation always succeeds. It might be possible, for example, that capital is not capable of sufficiently shifting the limits so as to avert catastrophic climate change. The point, however, is to understand that 'hard', objective limits do not exist for capitalism, in the sense that it will never recognise them (even if that would entail, in the end, the destruction of its own conditions of possibility), and that it is incredibly creative in turning these limits into new opportunities.

As we already showed in Chapter 1, green economy discourses equally focus on the idea that crises or problems should be considered as challenges and opportunities. The green economy, UNEP president Achim Steiner argues, 'is a positive message of opportunity in a troubled world of challenges' (UNEP 2012). The green economy, therefore, is also about inventing mechanisms through which obstacles can be turned into barriers, and new economic opportunities can be generated, namely through the sale of new products and the creation of new markets.

But this dynamic of limits and opportunities can take absurd and problematic forms. Global warming has sparked new opportunities in the tourism industry, with cruise lines offering expensive trips allowing tourists to see the melting ice in the arctic (Bennett 2014). More and more people suffer from work-related stress and depression, creating a gap in the market for the health farm and beauty industry. Capitalist civilisation knows no restraint, but capitalism can even make an industry out of moderation. Escaping the rat race is possible, if only it is by buying commodities. Reducing CO_2 emissions must happen through newly created carbon markets where significant profits can be made. Banks that have trouble selling mortgages in a context of crisis can still make a profit by speculating on the collapse of the housing market (which is what effectively happened in 2008). Even protest can apparently be turned into a market opportunity. Revolution has become an advertising slogan: there are 'cellulite revolutions', 'slimming revolutions' and 'car revolutions'. Capitalism tries to turn every obstacle that it encounters into an opportunity. This does not mean that it always succeeds, but it gives the system a survival dynamic that few other social orders have.

Neoliberal ideology even goes a step further: it treats every obstacle and every crisis as a result of too little capitalism, rather than too much. Poverty would be the result of the fact that markets are not yet sufficiently liberalised. Social inequality is seen as a by-product of government interference with the market. Ecological destruction would be the consequence of the fact that nature has not been priced and marketed correctly. Every boundary, every obstacle is thus the starting point for the creation of new markets and industries, which allow global capital to expand further.

In this context, it is worthwhile to stress that very often, 'green' and 'brown' forms of capital are intertwined. Again, capital is blind to the concrete sources of profit, and can easily switch from brown to green production, but also vice versa. Investment funds buy shares in green companies and in polluting companies at the same time. Like many other banks, BNP Paribas offers green investment bonds next to conventional ones: it is a matter of covering all market niches. If green sectors yield insufficient profit, capital flows will shift immediately. The Belgian bank KBC has its own environmental education agency, is proud of its reputation as a sustainable business and claims to screen its investments based on the UN Principles for Responsible Investment.[6] At the same time, the bank invested almost €120 million in Canadian tar sands in 2009.[7] A similar analysis can be made for several other major financial institutions: RBS, Citibank, ING, etcetera.

Capital can produce green commodities, but it thereby especially creates more of itself. Green(er) industries contribute to the overall accumulation of capital, which naturally finds its way to where most profits can be made. Take Umicore, for example, a Belgian multinational company that takes great pride in its position as a world leader in the recycling of rare materials from electronic scrap. It is certainly a very innovative company working with integrity to resolve the problem of scarcity of materials. But what happens to the profits which the company makes? In 2009, the largest shareholder of Umicore was FIL Limited, a typical investment firm with headquarters in Bermuda, a tax haven. Other major shareholders included the Australian investment bank Macquarie Group Limited, which is referred to as a 'millionaire factory' in the Australian media, and Barclays Bank, which has invested billions of dollars in Canadian tar sands.[8] The 'shareholder value' which was created by 'environmentally friendly' production thus fed financial speculation and the destruction of the environment.

This is not to suggest the environmental efforts of companies are vain or useless. Our aim is to draw attention to the general logic of capitalism as a global system, which overdetermines what individual companies (can) do. Although not every individual capitalist enterprise is necessarily and fundamentally anti-ecological, global interaction between capital and the ecosystems is (cf. Foster, Clark and York 2010).

Crisis

As we already suggested, capitalism creates enormous ecological havoc, but this does not bring it immediately into crisis. How can this be understood? Paul Burkett draws a distinction between two types of ecological crises, which helps us to understand why capital continues to thrive despite ecological destruction (Burkett 2006, 136). First, there are the crises that capitalism causes because it undermines its own ecological conditions. Take, for example, the speed at which fossil fuel supplies are becoming exhausted. The point is that capital can often work around such crises, by making use of nuclear energy or unconventional oil sources. This kind of ecological crisis brings problems for some capitalists, but for others it generates new opportunities. The end result is that the system continues to function, sometimes a little less dynamically than before, but its logic remains intact.

Second, there is the crisis of the quality of the ecosystem as such, and therefore of human life. Burkett speaks about the 'unitary, global, and permanent tendency toward qualitative deterioration in the natural conditions of human development' (Burkett 2006, 137). This crisis is becoming steadily sharper and more visible. Millions of people are suffering its consequences: climate change, biodiversity loss, pollution, all kinds of health problems. This crisis is not periodic but permanent.

These two types of crises are connected in a particular way. The first type can often be overcome, but it thus threatens to enhance the second type. Many 'solutions' to the crisis of capitalism increase the ecological impact of the economic system as a whole. Conversely, the second type of general ecological crisis does not lead directly to the first type of capital crisis. Capitalism can survive for a long time in the middle of an ecological wasteland. In principle, it does not need to take account of the deteriorating state of the ecosystems, just as it does not necessarily need to guarantee access to affordable and decent health care for the mass of the people.

Hence the phenomenon that we see today: the global ecological crisis is bigger than ever, while the capitalist machinery continues to turn without fail. Obviously capitalism in favourable ecological conditions will be more dynamic than capitalism in a wasteland. Nevertheless, the kind of 'nature' capitalism needs to continue to accumulate is another and poorer one than is needed for a humane and sustainable society. This analysis has important implications: capitalism will not simply 'collapse' due to ecological destruction. Neither will capitalism spontaneously 'green' itself.

Notes

1 For a critical analysis, see McAnany and Yoffee 2010.
2 See the opening page of TEEB's website: http://www.teebweb.org
3 On non-linearity and critical thresholds, see Jones and Jacobs (2007, 7). On the inability to express certain critical processes in money terms, see Burkett (2006).

4 Figures for the Netherlands are drawn from the Dutch Central Statistics Bureau (Centraal Bureau voor Statistiek), www.cbs.nl

5 This can only be corrected, so the report suggests, by increased use of carbon sequestration, nuclear energy and carbon capture and storage, but these techniques remain controversial. More about this in Chapter 5.

6 In 2011, KBC Belgium was placed 98th in *Newsweek*'s global ranking of the 500 largest publicly traded companies in the world. Regarding environmental performance, see https://www.kbc.com/MISC/D9e01/N/KBCCOM//BZIZTPN/BZJ07U9/-BZL2H0Z. It had even been raised to 83rd place in 2014; see http://www.newsweek.com/green/worlds-greenest-companies-2014

7 For more information about which banks invest in Canadian tar sands and other climate-destructive practices, see the Bank Track website: http://www.banktrack.org

8 Cf. http://www.banktrack.org

References

Alcott, Blake. 2005. "Jevons' Paradox." *Ecological Economics* 54:9–21.

Barnaud, Cécile, and Martine Antona. 2014. "Deconstructing Ecosystem Services. Uncertainties and Controversies around a Socially Constructed Concept." *Geoforum* 56:113–123.

Bennett, Drake. 2014. "The Melting Arctic Makes Way for $20,000 Luxury Cruises." *Bloomberg Businessweek*, 25 July. http://www.businessweek.com/articles/2014-07-25/climate-change-tourism-cruise-ships-will-cross-the-melting-arctic (accessed 19 November 2014).

Boltanski, Luc, and Eve Chiapello. 2007. *The New Spirit of Capitalism*. London: Verso.

Burkett, Paul. 1999. *Marx and Nature: A Red and Green Perspective*. New York: St. Martin's Press.

Burkett, Paul. 2006. *Marxism and Ecological Economics. Towards a Red and Green Political Economy*. Leiden: Brill.

Canadell, Josep G., Corinne Le Quéré, Michael R. Raupach, Christopher B. Field, Erik T. Buitenhuis, Philippe Ciais, Thomas J. Conway, Nathan P. Gillett, R. A. Houghton, and Gregg Marland. 2007. "Contributions to Accelerating Atmospheric CO_2 Growth from Economic Activity, Carbon Intensity, and Efficiency of Natural Sinks." *PNAS* 104 (47):18866–18870.

Castree, Noel. 2003. "Commodifying Nature." *Progress in Human Geography* 27 (3):273–297.

Chaffin, Joshua. 2010. "Economic Crisis Cuts European Carbon Emissions." *Financial Times*, 1 April.

Clark, Duncan. 2011. "Google Discloses Carbon Footprint for the First Time." *The Guardian*, 8 September.

Cleaver, Harry. 1979. *Reading Capital Politically*. Brighton: The Harvester Press.

Combiner, Joel. 2011. "Carbon Footprinting the Internet." *Consilience: The Journal of Sustainable Development* 5 (1):119–124.

Costanza, Robert, Rudolf de Groot, Paul Sutton, Sander van der Ploeg, Sharolyn J. Anderson, Ida Kubiszewski, Stephen Farber, and R. Kerry Turner. 2014. "Changes in the Global Value of Ecosystem Services." *Global Environmental Change* 26:152–158.

Coutrot, Thomas, and Jean Gadrey. 2012. "Green Growth Is Called into Question." *ETUI Policy Brief*.

Dale, Gareth. 2012. "The Growth Paradigm: A Critique." *International Socialism Journal* 134:55–88.

Daly, Herman E. 1996. *Beyond Growth: The Economics of Sustainable Development*. Boston: Beacon Press.

Daly, Herman E., and Joshua Farley. 2004. *Ecological Economics. Principles and Applications*. Washington, DC: Island Press.

Davis, Mike. 2007. *Planet of Slums*. London: Verso.

Diamond, Jared. 2005. *Collapse: How Societies Choose to Fail or Succeed*. New York: Viking.

EJOLT. 2012. *No Green Economy without Environmental Justice!* http://www.ejolt. org/2012/06/no-green-economy-without-environmental-justice/ (accessed 22 September 2014).

ENS. 2006. "World Economic Forum: No Looming Energy Crisis." *Environment News Service*.

Foster, John Bellamy. 1999. *The Vulnerable Planet. A Short Economic History of the Environment*. New York: Monthly Review Press.

Foster, John Bellamy. 2000. *Marx's Ecology. Materialism and Nature*. New York: Monthly Review Press.

Foster, John Bellamy. 2002. *Ecology against Capitalism*. New York: Monthly Review Press.

Foster, John Bellamy. 2009. *The Ecological Revolution*. New York: Monthly Review Press.

Foster, John Bellamy. 2011. "Capitalism and Degrowth: An Impossibility Theorem." *Monthly Review* 62(8).

Foster, John Bellamy, Brett Clark, and Richard York. 2010. *The Ecological Rift. Capitalism's War on the Earth*. New York: Monthly Review Press.

Foucault, Michel. 1997. *Subjectivity and Truth. Essential Works of Michel Foucault 1954–1984*. London: Penguin Books.

Frederici, Silvia. 2009. *Caliban and the Witch*. New York: Autonomedia.

Friedman, Thomas. 2008. *Hot, Flat, and Crowded: Why We Need a Green Revolution – and How It Can Renew America*. New York: Farrar, Straus and Giroux.

Gordon, Kate. 2014. *Risky Business: The Economic Risks of Climate Change in the United States Risky Business Project*. http://riskybusiness.org/uploads/files/RiskyBusiness_Report_WEB_09_08_14.pdf (accessed 22 September 2014).

Gore, Al. 2007. *Earth in the Balance. Forging a New Common Purpose*. London: Earthscan.

Hansen, James. 2009. "Coal-Fired Power Stations Are Death Factories. Close Them." *The Observer*, 15 February.

IBON. 2011. "Green Economy: Gain or Pain for the Earth's Poor?" *Policy Brief*.

IPCC. 2007. *Climate Change 2007: Working Group I: The Physical Science Basis*. http:// www.ipcc.ch/publications_and_data/publications_ipcc_fourth_assessment_report_wg1_report_the_physical_science_basis.htm (accessed 22 September 2014).

IUCN. 2009. *Wildlife Crisis Worse than Economic Crisis*. http://www.iucn.org/news_homepage/?3460/Wildlife-crisis-worse-than-economic-crisis—IUCN (accessed 15 August 2014).

Jackson, Tim. 2009. *Prosperity without Growth. Economics for a Finite Planet*. London: Earthscan.

Johnson, Bobbie. 2009. "Web Providers Must Limit Internet's Carbon Footprint, Say Experts." *The Guardian*, 3 May.

Jones, Peter Tom, and Roger Jacobs. 2007. *Terra incognita. Globalisering, ecologie en rechtvaardige duurzaamheid*. Ghent: Academia Press.

Kempf, Hervé. 2007. *Comment les riches détruisent la planète*. Paris: Seuil.

Kovel, Joel. 2007. *The Enemy of Nature. The End of Capitalism or the End of the World?* London: Zed Books.

Laube, Johannes C., Mike J. Newland, Christopher Hogan, Carl A. M. Brenninkmeijer, Paul J. Fraser, Patricia Martinerie, David E. Oram, Claire E. Reeves, Thomas Röckmann, Jakob Schwander, Emmanuel Witrant, and William T. Sturges. 2014.

"Newly Detected Ozone-Depleting Substances in the Atmosphere." *Nature Geoscience* 7:266–269.

Lebowitz, Michael A. 2003. *Beyond Capital. Marx's Political Economy of the Working Class*. Houndmills: Palgrave Macmillan.

Li, Minqi. 2008. "Climate Change, Limits to Growth, and the Imperative for Socialism." *Monthly Review* 60 (3):51-67.

Lievens, Matthias. 2005. *Het Neoliberaal Bedrog*. Brussels: Uitgave Formation Léon Lesoil.

Linebaugh, Peter. 2008. *The Magna Carta Manifesto. Liberties and Commons for All*. Berkeley: University of California Press.

Lööf, Jonas, and Mattias Goldmann. 2011. *Selling Environmentally Friendly Cars – Tap into the Green Economy*. SevernWye Energy Agency.

Magdoff, Fred, and John Bellamy Foster. 2011. *What Every Environmentalist Needs to Know about Capitalism*. New York: Monthly Review Press.

Marx, Karl. 1973. *Grundrisse*. London: Penguin Books.

Marx, Karl. 1982. *Capital. A Critique of Political Economy. Volume 1*. Harmondsworth: Penguin Books.

McAnany, Patricia, and Norman Yoffee, eds. 2010. *Questioning Collapse. Human Resilience, Ecological Vulnerability and the Aftermath of the Empire*. Cambridge: Cambridge University Press.

MIRA. 2012. *MIRA Milieurapport Vlaanderen. Indicatorrapport 2011*. Edited by Marleen Van Steertegem: Milieurapport Vlaanderen, Vlaamse Milieumaatschappij.

Monbiot, George. 2010. A *Ghost Agreement*. http://www.monbiot.com/2010/11/01/a-ghost-agreement/ (accessed 11 September 2014).

Moore, Jason. 2014. *The Capitalocene. Part I: On the Nature and Origins of Our Ecological Crisis*. http://www.jasonwmoore.com/uploads/The_Capitalocene__Part_I__June_2014.pdf (accessed 22 September 2014).

Mueller, Tadzio, and Alexis Passadakis. 2010. "Another Capitalism Is Possible? From World Economic Crisis to Green Capitalism." In *Sparking a Worldwide Energy Revolution. Social Struggles in the Transition to a Post-Petrol World*, edited by Kolya Abramsky, 554–563. Oakland, CA: AK Press.

Negri, Antonio, and Michael Hardt. 2000. *Empire*. Cambridge, MA: Harvard University Press.

Neuteleers, Stijn, and Bart Engelen. 2014. "Talking Money: How Market-Based Valuation Can Undermine Environmental Protection." *Ecological Economics*. Available online 19 July 2014. http://www.sciencedirect.com/science/article/pii/S092180091400202X (Accessed 4 February 2015).

OECD. 2008. *Environmental Outlook to 2030. Summary in English*. Paris.

OECD. 2011. *Towards Green Growth*. http://www.oecd.org/greengrowth/towardsgreen-growth.htm (accessed 22 September 2014).

OECD. 2013. *OECD Economic Outlook*, Vol. 2013/1. OECD Publishing.

Polanyi, Karl. 2001. *The Great Transformation. The Political and Economic Origins of Our Time*. Boston: Beacon Press.

PWC. 2012. *Too Late for Two Degrees? Low Carbon Economy Index 2012*. Pricewaterhouse Coopers.

Rockström, Johan. 2009. "A Safe Operating Space for Humanity." *Nature* 461:473–475.

Rockström, Johan, Will Steffen, Kevin Noone, Åsa Persson, F. Stuart III Chapin, Eric Lambin, Timothy M. Lenton, Marten Scheffer, Carl Folke, Hans Joachim Shellnhuber, Björn Nykvist, Cynthia A. de Wit, Terry Hughes, Sander van der Leeuw, Henning Rodhe, Sverker Sörlin, Peter K. Snyder, Robert Costanza, Uno Svedin, Malin

Falkenmark, Louise Karlberg, Robert W. Corell, Victoria J. Fabry, James Hansen, Brian Walker, Diana Liverman, Katherine Richardson, Paul Crutzen, and Jonathan Foley. 2009. "Planetary Boundaries: Exploring the Safe Operating Space for Humanity." *Ecology and Society* 14 (2). http://www.ecologyandsociety.org/vol14/iss2/art32/ (accessed 23 September 2014).

Rousseau, Jean-Jacques. 1997. *The Discourses and Other Early Political Writings*. Cambridge: Cambridge University Press.

Shiva, Vandana, ed. 1991. *Ecology and the Politics of Survival: Conflicts over Natural Resources in India*. Tokyo and New Delhi: United Nations University Press and Sage Publications.

Shiva, Vandana. 2006. *Earth Democracy. Justice, Sustainability and Peace*. London: Zed Books.

Shiva, Vandana. 2008. *Soil not Oil. Climate Change, Peak Oil and Food Security*. London: Zed Books.

Smith, Kevin. 2007. "Climate Change and Carbon Trade." *Critical Currents* 1:17–23.

Sohn-Rethel, Alfred. 1978. *Intellectual and Manual Labour. A Critique of Epistemology*. London: Macmillan.

Stern, Nicholas. 2006. *Stern Review on the Economics of Climate Change*. London: HM Treasury.

Tanuro, Daniel. 2010. *L'impossible capitalisme vert*. Paris: La Découverte.

TEEB. 2010. *The Economics of Ecosystems and Biodiversity: Mainstreaming the Economics of Nature: A Synthesis of the Approach, Conclusions and Recommendations of TEEB*. http://www.teebweb.org/publication/mainstreaming-the-economics-of-nature-a-synthesis-of-the-approach-conclusions-and-recommendations-of-teeb/ (accessed 22 September 2014).

The Economist. 2009. "Can the Spam." 15 June.

Thys, Bart. 2012. *Kilometers afgelegd door Belgische voertuigen in het jaar 2010*. Brussels: Federale Overheidsdienst Mobiliteit en Vervoer: Directie duurzame mobiliteit en spoorbeleid.

UN. 2008. *World Urbanization Prospects. The 2007 Revision. Highlights*. New York: UN Department of Economic and Social Affairs. Population Division.

UN. 2011. *The Great Green Technological Transformation*. New York: United Nations Economic and Social Affairs.

UNEP. 2011. *Towards a Green Economy: Pathways to Sustainable Development and Poverty Eradication*. http://www.unep.org/greeneconomy/GreenEconomyReport (accessed 19 November 2014).

UNEP. 2012. *Transition to Green Economy Could Yield up to 60 Million Jobs*. http://www.unep.org/Documents.Multilingual/Default.asp?DocumentID=2683&ArticleID=9145&l=en (accessed 8 August 2014).

UNFPA. 2007. *State of the World Population 2007: Unleashing the Potential of Urban Growth*. http://www.unfpa.org/swp/2007/english/introduction.html (accessed 22 September 2014).

Victor, Peter. 2010. "Questioning Economic Growth." *Nature* 468:370–371.

World Bank. 2012. *Inclusive Green Growth. The Pathway to Sustainable Development*. Washington: International Bank for Reconstruction and Development / International Development Association or The World Bank. http://siteresources.worldbank.org/EXTSDNET/Resources/Inclusive_Green_Growth_May_2012.pdf (accessed 22 September 2014).

Žižek, Slavoj. 2007. "Censorship Today: Violence, or Ecology as the New Opium for the Masses." http://www.lacan.com/zizecology1.htm (accessed 22 September 2014).

4 Reinventing capitalism

From crisis to opportunity

'There is only one thing bigger than Mother Nature and that is Father Profit,' Thomas Friedman states in his bestseller *Hot, Flat, and Crowded* (Friedman 2008, 244). '[W]e have not even begun to enlist him in this struggle,' he adds. The well-known columnist for the *New York Times* is undoubtedly one of the most intelligent and influential advocates of the green economy, although he prefers to speak of 'green revolution'. His idea is relatively simple: why can't we utilise market mechanisms and the innovative nature of capitalism to make the transition to a green future? Admittedly, the market will have to be corrected by governments in order to price externalities and make polluting products more expensive than environmentally friendly alternatives. Any correction will do, according to Friedman, whether it is a carbon tax, a gasoline tax, or a cap and trade system, 'as long as the effective tax is high enough and long-term enough to really change behaviour' (Friedman 2008, 261).

But for Friedman, more is at stake than warding off catastrophic climate change. The green economy is not only the solution to global ecological problems, such as climate change and biodiversity loss. It is the unique opportunity for the US to regain its hegemonic power, and reinstate itself as the moral leader of the world. The prestige of the US has obviously been severely dented by the subprime crisis and the failures in Iraq and Afghanistan. According to Friedman, the green economy can help the US win back its prestige. Furthermore, it could also help to reduce US dependence on autocratic oil-producing countries such as Saudi Arabia, which finance various forms of Islamic fundamentalism. Hundreds of billions of dollars currently flow every year from energy-consuming to energy-producing countries. This flow may stop if we play the green card, Friedman argues. Even wars for oil would become redundant. 'Making America the world's greenest country is not a selfless act of charity or naive moral indulgence,' he says. 'It is now a core national security and economic interest' (Friedman 2008, 23). 'What could be more patriotic, capitalistic, and geostrategic than that?' he asks rhetorically (203).

Friedman's green revolution seems to be the way forward for a capitalism beleaguered by crises. As Mueller and Passadakis argue, we are not only confronted with a biocrisis and a global economic crisis, but there is also a legitimacy crisis:

even though neoliberal ideology continues to dominate, its credibility has been dealt a severe blow (Mueller and Passadakis 2010). As Friedman acknowledges, America is viewed less as the promised land, and global institutions such as the World Bank and the International Monetary Fund (IMF) have been strongly contested during the past decade. The most intelligent defenders of the market seem to have understood that this is not just a series of crises that exist next to each other. The links between them could pose a threat to the core of the system. Unless the climate crisis is addressed with the help of market mechanisms, as Mueller and Passadakis argue: 'the biocrisis is the opportunity that might just allow capitals and governments to at least temporarily deal with the legitimation and accumulation crises' (Mueller and Passadakis 2010, 558). In a paradoxical way, it seems that climate change might provide an opportunity for capitalism to overcome its current deadlock.

The argument is ingenious. The 'green economy' seems to be the way out of the current economic crisis. That crisis is fundamentally one of overaccumulation: there is a huge amount of capital in the world, and it is difficult to find sufficient profitable investment opportunities (Callinicos 2010, Foster and Magdoff 2009, Joshua 2009). The best way to solve such a crisis is through the creation of new markets. The problem is that very few opportunities for marketisation remain. Financialising debt was not the best strategy, as it has generated the largest economic crisis in half a century. There is no longer an Eastern bloc that can be opened up to international capital, and virtually all developing countries have become capitalist. Many public sectors have already been privatised.

Climate change, or broader, the ecological crisis, seems to provide a potential way out, at least in the eyes of intelligent investors, politicians and policymakers. It opens up possibilities for the creation of new markets which make profit and growth possible once again. This probably brings to mind markets for all kinds of new green products such as wind turbines, solar panels, organic food and electric cars. But this is small fry compared with another huge opportunity that presents itself: the further development of various types of emissions trading (which will be discussed in detail below). It has been argued that if there would be a serious successor to the Kyoto Protocol, which the US signed, then the carbon market could be worth a mammoth $4,500 billion within a decade (Energy Business Reports 2012, Tickell 2010).[1] If one adds the potential bubble of all kinds of derivative products on the basis of carbon credits, this figure could perhaps be multiplied several times (Bond 2012, 33). This is a gigantic opportunity for capital accumulation. The stakes are high: if the market becomes the instrument to solve the problem of climate change, the fight against climate change might become the royal road to solving the problems of the market. Certain companies and sectors (e.g. the oil industry) will perhaps suffer, but elsewhere other promising opportunities await.

Intelligent investors are already targeting green niches of the market. But the type of green capitalism that is emerging now not only is supposed to provide opportunities for individual investors, but might also represent a way out of the different crises of capitalism as such. Means and ends are again reversed, as is typical of a market logic: stabilising the climate becomes a means to ensure growth and rescue the hegemony of the market. But is it that simple? Is such an end result achievable, let alone desirable? What form of society would result from such a strategy? What kind of social relations, power concentration and distribution mechanisms would prevail if such a project would be realised? Would it help us address climate change in an effective and democratic way?

Green New Deal

A similar threefold combination of the climate crisis, peak oil and economic crisis is also the starting point for the so-called Green New Deal (GND), which could be seen as a less market-oriented variant of the green economy narrative, or as 'the left wing of the project' (Mueller and Bullard 2011). The Green New Deal is a policy package that was developed by the UK Green New Deal Group, including the leader of the British Green Party and representatives of Greenpeace and Friends of the Earth. The idea of a Green New Deal was quickly adopted by a range of actors, and the term is even used by UN Secretary Ban Ki-moon and the United Nations Environment Programme (UNEP) (UN News Centre 2008, UNEP 2009). In the US, the Green New Deal was promoted by (amongst others) the Blue Green Alliance, a partnership of labour unions and environmental organisations.[2] In Europe, mainly green parties and some non-governmental organizations (NGOs) advocate the Green New Deal.

The term has been appropriated by very diverse forces, which have also given it quite divergent meanings. Several versions are circulating: from a '*Green New Deal Light*', which is often limited to government investments in green sectors as a means of combatting the economic crisis, to a '*Green New Deal XXL*', which aims to profoundly readjust international, financial, economic and tax structures (Vandaele 2009).

The original ambition of the Green New Deal Group was to offer a policy package of financial re-regulation, the greening of taxation and investment in renewable energy in order to solve simultaneously the credit crisis, climate change and the energy crisis. The report of the group has a certain Keynesian flavour, and seeks to stimulate demand particularly through wages and government spending. The package contains several progressive and democratic demands, such as the introduction of controls on capital flows, tackling tax havens, the cancellation of the debts of millions of individuals and of governments, the introduction of taxes on capital and the realisation of a single corporate tax rate in Europe.

The European green parties gave this policy package a central place in their 2009 European elections campaign. In the words of Bart Staes, a green Member of the European Parliament from Flanders (Belgium):

> By investing 500 billion in renewable energy and green technology across the European Union over the next five years, at least five million sustainable jobs will be created. This is good for future economic growth and good for the fight against climate change.

(Groen 2009)

The name 'Green New Deal' refers, of course, to the New Deal which was introduced in the US in the 1930s under the presidency of Franklin Delano Roosevelt. The New Deal was a turning point in socio-economic policy, which became increasingly Keynesian. It is often claimed that this laid the foundation for the golden 1950s and 60s, a period of economic prosperity and social progress. While the New Deal is sometimes presented as an intelligent set of policy interventions, envisioned by a great politician, Antonio Negri (amongst others) has shown that a crucial element of the New Deal is that the government began to take a new approach regarding the wage demands of workers, as we already argued in Chapter 1 (Negri 1988). Where these had previously been rejected, they were now met to a certain extent by a state pursuing 'planned development' by seeking a balance between the different elements of production and establishing 'an organic relation between the working class and the state' (Negri 2005, 21). As argued by the regulationist school of political economy, by letting part of the growth in productivity flow back to the workers in the form of higher wages, the workers would have more purchasing power to buy the goods they produced. This would make mass production for mass consumption possible, and this mechanism was indeed partly responsible for the enormous economic growth after World War II (Boyer and Saillard 2002, Husson 1999).

This analysis should ring a bell. If green investments and adjustments to the market are aimed at achieving a new cycle of economic growth, will that not lead to an increasing pressure on ecosystems once again? The authors of the Green New Deal are very critical of neoliberalism. But they seem to overlook the fact that the period of economic growth that preceded the neoliberal turn was also ecologically catastrophic. CO_2 emissions in Western Europe increased faster during the period from 1945 to the 1960s than in any other time in history.[3] As we argued in Chapter 3, whether it is green or otherwise, economic growth goes together with an increased pressure on the ecosystem. Of course, it is better that growth is realised through investments in wind turbines than in coal factories, but even green growth requires extra input of energy and materials.

Moreover, the political context today is very different from that of over seventy years ago. The 1930s marked a high point of working-class struggle in the US. Massive factory occupations took place, something that it is hard to imagine happening today. The New Deal was not simply the brainchild of the American president, as it is often presented, but came following pressure from below. This does not mean that the New Deal simply delivered the workers' demands. Far from it: in a sense, the government sought to channel their struggle and to integrate it into a new regime of capital accumulation that appeared to be very successful for several decades. Wage increases forced by the workers became the engine behind a new growth dynamic of capital.

There seems to be a similar role for the 'green economy'. What is at stake this time is to turn ecological struggle into the motor force of a new 'green' regime of capital accumulation, as Mueller and Passadakis have also argued (Mueller and Passadakis 2010, 558). This should entail real social and ecological improvements, at least in theory. However, the question is how far reaching these improvements will be in practice, how democratic they will be and whether they will be enough to turn the tide. Furthermore, such a process also presupposes the depoliticisation of this struggle and its integration into the consensual logic of green economy governance. Partly because of the current weakness of the labour movement and the left more in general, many environmental organisations seem to be easily seduced by new potential allies amongst 'green' and 'socially responsible' businesses. They finally see an opportunity to mainstream their concerns.

Admittedly, different interpretations of the Green New Deal cover very diverse alliances of social and political forces. The poison is often in the practical implementation, and this risks being the case with the original Green New Deal too. Just as with Roosevelt's plans, the Green New Deal report suggests a deal that amounts to about 3.5% of GNP. Roosevelt used public funds, but in the Green New Deal report, we read: 'The Green New Deal will, however, differ from its 1930s predecessor in that there will be a much bigger role for investments from private savings, pensions, banks and insurance' (Green New Deal Group 2008, 35). Moreover, public investments included in the package would be paid for with the proceeds from special eco-taxes and emissions trading. This reliance on mechanisms such as carbon trading is a red thread running through the different variants of the green economy (e.g. UNEP 2011, World Bank 2012a). Therefore, it is to these market mechanisms that we should first turn in order to grasp the core of the green economy.

Defining property rights

To create a favourable context for green investments, UNEP advocates a whole range of policies, including regulation, product standards, taxes and systems of tradable certificates (e.g. cap and trade). While UNEP does not refrain from government regulation, its main focus is on greening the market. 'UNEP's green economy concept contains nothing that could revolutionise the (global) economy, or that could transform the main macroeconomic parameters (money, currency and trade policy) into an eco-social direction,' Barbara Unmüßig from the German Heinrich Böll Stiftung critically concludes (Unmüßig 2012, vi). A similar observation can be made for most other variants of the green economy. In most versions, technological innovation is the alpha and omega of the project (more about this in Chapter 5), which will have to be delivered through market competition. To make sure market competition leads to green results, two elements are key: first, the establishment of new property rights with regard to nature, and second, the correction of market prices in order to account for the value of 'natural capital'.

As is summed up by the World Bank report *Inclusive Green Growth*:

> Much of green growth is about good growth policies, addressing market failures and 'getting the price right' by introducing environmental taxation, pricing environmental externalities (such as carbon pricing), creating tradable property rights, and reducing inappropriate subsidies. These measures

are critical for enabling the private sector to undertake needed investments and innovations and for getting consumers to internalise the true costs of their behavior.

(World Bank 2012a)

We will turn back to this notion of correcting prices below. First, we will delve into the introduction of new property rights which are supposed to enable a better 'management' of natural capital. As the report by the Organisation for Economic Co-operation and Development (OECD) *Towards Green Growth* states: 'Examples of the cost of mismanagement [of natural resources] are perhaps most stark in the case of resources with undefined or unenforced property rights, and incentives to "free-ride"' (OECD 2011, 25). Natural capital can best be managed by establishing clear property rights, which will help avoid overexploitation, so it is suggested. The World Bank report on *Inclusive Green Growth* argues that the inefficient management of natural capital

> stems partly from the fact that many natural resources are common property, so consumption by one person precludes consumption by another, and it is hard to exclude potential users. Open access regimes for common property create incentives to use up such resources as quickly as possible.
>
> (World Bank 2012a, 8)

The paradigm of privatisation, which has been central to World Bank thinking for many decades, is thus reaffirmed, while it is being applied on novel terrains. This call for the introduction of property rights in the environmental domain is not new in itself, but gets a new impetus in green economy projects. One of the most influential articles ever published on the fight against environmental pollution had exactly this theme as its core topic. We refer, of course, to the famous article 'The Tragedy of the Commons', written by Garrett Hardin and published in December 1968 in *Science* (Hardin 1968).

Hardin's starting point is the exact opposite of what we explained in Chapter 3. There, we argued that the privatisation of communal lands helped to lay the foundation of capitalism and the current ecological crisis. Hardin turns this history on its head: according to him, it is not privatisation which leads to ecological crisis, but the fact that too much of nature is still under common ownership.

'Picture a pasture open to all,' Hardin writes. 'It is to be expected that each herdsman will try to keep as many cattle as possible on the commons' (Hardin 1998, 6). According to Hardin, every individual farmer stands to gain from adding an animal to his flock and letting it graze on the common land. The farmer keeps all the profit the additional animal brings him, while the impact of the additional grazing is shared by all the farmers. Because all shepherds will follow this logic, Hardin concludes that the grazed pastures will be bare in next to no time.

Hardin believes that the same applies to different types of environmental pollution: for instance, every individual benefits from dumping her waste, because that is easiest, while the community pays the price. As a consequence, massive amounts of waste are piling up, and a profound ecological crisis is the result. Hardin also addresses 'overpopulation' in his article. As long as everyone is allowed to reproduce freely, many families will benefit from this and 'overbreed' in order to 'secure [their] own aggrandisement', relying on resources provided by the Welfare State (Hardin 1998, 10). As a result, Hardin claims, our natural resources will be rapidly exhausted: a real tragedy. Therefore, he argues not only for giving up the freedom to 'procreate', but also for the privatisation of the commons. If the natural commons would be private property, he argues, at least someone will look after them. Private property is unjust, he acknowledges, but '[i]njustice is preferable to total ruin' (Hardin 1998, 14).

If one accepts Hardin's assumptions, the theory sounds quite robust. But one thing strikes the reader of his article immediately: he offers no empirical evidence at all for his theory! He gives not one historical example of a situation in which his infamous tragedy occurred. His story about shepherds in rural England is purely speculative. It is merely based on a thought experiment. Interestingly, historical research provides a very different story: both in pre-capitalist societies and today, the commons are often managed by local communities in a sustainable manner (e.g. Ostrom 1990, 2010, Wall 2014).

How should we then understand Hardin's article? If one looks a bit closer, Hardin's piece is not about shepherds in rural pre-capitalist England, but about the mentality of growth and profit ingrained in contemporary capitalism. Hardin seems to basically project his own cultural framework on other people, assuming there is a necessary and universal logic underlying human action. He thus misrecognises the contingency and variety of ways in which people can relate to each other and organise society. David Harvey turns Hardin's viewpoint on its head: are the commons really the problem, or is it rather private property? 'If the cattle were held in common,' he argues provocatively, Hardin's 'metaphor would not work.' He concludes: '[t]his shows that it is private property in cattle and individual utility-maximising behaviour that lie at the heart of the problem, rather than the common-property character of the resource' (Harvey 2012, 68).

Hardin's article has become more than an academic exercise. It has underpinned policies of governments and international institutions such as the IMF and the World Bank, and has provided them with scientific legitimacy. In recent decades, large parts of the public sector were privatised around the world, and in many instances principles of private property also became the basis for environmental policy. The green economy project is the current inheritor of this strand of thinking. Even the World Wildlife Fund (WWF) has endorsed similar ideas. 'Until now, natural wealth or capital has been considered as "global commons" and therefore treated as a "free good"', it states on its website, calling for natural capital accounting systems to be set up both by states and by companies (WWF 2012).

This logic can be taken quite far. As Bram Büscher argues, for example, this can ultimately even lead to 'green grabbing': 'the appropriation of land and resources for environmental ends' (Morrissey 2012). This 'happens in many different contexts, from the imposition of protected areas to forest enclosures under REDD schemes' (more about which below). Furthermore, many critical environmentalists are concerned about new developments in intellectual property rights in living species, a topic which is especially relevant in the increasing focus on biomass as an alternative resource for a post-petroleum economy (Attac 2012, ETC-Group 2011, ETC-Group and Heinrich Böll Foundation 2013). At several levels, therefore, new, qualitative steps are being made in the privatisation of nature.

Getting prices right

This brings us to the second point. As we argued above, two elements are core to the project of the green economy: first, the establishment of property rights, and second, correcting market prices. Indeed, if nature is seen as 'natural capital', it ought not only to be 'protected' by its owner, but its use or consumption should also be paid for. The idea is that putting a price on nature's contributions to economic production will lead to an incentive structure which will reduce overconsumption or overexploitation. As the OECD argues, '[i]n the presence of externalities and/or incomplete property rights the economic "value" of natural capital will not be fully reflected in the prices faced by agents in the market, and as a result the natural capital base will be over-exploited' (OECD 2011, 27). To remedy this, nature must be given a price, so the argumentation goes. Basically, this is done in three steps: first, the ecosystem is broken down into specific 'goods' and 'services', second, a price is attached to these, and finally, new markets are created where these goods and services can be bought and sold. The goal is to remediate the problem of the 'externalisation' of the environmental costs we spoke about above.

According to many environmental economists,[4] as long as nature is nobody's possession, the cost of pollution will not be borne by the polluter, but by society at large: the cost is 'externalised'. They consider this a form of market failure, in the sense that the market price does not cover the real environmental cost of a product. In order to adjust the market to make sure it accounts for pollution, it is argued one should put a price on nature. On this basis, the 'real environmental costs' of a certain good or service would be internalised in its price.

At first sight, this might sound perfect. The first problems start to emerge, however, when the principle is being translated into practice. The first question is *how* environmental costs should be 'internalised' in the price. This is not an easy task. To start with, how can one determine the value of nature and thus the cost of pollution? Second, how should one internalise this cost or value in the final price? According to the OECD,

> value is reflected in people's 'willingness-to-pay' – the amount of money an individual is willing to pay for a good or service – or 'willingness-to-accept' – the amount of money an individual is willing to accept as a compensation for [forgoing] a good or service.
>
> (OECD 2011, 27)

Value, in other words, expresses subjective preferences. The World Bank makes a similar argument: 'Environmental valuation,' as the bank calls it, 'estimates people's willingness to pay for environmental goods and services or willingness to accept compensation for the loss of an environmental asset' (World Bank 2012a, 52). However, if value expresses subjective preferences or willingness to pay, one should find ways to determine these. Environmental economists have developed a method to determine nature's value via what they call *contingent valuation studies* (Alberini and Kahn 2006, Burkett 2006, 56 ff, Whittington and Pagiola 2012). Basically, these studies involve interviewing people in order to determine their preferences in relation to the environment. How much compensation do residents think they should receive from a company that pollutes the river along which they live? How much money are people willing to pay to go walking on a Sunday in a local nature reserve, or for the protection of natural resources, such as forests or oceans more generally? Surveys like this are even carried out to estimate how much people are willing to pay to avoid certain risks. On this basis conclusions are drawn regarding, for example, the acceptability of genetically modified organisms (GMOs) (Musk et al. 2005).

The argument goes that the more importance people attach to a healthy environment, the higher will be the price they are willing to pay for it, or vice versa, the more money they want to receive for accepting pollution. In theory, this would lead to an additional cost to polluting companies, which they will pass on to their customers. In this way, the cost of pollution would be 'internalised' in the market price of the final product.

Despite their seemingly scientific nature, such methods are highly questionable. To start with, as Paul Burkett argues, such reasoning contrasts starkly with people's commonsense perception of the problem. As a result, contingent valuation studies often yield hilarious responses (Burkett 2006, 56). In about half of all cases, Burkett shows, economists get a different type of response than the one they expected. Many respondents state they believe there should not be pollution at all, and that this is not something which you can make a financial judgment about. There appears to be a spontaneous resistance both to the tendency to express everything in terms of money and to the idea that it is the individual, rather than society at large, who should take care of this. Expressing nature's worth in monetary terms is indeed a contingent choice. As Neuteleers and Engelen argue, 'converting all goods to a single scale can only be done by favouring one comparative value,' and this is 'inevitably reductionist with regard to the spectrum of values', which also includes aesthetic, health or cultural values, for example (Neuteleers and Engelen 2014, 2).

Furthermore, such a method is inevitably socially biased, as poor people will be much more ready to accept pollution in exchange for some money. It is well documented that poor or coloured people often live in neighbourhoods with higher rates of pollution, which amounts to a form of environmental inequality, or even environmental racism (Keucheyan 2014). Even if they are intended to correct environmental harm, such methods might actually reproduce environmental inequalities.

Finally, the fundamental question is not solved by these efforts to calculate or estimate the price of environmentally destructive practices. As we already argued in Chapter 3, whatever method is used, the real question remains whether it is possible and meaningful at all to put a price on nature and on environmental destruction. Can one ever put a price on the disappearance of a bird species, the destruction of a landscape, or the contamination of ecosystems with GMOs? How can one put a price on system crises such as climate change, desertification, deforestation and acid rain? Even if one would be able to make exact calculations of the factual costs which these crises cause to the economy, the question remains whether 'the price of the crisis' itself is thereby determined.

In a remarkable passage of UNEP's green economy report, it is suggested that carbon markets might represent a solution for finding a correct price for, in this case, carbon. 'Carbon markets comprise one of the key areas of green finance and provide an important discovery mechanism for the price of carbon,' it is stated (UNEP 2011, 599–600). In other words, there *is* a price for carbon – we only need a mechanism to *uncover* it, and this is what carbon trading is supposed to do. The philosophy behind this is that the market *discovers* the price, rather than it being determined, as if the market is a transparent mechanism through which underlying values can be adequately represented. As we showed in Chapter 3, this way of speaking covers up the blindness which is inherent in the market's mode of operation. In a way, it blinds us to the very blindness of the market.

Of course, this critique on putting a price on nature does not suffice to dismiss policies which correct market prices via taxes or subsidies as such. The argument that the incentive structure of economic agents can thus be transformed makes sense. The idea is that as a result, businesses, but also consumers, will spontaneously opt for the most environmentally friendly options. Without any doubt, it is odd that flying from Brussels to Nice is often much cheaper than travelling by bus or by train. In the same way, it is difficult to convince business to opt for renewable instead of fossil fuel energy as long as the latter is cheaper. An adaptation of the cost structure can thus be needed in a number of cases. However, this does not mean that such approaches suffice, or provide the only or best possible method to tackle ecological destruction.

One of the problems relates to the way such measures are often portrayed. As we explained earlier, they are represented in a way that appears neutral, and thus conceals certain things. For example, correcting market prices can have socially unjust effects, depending on how the fiscal burden is distributed. But there is more: the idea that externalities can be completely internalised and market failure can thus be overcome is problematic in itself. The market economy always and by definition relies on practices and (re)production processes which take place outside of the market, and therefore it inevitably externalises certain costs. No future economic activity is possible without the education of children or the development of moral standards or language through everyday interactions. Numerous similar practices are essential preconditions for the market economy. They represent a certain 'cost' for society, but this cost is not expressed in market prices. Even if one would consider this desirable, it is impossible to internalise all such 'costs', especially given the complexity and the non-market nature of many essential social practices. How should we determine the 'cost' of raising children and educating new work forces, which the market now 'externalises' to (mainly) women? How to determine the cost of building a social fabric, including traditions, symbols and forms of morality which hold society together and without which the market could not possibly exist? It is not feasible to put a price on everything, including all aspects of natural and human life, through processes of market valuation.

The point is that the market and society can never completely coincide, as Karl Polanyi showed: the market can only hold sway when embedded in the larger context of society, even though it tends to disembed itself from society (Polanyi 2001). The crises which result from the latter attempt testify to the fact that the market never suffices on itself and that it always needs non-market social relations as its precondition. When it starts to integrate these relations within its own logic, by giving them a price or commodifying them and thus turning them into market relations, it threatens to destroy these relations.

We should be wary, therefore, of the idea that a market equilibrium without externalities can be restored through the correct pricing of all possible goods and services. There is always a sphere outside of the market to which certain costs are externalised, and to which the market stands in a tense relation. As we want to argue in this book, we cannot solve this by expanding the reach of the market. This tension is there to remain, and we have to acknowledge it and deal with it in a political way, by recognising that clashing values are at stake (more about this in Chapter 6).

A similar, political approach should be adopted to the issue of climate debt. The attempt to develop some kind of accounting system that could help calculate the economic value of ecological debt is not without merit, but we should not be mistaken about what is the real, political stake of the concept (Sharife and Bond 2013, Simms 2005). The notion of ecological debt should be understood as a critique of the way the global political and economic system is organised with a view to radically transforming it. It does not just underpin an invoice which the global South presents to the global North, and which the latter could ever pay back as if a normal indemnisation were involved.

As we already stated, this critique of the idea that nature can be correctly priced is not to suggest that adjusting the incentive structure is meaningless as such. Yet, there is not only the difficulty or even impossibility to decide which prices should be put on environmental goods and services, it is also an illusion to think that thereby all problems would be solved and market equilibrium restored. Suggesting it is possible to put a 'right' price on nature or natural destruction has deeply depoliticising effects: it suggests that a neutral, technical or scientific solution for market failures is possible. More precisely, the suggestion is that there is indeed one right solution. We would argue, instead, that we are dealing here with deeply political choices: both the decision to correct prices as such and the magnitude of their correction are contingent and value laden. They are far from neutral, and involve important distributional effects.

Indeed, the problem is that within the logic of correcting prices, sustainability remains subordinated to the criterion of cost-effectiveness. Even when prices are adjusted, a business will only make a change to its ways of working if the costs of the environmental taxes are higher than the benefits of producing polluting products. This means not only that business practices will immediately turn back to business-as-usual on the moment the cost-benefits calculation (for whatever reason) changes again. It also means that mostly relatively high prices have to be put on pollution if one really wants to change the cost-benefits calculation. As we will show below, this could have such a far-reaching effect on many existing industries that economic shocks might result, at least as long as we remain within a market framework. Not surprisingly, this is something most politicians and policymakers are very reluctant to risk.

Balancing values: the climate and the market

One of the most influential statements of the economic importance of tackling climate change is the famous report drafted by the British economist Nicholas Stern and commissioned by the Blair government (Stern 2006). Stern's conclusion is clear: it costs much less to implement ambitious policies to address climate change than to pay for the damage caused by all kinds of climatic disasters in the future. Stern initially believed that about 1% of global GDP per year would be needed to limit climate change. In 2008, when it transpired that the Earth is warming much faster than expected, Stern raised this to 2%. In comparison, Stern estimates that coping with the impacts of climate change in the future will cost up to 20% of global GDP. Stern's conclusion is very clear: 'Tackling climate change is the pro-growth strategy for the longer term' (Stern 2006, viii).

Even if this economic approach could convince some actors to take action on climate change, Stern's approach is not as neutral as it may seem. Many climate scientists, including the Intergovernmental Panel on Climate Change (IPCC), have argued that it is important to limit global warming to a maximum of 2°C. If we go above this threshold, we risk runaway climate change.[5] The question is therefore what should be done to keep temperature rises below this threshold. Environmental economists, in contrast, ask a very different question, namely 'how much' climate change is 'economically optimal'. Their criterion is cost effectiveness, not the sustainability of human, let alone non-human, life as such. Basically, this means that they accept that our society is causing climate change and that this entails a cost. This cost is not considered as a problem, as long as the economic benefits are higher. In other words, you need to weigh up the relative costs of different scenarios.

Even if this would be an appropriate approach (which we think it is not), weighing up different scenarios is not as easy as it might seem. First, one has to know how to express the consequences of climate change in economic terms. And second, complex calculations are needed to determine the costs of taking action. It is only when the expected costs of dealing with the impacts of climate change exceed the costs of climate mitigation and adaptation that measures will be taken.

According to most environmental economists, the ideal measure is to put a price on CO_2, which would enable businesses and consumers to 'spontaneously' make green choices. As we pointed out before, the key question is how high that price should be. On the one hand, the price of carbon must be high enough to ensure that businesses and consumers do make climate-friendly choices. On the other hand, from a market standpoint, the price should not be too high, because this could lead to economic turbulence and even crisis.

As Tanuro points out, in his famous report Stern proposes a climate target of 500 to 550 parts per million CO_2 equivalent (ppm CO_2eq), while the IPCC aims at 445 to 490 ppm CO_2eq (Tanuro 2006). How can this difference be explained? A greater reduction in emissions entails risks for the normal functioning of the market, Stern admits: '[d]igging down to emissions reductions of 60–80% or more relative to baseline will require progress in reducing emissions from industrial processes, aviation, and a number of areas where it is presently hard to envisage cost-effective approaches' (Stern 2006, 247). Stern also believes that '[p]aths requiring very rapid emissions cuts are unlikely to be economically viable' (Stern 2006, 203). Stern thus seems to warn against economic shocks if one would put forward more ambitious emission reduction goals (Foster, Clark and York 2010, 155). He prefers a gradual, market-driven transition to a low-carbon economy.

But in view of such a gradual transition, Stern initially disregarded the figures the IPCC put forward (Tanuro 2006). According to Stern, only the 550 ppm target would be economically feasible because 'it is difficult to secure emission cuts faster than about 1% per year except in instances of recession' (Stern 2006, 204). However, according to climate scientists, we must aim for annual reduction scenarios of 2% in order to keep atmospheric CO_2 concentrations below the 450 ppm threshold which is needed to limit global warming to 2°C (e.g. Kasibhatla and Chameides 2007). This suggests that holding on to market mechanisms makes it virtually impossible to reduce CO_2 emissions quickly enough. In more recent work, Stern acknowledges that a higher target is needed, and advocates a global target of 500 ppm CO_2eq (450 ppm CO_2) (Stern 2009). But in the meantime, a number of climate scientists also adapted their views. For instance, James Hansen suggests that even this latter figure is too high, as he advocates a limit of 350 ppm CO_2. In a 2013 interview, Stern acknowledges: 'Looking back, I underestimated the risks. The planet and the atmosphere seem to be absorbing less carbon than we expected, and emissions are rising pretty strongly. Some of the effects are coming through more quickly than we thought then' (Stewart and Elliott 2013). The longer decisive action on the climate is postponed, the greater the tension will become between the radical transformations required to stabilise the climate, and the gradual changes of prices which the market can tolerate.

As we stressed already several times, the price mechanism can, of course, make a difference. The massive rise in oil prices in the 1970s encouraged many countries to become more energy efficient. However, when oil prices fell again, these plans were immediately shelved (Verbruggen 2008). The problem is thus how to hold the price of carbon high enough. The point is that in order to stop climate change, the price might need to be so high that this could cause serious economic shocks and even recession. Yvo de Boer, former executive secretary of the UN

Framework Convention on Climate Change (UNFCCC), in 2012 advocated a carbon price of €150 per tonne CO_2 (EurActiv 2012). Compared with the average carbon price of €4–7 per tonne in the emissions trading system in 2013, this is huge. According to a 2014 World Bank report, the majority of prices of CO_2 in carbon taxation systems are below $35 (about €27) per tonne (World Bank 2014, 18). In a recent report, Stern and Dietz argue the price of carbon should be between $32 and $103 per tonne in 2015, and should increase to between $82 and $260 per tonne CO_2. 'Doing so,' they argue, would 'keep the expected atmospheric stock of carbon dioxide to a maximum of c. 425–500ppm' (Dietz and Stern 2014, 22).

Others argue that to generate sufficient changes in certain sectors, the price should even rise to hundreds of euros per tonne CO_2. As a report of the UN Department of Economic and Social Affairs states:

> With respect to individual behaviour, calculations done by MacKay (2008) suggest that only with very high carbon prices would there be a noticeable impact on activities like driving and flying. For instance, he concluded that at $150 per ton, domestic users of gas would notice the cost of carbon in their heating bills; a price of $250 per ton would increase the effective cost of a barrel of oil by $100; at $370, carbon pollution would cost enough to significantly reduce people's inclination to fly; and at $900, driving habits might be significantly changed.
>
> (UN 2011, 48)

Moreover, the longer the imposition of a carbon price is delayed, the higher the price will have to be to realise the steeper CO_2 reductions which will be needed to prevent runaway climate change. It is to be feared that such mechanisms will generate economic, and therefore social, shocks.

Carbon trading

In a 2014 report, the World Bank argues that 'about 40 countries and over 20 sub-national jurisdictions are putting a price on carbon. Together, these carbon pricing instruments cover almost 6 gigatons of carbon dioxide equivalent (GtCO2e) or about 12% of the annual global [greenhouse gas] emissions' (World Bank 2014, 14). A major role in this is played by carbon trading.

The idea originally comes from the US, where so-called flexible mechanisms had been used in the 1970s to tackle air pollution (Bernier 2008). The government had enacted the Clean Air Act in 1963, but many companies failed to follow the rules. As a response, the rules were relaxed: it was no longer a problem if a factory caused too much pollution, as long as this was compensated by other, more modern and less polluting factories belonging to the same company elsewhere. This was the first time the principle of *offsetting* of pollution was introduced.

In 1990, a further step was taken, this time in the name of the fight against sulphur dioxide, which causes acid rain. The then US government decided to issue companies emission licenses which they could trade. The idea was the following: suppose two companies each emit too much, but one company has a possibility to reduce emissions in a cheaper way than the other. From an economic point of view it is more profitable that this company makes the necessary investments, and sells the surplus emission licenses it thus acquires to the other company. The overall pollution targets would in this way be achieved at the lowest cost, at least in theory.

These experiments remained on a relatively small scale. But the precedent was set, and it was no coincidence that the US, represented by Al Gore, lobbied heavily for the principle of emissions trading to be included in the Kyoto Protocol (which the US did not ratify in the end). This happened notwithstanding the fact that European measures against sulphur dioxide, based on government regulation, had proven much more effective: emissions in Europe decreased by 87% in the 1990s, while the US system accounted for a decrease of only 31% (Bond 2012, 38).

Since then, a number of carbon trading systems have been up and running. In 2013, the World Bank reports, no less than eight new carbon markets were launched (World Bank 2014, 15). The most well-known carbon trading system is, of course, the EU Emission Trading System (ETS). It is extraordinarily complex, but broadly speaking, it works as follows.[6] States are given an emissions reduction target on the basis of international negotiations. National governments then publish a list of installations and factories on their territory that produce greenhouse gases, such as power plants, steel mills, cement factories and so on. Each of these companies will be given a certain number of allowances (often on the basis of negotiations with the government), with one allowance corresponding to the emission of one tonne of CO_2 (or CO_2 equivalent).[7] Companies must then be able to present an allowance for every tonne of CO_2 they emit. If they emit more than the number of allowances they received, they have to buy additional allowances on the international market from other companies. If they emit less, they can sell the excess allowances and make an additional profit. This is called a *cap and trade* system: first, a limit is set to the amount of emissions that may be emitted (cap), and these emissions can then be traded (trade). The *cap* is reduced each year, so as to gradually decrease total emissions.

The operation of the EU ETS predates the actual launch of the UNFCCC Kyoto Protocol, but integrated key aspects of it, notably the two 'flexible mechanisms' the protocol established. The first is called Joint Implementation (JI), and involves setting up projects in a number of former Soviet bloc countries to reduce CO_2 emissions. Since these industrial facilities are often outdated and emit more than those in the West, this can be done relatively cheaply. In addition, there is the Clean Development Mechanism (CDM), which focuses on developing countries, where emissions reduction can often be achieved at an advantageous price. Projects realised within the Joint Implementation and the Clean Development Mechanism frameworks allow countries or companies to acquire additional carbon credits. They can use these extra credits to offset their own emissions, or they can sell them on the international carbon market.

In itself, the launch of the EU ETS and the Kyoto Protocol appeared promising. The initial targets were too low and the timing too slow, but carbon trading had at least the merit of putting forward quantified targets and strict deadlines. From an ecological point of view, the cap is crucial, as it sets a strict limit on the amount of CO_2 that can be emitted. This is an advantage compared with taxes, which in theory allow continued pollution, as long as the polluter is willing to pay.

But very soon, the system started to reveal its flaws. These were related both to how it was practically implemented and to intrinsic problems of the cap and trade principle. The theory behind it appears quite ingenious at a first glance. It does not actually matter to the climate how or where greenhouse gas emissions are reduced. It seems logical therefore to realise reductions where they can be achieved most economically. Instead of forcing companies to achieve the reduction targets themselves, they can choose where and how they do this. If companies prefer not to modify their own installations, they can always set up projects elsewhere to offset their emissions, or they can purchase additional allowances on the market. Technically speaking and considered from the perspective of climate science, this is completely correct. But there are some snakes in the grass.

When the system was launched in 2005, about 12,000 sites in Europe received a total of 2.19 billion allowances. Especially energy-intensive industries were covered by the system, such as cement, oil refineries, iron and steel production, paper and glass (though the system also excluded some heavily polluting sectors such as transport and aviation). Because such a large number of plants are involved, advocates of emissions trading claim that it is impossible for the government to directly regulate all of them. It would therefore be better to leave it to the industry itself to decide what action to take. However, in France, for example, at least 83% of total emissions were produced by only 18% of the installations (Bernier 2008, 39). Almost half of the emissions (46%) came from only 21 installations. Critics argue that government regulation, coupled with a good inspection regime, would be much easier in such a situation.

There is obviously more at stake behind the choice to opt for the emissions trading approach. It is not so much a matter of efficiency, but involves a real societal choice. Who has the initiative? Who is driving climate politics? These are the key questions. Is it the government or corporations, democracy or the market? Do we realise a sustainability transition by taking decisions following a social and political or an economic rationality? For the proponents of emissions trading, ultimate decision-making power on investments should lie with business owners. The only relevant criteria are cost efficiency and profitability.

The fact that private actors thus acquire a central role in the system has profound political implications which remain concealed behind an economic and technical discourse. For a start, it is quite remarkable that it is the companies that historically polluted which received emissions allowances from their governments. In other words, companies that have contributed to climate change in the past are not sanctioned for having emitted huge quantities of greenhouse gases. On the contrary, they received free allowances in proportion to their actual emissions on the date when the EU ETS came into force. Indeed, initially industries were given a number of allowances on the basis of their actual level of emissions, as they reported these themselves.

A measure such as carbon trading is never merely technical. It always embodies a conception of how society should be organised. It could have made sense, for example, to allocate each citizen an equal amount of allowances, which companies would have to buy if they wanted to emit CO_2. Such an approach would at least have vindicated the principle of equality. The principles underpinning EU ETS, in contrast, stand in radical contrast to this. The system not only distributes allowances unequally, but also introduces an apparently new principle in environmental policy: not 'the polluter pays,' but 'the polluter earns,' as it is only the polluter who receives free allowances.

At the start of the EU ETS, companies in most European countries (excluding Denmark, Hungary, Ireland and Lithuania, where auctioning took place) were given permits for free. More than 95% of allowances were distributed for free in the period 2005–2007, and at least 90% in 2007–2012 (Vlachou 2014). In 2013, an important shift took place: about 40% of allowances were auctioned, an amount which is set to increase gradually, as a response to the fierce critique of the free distribution of emission permits. Critics argue that auctioning is a much more just and environmentally favourable option. As a response, the EU intends to completely phase out free allocation in favour of auctioning, but only by 2027.

Attempts to modify the system in that direction were fiercely opposed by industry lobbies. Companies argue that if they would have to pay for allowances, *carbon leakage* would be the result. Carbon leakage is the phenomenon whereby companies move to countries without or with less strong climate regulation. The result is that while emissions in the original country might fall, they would remain roughly the same overall or possibly even increase. Although the risk of carbon leakage is real, it is often overblown by lobbyists in order to ward off environmental regulation (Gilbertson and Reyes 2009, 47). Interestingly, the rate of auctioning applied in different sectors seems to express their relative power positions. The aviation sector, for example, will have only 15% of its allowances auctioned in the period 2013–2020.[8]

At the beginning of the EU ETS, emissions allowances were not only given out for free, but too many were distributed. In the first phase, the surplus amounted to 5.6% of allowances, leading to falling prices once market actors became aware of this overallocation (Vlachou 2014, 130). In April 2006 a tonne of CO_2 still cost about €30. By the end of that month, when it became known that there were too many allowances on the market, the price dropped to €11 in the space of a week (Lohmann 2006, 88). In February 2007, a tonne of CO_2 was worth less than €1.[9] Evidently, the overallocation of allowances and their volatile prices do not stimulate companies to plan long-term investments in cleaner technology. Therefore, one of the main objectives of the system seemed to be put in jeopardy from the very beginning.

This overallocation should not come as a surprise, given the fact that businesses and governments had to indicate themselves how many allowances they needed. This method naturally opens the door to all kinds of behind the scenes lobbying and manoeuvring. What happened in Lithuania, for example, is a case in point (Gilbertson and Reyes 2009, 38). The EU had requested that an old nuclear reactor, which used the same technology as in Chernobyl, would be shut down. The Lithuanian government demanded, in turn, that it should be given additional allowances for the coal plants that would replace the nuclear power station. The government exaggerated the number of allowances needed, as a result of which Lithuania acquired a large surplus of allowances. In fact, only 3 of the 93 Lithuanian installations falling under the EU ETS emitted more CO_2 than they had received allowances for. All others had a surplus which they could sell on the market.

Many such practical problems soon came to the surface. The system's proponents argue these were childhood diseases which could be cured. However, the complexity and intransparency of the system make it very liable for fraud and all kinds of operational problems, which should be a warning for green economy proponents who want to establish similar mechanisms in other terrains.

A number of big polluting companies have been able to make huge extra profits thanks to the system. In 2005 alone, the European steel industry made a tidy €480 million additional profit by selling surplus allowances. A company like ArcelorMittal could cash in significantly under this system. Its emissions rose by 6.7% in 2006 and 15.5% in 2007 before decreasing by 8.4% in 2008 as a result of the economic crisis. But the company consistently obtained more allowances than it needed: an excess of 36.9% in 2005, 26.9% in 2006, 25% in 2007 and 31.7% in 2008 (Gilbertson and Reyes 2009, 43). Between 2008 and 2012, it received 435.57 million emission rights from eight governments, an overallocation which was aimed at avoiding steel plants from closing down and represented a potential windfall profit of €808 million (Belga 2014).

Electricity producers play a special role in this story. They have been able to pass on the price of the allowances to their customers, even if they obtained these for free (World Bank 2012a, 48). In the first phase of the European emissions trading system, the cost of electricity increased by €10–20 per megawatt hour as a result (Lohmann 2006, 92). In 2008, British families paid on average £117 for EU ETS, especially due to higher electricity prices (Vlachou 2014, 141). A study by the WWF estimates that the additional profits that the European energy sector made in this way during the second phase of the Kyoto Protocol (2008–2012) totals €23–71 billion (PointCarbon 2008).

The emissions trading system can also change companies' business strategies. In addition to their actual production, several companies developed a new profitable activity by trading and speculating in emission rights. In a certain way, emission allowances represent a new type of security or money (Descheneau 2012). The tradable quotas which are issued under EU ETS and are called European Union Allowances (EUAs) can be traded on the stock exchange and even speculated upon. A company like ArcelorMittal knows how to engage creatively with this opportunity. Since the 1990s it has been one of the many multinationals with a separate financial department specifically concerned with investment and speculation in financial markets. Its activities are increasingly orientated towards the carbon market. For such companies, CO_2 is no longer a waste product, but an investment. It is a sort of by-product, around which all sorts of profit-making strategies can be developed. For example, one can threaten to delocalise, in order to get extra allowances from the government (which has actually happened in a number of countries, as argued above). One can also reduce polluting activities in a country that is within the ETS, and compensate for this by additional production in a country that falls outside this system. The allowances that are released by reducing the pollution in the first country can then be sold at a profit on the stock market, while the total amount of emissions does not change.

Especially since the financial crisis, the EU ETS system has been in crisis due to a surplus of allowances in the system. In 2013–2014, prices of allowances within EU ETS were historically low: about €4 to €7. Prices of 'certified emissions reductions' or CDM credits (about which more below) were only about €0.37, as a result of which many companies started to exit the CDM market. The EU has attempted to address this crisis by postponing ('backloading') the auctioning of a number of allowances, and aims at establishing a 'market stability reserve' at the beginning of a new trading period in 2021.

Although the infrastructure set up through the Kyoto Protocol is in crisis (with several countries pulling out), the principle of cap and trade is nevertheless slowly gaining acceptance. In terms of the amount of greenhouse gases covered, the biggest market is still the EU ETS, with a cap at 2,084 megatons of carbon dioxide equivalent in 2013, but it is closely followed by a market of 1,115 megatons of carbon dioxide equivalent in China.

Carbon colonialism?

How will developing countries acquire access to sufficient resources and technologies to also keep their emissions within limits? This is a key question in any international climate agreement. During the Kyoto negotiations, the Brazilian government proposed to set up a clean development fund. The fund would be financed using fines imposed upon countries that did not meet their emissions targets, and would be used to help developing countries towards a sustainable path. The US, however, did not want any penalties, and suggested an alternative: countries that were not able to reduce their emissions sufficiently would instead have to invest in green technologies and other projects in the global South. This system would allow countries to *offset* their own emissions, and would therefore create a win-win-win situation: for companies, for the global South and for the climate. This proposal paved the way for the *Clean Development Mechanism* to be included in the Kyoto Protocol. Interestingly, a key role in this process was played by Al Gore, who would himself later become a major player in the emissions trading market. 'Most of the other governments insisted that the cuts be made at home,' writes British journalist George Monbiot on the Kyoto negotiations. 'But Gore demanded a series of loopholes big enough to drive a Hummer through' (Monbiot 2007).

Once again, at first glance, the principle seems to make sense: to reduce emissions in Europe by a tonne of CO_2 requires an average of €80 in investment (Bernier 2008, 65). In China, some projects are able to achieve the same reduction for €3 per tonne. Climate-wise it makes no difference where emissions are reduced. So, why would you not do it in China? Moreover, as CDM credits can usually be bought more cheaply than allowances within the EU ETS, clever investment and trading strategies can yield a handsome profit.

Various projects are eligible for CDM credits: the replacement of fossil fuels with renewable energy in industrial facilities, methane capture, re-afforestation, construction of wind turbines or hydropower, etcetera.[10] Nuclear energy is excluded. But the construction of a gas-fired power station, with lower emissions than a coal plant, for example, is not. The profits from these investments are twofold, as one can sell electricity and acquire emission rights. One can even get CDM credits for investments in new coal plants, provided that the technology emits less CO_2 than the norm.[11] This is remarkable at the very least: a Western company can offset its own emissions by investing in the construction of coal plants, which, although they are more efficient than average, will still emit large quantities of CO_2 over the coming decades.

The philosophy behind CDM is that it should benefit the development of poor regions. However, according to figures from UNEP, in 2012 only 2.9% of the projects were implemented in Africa, which has the greatest development needs, compared with more than 80% in Asia and the Pacific. Within Asia, more than 70% of CDM credits issued go to China. In 2012, only about 26% of all CDM carbon credits had been allocated to renewable energy projects.[12] The bulk of these were generated by hydroelectric plants involving large dams (which often have detrimental social and ecological effects). Only 0.12% went to solar energy projects. Remarkably, 54% of the total amount of credits went to projects aiming to reduce emissions of nitrous oxide and gases such as hydrofluorocarbons (HFCs).

Especially around the gas HFC-23, there has been a lot of controversy. HFC-23 is a very strong greenhouse gas: 11,700 times the power of CO_2. It is released during the production of refrigerant gases (which are used in the manufacture of refrigerators) and Teflon (which serves as a non-stick coating for pots and pans). Since a carbon certificate is equivalent to one tonne of CO_2, the destruction of one tonne of HFC-23 delivers 11,700 emission credits.

Many companies have funded HFC-23 CDM projects, as there is a lot of money to be made.[13] The destruction of one tonne of HFC-23 costs a lot less than avoiding more than 10,000 tonnes of CO_2 emissions. This evidently explains the high percentage of HFC-23 projects within CDM: in 2012, about 35% of CDM credits went to such projects.

When the controversy around this gas erupted in 2007, HFC-23 processing had led to around €4.7 billion worth of allowances (Harvey 2008, Wara 2007). However, the installations required to capture and destroy this HFC-23 had cost a mere €100 million in total. This means that a number of companies had been able to make €4.6 billion in profit through CDM projects involving this gas.

This business was even so profitable that refrigerator manufacturing in Asia boomed. It seemed HFC-23 was no longer a by-product of the production of refrigerators, but it was produced in order to gain emission rights via the Clean Development Mechanism. The profits that could be achieved through CDM proved far higher than those made with the production of refrigerant gases or Teflon itself. This scandal threatened to put the CDM in such a bad light that eventually it was decided that factories that were built after 2004 had to be excluded from the system. Older plants have still been able to reap additional profits after this intervention.

What does the destruction of HFC-23 deliver for the climate? This is not only a scientific problem. Also from a social and political point of view, one may wonder whether CO_2 and HFC-23 can be made equivalent. The fact that so much CO_2 is emitted is the result of an entire economic system which is based on fossil fuels. In contrast, HFC-23 is a specific product that is released by certain industrial processes. These are two totally different things. It would be much simpler, and better for the environment, if governments simply regulated HFC-23 emissions, just as happened with gases that deplete the ozone layer. Furthermore, offsetting CO_2 emissions from European factories by processing HFC-23 in India is extremely problematic if our aim is to get rid of the fossil fuel system. Such practices actually extend the life of that system even longer.

Processing HFC-23 does not in any way contribute to the transition to a society that is no longer dependent on fossil fuels. In fact, that is also the fundamental flaw in the whole system of emissions trading, as we already suggested in Chapter 2. It equalises things which in fact are completely different in social terms: CO_2 emissions from a steel plant, CO_2 absorbed by newly planted forests or emissions of industrial gases avoided by processing HFC-23, CO_2 emitted by a hospital or by an artificial ski slope. These all have the same value within the logic of emissions trading. But socially and ecologically, they are obviously completely different. In recent years, numerous steam and gas power stations (combined cycle gas turbines [CCGTs]) were built in China, which enabled companies to acquire carbon credits through the CDM.[14] These carbon credits are worth the same as those acquired by companies engaged in the construction of wind farms in Morocco. But the two projects differ as clearly as day and night: the construction of wind turbines is a step towards a society that is no longer dependent on fossil fuels, while the construction of CCGTs represents just a small change within the fossil fuel system, which is kept in place. These are fundamentally different social and political choices, but they are hidden behind the game of emissions trading, where only the number of emission credits acquired counts. If there is one mechanism through which fundamental political choices and stakes are evaded, then this is it.

This depoliticisation is a problem not only of offsetting, but also of carbon trading as such. Indeed, all allowances within EU ETS represent the same value, but not all activities emitting CO_2 are equivalent, at least not from a social and political point of view. In this sense, the distribution of allowances is not a neutral affair. If it turns out that big oil companies are able to make additional profit while public utilities or institutions (including universities, as was the case in the UK) have to buy extra allowances on the market, this reveals social, ethical and political tensions which ought to be the object of public debate about society's priorities (Open Europe 2006).

In Chapter 3, we referred to the 'real abstraction' operated by the logic of capital, which blinds us to certain (qualitative) realities. What carbon trading basically does is to bring this process of abstraction to an even higher level. It not only makes everything quantitatively equal, but it also dissolves processes or things in order to turn specific aspects of it into a commodity. In this case, a production process is disaggregated into a number of aspects, one of which (the fact that it emits CO_2) becomes a commodity.

This opens the door for a mode of representation of the world which makes it possible to circumvent the fundamental question, namely how to make the transition to a society that is no longer dependent on fossil fuels. Instead, a quantitative and abstract logic sets in, which is about the search for the cheapest CO_2 reductions. It is to be predicted that this search leads to completely other results than rationally organising a transition to a sustainable future.

Teething problems?

In principle, projects can only get CDM accreditation if they would not have occurred in the absence of the scheme. This criterion of additionality is a sound principle, but it is extremely difficult to monitor. To give one example, one tonne of CO_2 saved by building a wind turbine in, say, Brazil, is intended to offset one tonne of CO_2 emitted in a French coal-fired power plant. This is based on the presumption that if these wind turbines had not been built in Brazil, then power plants based on fossil fuels would have been built instead. But does this make sense? How can one offset European emissions by preventing what may have taken place on the other side of the world in a business-as-usual scenario? Actual emissions here in Europe are considered equivalent to potential emissions in the future in Brazil. Total emissions will not decrease because of such practices. At best, emissions may grow less rapidly than could be otherwise expected in a business-as-usual scenario. But how can one know what that scenario would look like? This is one aspect of how abstraction makes us blind: as if one can exactly calculate and predict what the business-as-usual scenario would have given.

Seventy-six percent of the projects approved by the CDM Executive Agency before 1 October 2008 were at the time of approval already in operation (Gilbertson and Reyes 2009, 54). This suggests that they would have occurred anyway, whether or not the CDM existed. More fundamentally, there is an intrinsic problem with the criterion of additionality that is used by the CDM Executive Agency. As Larry Lohmann argues, '[s]cientifically speaking, there is no such thing as "additionality" or "non-additionality", and thus no standard that either market participants or regulators could use either to clarify the accounting rules or to prevent scamming' (Lohmann 2010, 5). The criterion is inevitably vague, although it is portrayed as if it would be technically precise.

The importance of the CDM should not be underestimated. The Kyoto Protocol states that CDM credits may be used to only a limited extent to offset emissions and that the greatest efforts must therefore be done domestically. However, this principle is often ignored in practice. In May 2009, the EU claimed that the emissions from the sectors covered by the EU ETS were 3.06% lower than in 2007. This is a reduction of approximately 50 million tonnes of CO_2. However, closer examination revealed that this figure was achieved by the inclusion of 80 million carbon credits from CDM projects (and to a lesser extent JI projects) (Gilbertson and Reyes 2009, 41). Although flexible mechanisms such as the CDM were originally intended to play only a limited role, in practice they have turned out to be very important. As a result, it is to be feared that 'the CDM/ JI credits might be quite close to the reduction target, limiting domestic action' (Vlachou 2014, 134). Since the onset of the crisis of the carbon trading system, due to the glut of allowances available, the importance of CDM has dwindled. Still, its underlying principle continues to be part of the DNA of green economy discourses.

It is sometimes argued that these are all teething problems, and that a distinction should be made between 'good' and 'bad' CDM projects. And indeed, a number of reforms have been undertaken to correct the system, including the problems with regard to processing HFC-23. At the same time, however, all over the world resistance has been mounted by local inhabitants against offsetting projects, and not only against the 'bad' ones involving industrial gases. From the construction of new coal plants to the creation of forests on agricultural land, from the maintenance of harmful landfills in view of energy production to the building of waste incinerators, from large hydropower plants to projects involving the use of biomass: a significant number of offsetting projects generates forms of injustice or disempowerment which trigger legitimate popular resistance (Böhm and Dabhi 2009, 2).[15]

What we again witness is that the abstraction operated by the carbon trading system is incapable of accounting for complex social and political realities. The way carbon credits are calculated is based on a social and political construction which is only neutral or technical at first sight, but which hides deeply political choices. Indeed, what 'offsetting', emissions reduction, development or sustainability mean is inevitably the object of contestation.

Save a forest

Similar controversy exists around Reducing Emissions from Deforestation and forest Degradation (REDD), a mechanism developed to reduce deforestation and one of the most contentious points of discussion within the framework of the UN negotiations on climate change. Without any doubt, the conservation of existing forests is crucial in the fight against climate change: deforestation contributes more to climate change than does the global transportation sector (all cars, planes, lorries, trains and ships included). However, a number of companies and investment funds have sensed here an opportunity to acquire carbon credits from forest conservation and in doing so turn a handsome profit. The cost of planting or not exploiting a forest is usually much lower than the value of credits on the international markets (Tanuro 2010, 168). A small investment can thus quickly bring in a lot of money.

Saving the existing forests is extremely important. But if it becomes part of the market game, by being turned into the centerpiece of systems based on the principle of payment for ecosystem services (PES), or even markets for ecosystems services (MES), it might generate a number of negative effects.

Significantly, because of these mechanisms, REDD is no longer merely about protecting and preserving nature. It is increasingly about producing and marketing nature. Through REDD and the Clean Development Mechanism, planting a forest could yield carbon credits. One of the problems is that in this way, forests are reduced to forms of carbon storage. The 'nature' that is so produced might turn out to be a poor form of nature: monocultures of fast-growing trees, resulting in biodiversity loss, soil depletion and erosion. In other words, it is abstract nature corresponding to the abstraction process involved in offsetting.

In this process, 'nature' is capitalised more than ever, and in a very particular way becomes part of capital itself. This is not an innocent process. As we showed, capitalism has a tendency to intervene ever more deeply in ecosystems, but here we see that a qualitative leap is being made. 'Nature' is no longer a source of raw materials or a sink where one can dump waste, but has become *the product itself*. Capitalist companies are now actually creating 'nature' as a commodity (Smith 2006). The result is that this (often very poor form of) 'nature' becomes subject to the laws of capitalism, which, over time, goes through periods of boom and bust. In times of crisis, companies go bankrupt, and large numbers of workers lose their jobs. Crises are times when capital destruction takes place on a large scale. Until now, economic crises often led to a decrease in pollution, simply because economic growth was faltering. Now the opposite is possibly to happen: when companies that produce 'nature' go bankrupt, there is a threat that capital destruction will be accompanied by the destruction of nature.

But REDD also causes problems within the emissions trading system itself. There is a fear that the introduction of REDD into the system will increase the number of carbon credits on the market tremendously. This threatens to put further pressure on the price of carbon. REDD could 'undermine the whole carbon market', according to European Climate Commissioner Connie Hedegaard, who in recent years has been a strong advocate of European emissions trading (Cheam 2010). In fact, this is also a more fundamental problem with the CDM: it introduces additional allowances into the system, on top of those that are distributed to companies by governments. In other words, it bursts the cap on emissions, or pushes it up to a higher level. This not only creates a downward pressure on the price of allowances, it also puts one of the few positive elements of emissions trading under pressure (Bernier 2008, 43).

Cash

Emissions trading was a very fast growing market until 2011, representing a total value of $176 billion in that year, after which the system got into a crisis (World Bank 2012b). The EU ETS represents the lion's share of it. As already stated, if there is a successor to the Kyoto Protocol, then this market could become within a decade the size of the financial derivatives market, which is currently the largest in the world. It is not surprising, therefore, that large banks such as BNP Paribas Fortis, Morgan Stanley, Barclays Capital and Deutsche Bank have all become active on carbon markets.

It is striking that the main buyers of CDM credits are often large companies and states or institutions such as the EU or the World Bank.[16] In fact, a government can have only two motives for doing this: to speculate on profits made from CDM projects, or to avoid efforts at home and deliver additional carbon credits to national industry. Such practices are therefore a tool for many states to discreetly support their own businesses.

Several exchanges specialised in emissions trading have been set up during the last decade, including the Chicago Climate Exchange (which closed in 2010) and the European Climate Exchange in the City of London. There are even specific carbon rating agencies.[17] In these markets, the same mechanisms are used as in the financial markets. For instance, there is extensive trading in derivatives such as futures and options, and arguments are made to go further. Blythe Masters, who previously worked for JP Morgan and is the inventor of the infamous credit default swaps (which were at the centre of the financial crisis), advocated a few years ago that more complex financial derivatives such as swaps should also be allowed in emissions trading (Teather 2008). This would enable carbon credits to be repackaged several times into a new financial product and be resold (Kassenaar 2009).

Before the crisis of the carbon trading system fully set in, modest steps were also made in this direction. Shortly after the outbreak of the financial crisis, some hedge funds started to shift capital towards carbon markets as they could not find profitable outlets elsewhere (Kwong 2008). New, complex financial products were created, amongst which were structured products. These products function according to the same principles as collateralised debt obligations (CDOs), which played a key role in triggering the financial crisis in the US. One such product was issued by Credit Suisse, for example. It was composed of 25 offset projects in different countries and at various stages of approval by the CDM Executive Board. There is, of course, a risk that the carbon reduction projects which generate the carbon credits included in these products, do not produce the amount that is hoped for. Therefore, the insurance industry is getting involved to offer products in case the credits concerned are not delivered (Kwong 2008).

The problem is that such derivatives cut the already very dubious bond with real emissions reductions completely. These securities are completely blind to the underlying emissions reductions. The buyer of such a product has almost no idea whether and how much emissions reductions it really represents. If such carbon derivative products are sold on a large scale, although they do not actually represent real reductions, this could result in a situation similar to that of 2007–2008 in the subprime market: collapse of the market, foreclosures of funds that invest in emission allowances and an explosion of distrust in the whole system.

A fraud scandal could be the first push that brings down the entire house of cards. The ETS is particularly vulnerable to fraud, and there has been a number of scandals (Chaffin 2011). In the summer of 2012, it came to light that Poland had applied to the European Union for 33 million allowances for a coal power plant which simply did not exist (Neslen 2012a). In 2010, Europol estimated that VAT fraud in European emissions trading amounted to €5 billion per year (Van Cauwelaert 2010).

Carbon credits constitute a form of private property of a part of the atmosphere (Vlachou 2014, 139). Through the Kyoto Protocol, governments have actually created artificial instruments which allow companies to appropriate parts of nature that for a long time were considered impossible to privatise. In the words of Carbon Trade Watch: 'This free gift of pollution rights to some of the worst industrial polluters amounts to one of the largest projects for the creation and regressive distribution of property rights in history' (Gilbertson and Reyes 2009, 10).

Therefore, emissions trading can be seen as the pinnacle of the neoliberal project that changes everything into a commodity. After decades trawling the world in search of cheap raw materials and labour, multinationals are now looking for cheap carbon reductions. In this way they are trying to appropriate the 'low hanging fruit'. This is a term used in the financial press to refer to the cheapest ways to reduce emissions. These are methods which require little effort or investment, just as you do not need a ladder to pick low-hanging fruit. As a result, structural changes are postponed. But there is also another problem. It is very likely that at least a number of developing countries will eventually also have to make efforts to significantly reduce their emissions. However, when the time comes for them to have to make real commitments, the low-hanging fruit is likely to have already been picked by governments and companies from rich countries. In other words, carbon trading and especially offsetting opens the door for a 'cheap emissions reductions' grab, after we have also witnessed land grabs, resource grabs, etcetera. This is a new form of what Marx once called 'primitive accumulation' or what David Harvey referred to as 'accumulation by dispossession', which a number of authors have shown plays a crucial role in contemporary market globalisation (De Angelis 2007, Harvey 2005, Marx 1982).

While in the global North accumulation continues unhindered, land is being grabbed in the global South for emissions reduction projects. Mechanisms such as carbon offsetting thus open the door for the global South to become the provider of cheap CO_2 certificates. Companies from industrialised countries buy these certificates in an attempt to outsource their responsibility. Carbon offsetting thus potentially represents a new and ingenious type of ecological imperialism. Previously, this imperialism was based on the plundering of resources and dumping of waste. Now it threatens to be about using the ecosystems of the global South to offset the emissions of the global North.

Buy a clear conscience

Carbon offsetting goes beyond Kyoto and the EU ETS. Many genuinely concerned people who want to do something for the climate voluntarily take part in all sorts of projects to compensate for their own emissions. If you are travelling by plane, for example, it is possible to buy what is called a *green seat*. The airline then uses the profit made from this sale to, for instance, plant trees to capture CO_2, often in the global South. Even rock groups like the Rolling Stones pay for tree planting to offset the emissions of their concerts (Rogers 2010, 3). Given the state of the negotiations about REDD in 2014, almost all REDD projects until then were part of the voluntary market (World Bank 2014, 43).

The market for voluntary offsetting is still relatively small compared with the emissions trading system, but has grown steadily over the past decade. In 2011, the market had a value of $569 million, representing more than 90 million tonnes of CO_2eq (World Bank 2012b, 10). The market reached a high point in 2012, representing more than 100 million tonnes of CO_2eq, but declined again in 2013. Still, its importance is not to be underestimated – not only or primarily because of the amount of CO_2 reductions it represents, but especially for the kind of environmental consciousness that it helps create (more about this in Chapter 5).

The market for voluntary offsets is sometimes called the 'Wild West' of emissions trading because for a long time, there was hardly any regulation. A number of projects run by NGOs include attention to social and environmental aspects, which the CDM is not always concerned with. But questions can even be asked about these projects. One of the problems is that there is often a significant difference between the time at which the emission occurs (for example, during air travel) and the time at which the emissions will be compensated. This is a more general problem with carbon offsetting: offsets are actually anticipations of future emissions reductions. In this sense as well, one might question if what is rendered equivalent through carbon trading is really equivalent.

Climate Care is a company that deals with this kind of offsetting, and was bought by JP Morgan several years ago. It allows one to offset a return flight between Brussels and New York (which represents approximately 1.63 tonnes of CO_2) for a bit more than €15. This money is used, for example, to plant trees, build wind turbines or provide poor people in the global South with more efficient cookstoves. As Aurélien Bernier argues, it will take roughly 100 years to fully compensate the CO_2 emissions from the plane trip by planting trees. Not only should the question be asked whether emissions should not be reduced right now instead of in 100 years, but it is also far from certain whether the trees will still be alive then, or who will check this (Bernier 2008, 97, Carbon Trade Watch 2007).

The green seats industry is scarcely regulated or controlled. In many countries one can even get tax deductions when buying green seats. This is perhaps the most far-reaching attempt to date to give capitalism a moral face. Critics have therefore called it a modern form of the trade in indulgences (Altvater and Brunnengräber 2008).

Kyoto has created a precedent. New, similar systems have been put in place over the last years. During the summit on biodiversity in Nagoya (Japan) in October 2010, the establishment of a system of tradable biodiversity credits was discussed, whereby it would be possible to offset ecological loss instead of preventing it. In its green economy report, UNEP argues the market-based mechanisms that can be used to stimulate the green economy include 'the development of offset schemes, the trading of pollution permits and the trading of access rights to water' (UNEP 2011, 138). UNEP gives the example of a water treatment plant that can continue polluting a river if it helps a nearby dairy farm reduce pollution. Another example is the trade in wetland banking schemes, which is already taking place in the USA. In such systems, third parties quickly become active as intermediaries between the original two parties, and for whom this trade becomes a goal in itself. Similarly, since 2014 landholders can trade forest credits on a new, specially created green exchange in Rio de Janeiro (Reuters 2014). The idea is similar to carbon trading: if one cuts more trees than one is allowed on one's piece of land, extra forest credits will have to be bought to compensate for this.

The problem with such systems is that from the point of view of the (speculative) trader, the underlying asset is of less importance than the financial gain that can be won. This results from the blindness of the economic way of calculation which we explained previously. Moreover, speculation can go in both directions: one can speculate both against the maintenance of biodiversity and against biodiversity loss. Such systems again makes us blind to how processes of ecological, social and political change actually take place.

Alternatives?

Many advocates of carbon trading would probably concede that the system is not perfect, and that its negative side effects should be corrected, but would argue that it is better than nothing. One argument is that even though carbon trading does not reduce emissions fast enough, it helps a bit, and we can still set up other initiatives alongside it. In actual fact, however, it is not as simple. Once an emissions trading scheme is put in place, it threatens to undermine any additional measures. Suppose that a government wants to impose legal standards for certain industrial processes, in order to reduce power consumption and CO_2 emissions. The result is that the affected sectors will have excess allowances. These surplus allowances coming onto the market, especially in large numbers, threaten to cause the price to collapse. Cap and trade systems are actually a double-edged sword. On the one hand, imposing a cap on emissions has the merit of at least putting a limit to how much greenhouse gases can be emitted. But on the other hand, this also means that total emissions will inevitably (almost) be as high as the maximum set by the cap. Not higher, but also not lower, because if one goes too much below the cap, the market threatens to collapse. In other words, the cap works in two directions: one should not emit more, but one cannot emit (much) less.

The EU is aware of the problem: discussions on the implementation of European Directives on energy efficiency or renewable energy run into this issue time and time again.[18] The only way to circumvent the impasse is to remove emission allowances from the market, but this faces fierce opposition by businesses, and technical problems. Each additional measure to tackle climate change thus becomes a highly technical tangle which business lobbyists pounce on. In this way, the emissions trading scheme puts a straitjacket around the EU's environmental policy, and threatens to displace other policies and strategies. This is a fundamental problem for future climate and other environmental policies. The risk is that a choice for cap and trade systems is combined with a cap that is too high, and whereby additional measures are counteracted by the very logic of emissions trading.

Proposals are made to reform the system and improve it, or fundamentally redesign the system. For example, some people advocate the introduction of an individual carbon credit card (Fawcett 2010, Fawcett and Parag 2010). Under such a system, everyone would be entitled to a certain amount of emissions. Every time you make a purchase, an amount is deducted from your carbon credit. If you have a shortage of allowances, you can then buy them from those who consume less, as is the case with the EU ETS.

Individual carbon trading is politically neutral, claims Tina Fawcett, an expert in personal carbon trading at Oxford University. 'It is not really a policy of the left or right' (Neslen 2012b). Admittedly, such a system has an egalitarian side, and that is in a sense revolutionary in comparison with existing emissions trading schemes. But the principle of tradable emissions remains problematic. For a start, this kind of system ignores the social context. People who can afford well-insulated housing in the centre of the city will spend less of their carbon allowance (unless they often take the plane) than poor or unemployed people who live in badly insulated houses in poorer neighbourhoods and who get around in rickety old cars. It may be unfair, concedes Fawcett, but 'that's capitalism really. The rich are richer' (Neslen 2012b). She argues this is true whether or not you introduce this kind of system.

Progressive advocates of such systems suggest that in this scenario poorer people can acquire an extra income by selling part of their allowances. But are there no other and better ways to redistribute wealth? With tradable systems there is always the risk that the redistribution takes place in the opposite direction. The question also remains of how one can practically organise such a system, and whether it is possible to compare completely different activities in one single carbon credit card.

There are also types of certificates which do not necessarily have anything to do with the Kyoto system, but fit more or less within the same philosophy. In Flanders (Belgium), a system of Green Electricity Certificates was launched in 2002.[19] From that moment on, each electricity producer was obliged to deliver a minimum share of electricity from renewable energy sources (about 2% in 2004, 6% in 2010). The producer could seek to achieve this by producing green electricity itself, or through buying certificates on the market. The value of these certificates fluctuates according to supply and demand. Private individuals can also get certificates when they put solar panels on their roof and share excess electricity via the electricity network. They can then sell these certificates to the electricity distributor. A scandal broke out in 2011 when it appeared that the distributor Eandis had been passing on the cost of purchasing these green certificates to consumers, even those who did not have solar panels. The indignation grew further when it transpired that a number of companies had earned a significant amount through the system. They had installed massive arrays of solar panels, and had earned large numbers of Green Electricity Certificates. On average, the price of electricity for a Flemish household had increased by €72 per year, but in some regions this was a massive €147 per year (PVDA 2011). When this form of inverted redistribution from the less well-off to those who had the means to invest in solar panels became apparent, strong discontentment emerged amongst lower classes.

Numerous similar examples exist of green market systems which result in socially unjust forms of redistribution, and thus often undermine the support base for green policies amongst citizens. Significantly, better insulation of houses would have created a much greater impact on the climate than installing solar panels, as Belgium has one of the worst insulated housing stocks in Western Europe.[20] But it is much more difficult to figure out a market system for dealing with this. Moreover, the people living in the worst insulated houses are usually the least well-off, and do not have the financial means to take part in these (often complex) systems, which demand an initial investment of several thousands of euros to be earned back only after a number of years.

Interestingly, the critics of market-based systems such as carbon trading are not only radical or progressive activists. *The Economist* also rejects carbon trading and prefers a carbon tax (*The Economist* 2010). It has good arguments for this. Taxes are said to be much simpler and much less susceptible to fraud than the ETS. A carbon tax makes it possible for businesses to make long-term plans, since it remains more or less constant, while the price of allowances fluctuates very strongly, as experience has shown. The main drawback of a tax is that there is no cap. Whoever pays the tax can keep polluting indefinitely.

However, the main reason to argue against a tax resides somewhere else for most economic actors: whereas, from a certain perspective, carbon trading can be seen as a tax whose proceeds go to private actors, a normal tax usually entails a transfer from businesses and consumers to the government, something which is considered as ideologically unacceptable to many powerful economic actors. Governments have therefore often been forced to compensate for a tax with a reduction in social security contributions by employers. Or companies pass on the tax to consumers.

That brings us to a crucial strategic problem: how can a critical mass be found supporting a tax? While emissions trading mainly affects the poor in the global South (although energy prices also went up in Europe as a result of the EU ETS), such a tax will possibly encounter a lot of protest from the mass of working people in the global North. Although a carbon tax can have beneficial effects on emissions (a tax of 1% on fuel reduces its consumption by 0.6%–1% [Sterner 2007]), it is likely to be an unpopular way to fight climate change, as it makes working people pay the bill. The OECD admits: '[e]nvironmentally-related taxes are likely to be passed on into higher prices to some degree, so they may involve a reduction in real wages' (OECD 2011, 40).

That does not mean that any type of carbon tax should be dismissed. It is possible to conceive of carbon taxes that are accompanied with social redistribution. The well-known climate scientist James Hansen argues in favour of a '*tax and dividend*' system, for example (Hansen 2009). The idea is to impose a tax on fossil fuels, whereby the proceeds are distributed amongst the population, in order to compensate for the fact that companies, which have to pay the tax, will pass on the cost to consumers. Since it is expected that the majority of people have a lower carbon footprint than average, the yield per individual would be higher than the higher price that companies impose due to the tax. Of course, the relation between income and energy use is not perfectly linear, as poor people often are obliged to make use of inefficient apparatuses, for example. It is important to take that into account and to add correcting measures. If implemented in a good way, such a tax would be relatively easy to organise, and could potentially benefit lower social classes.

Of course, a carbon tax cannot be the only element in a strategy for a low-carbon society. Corrections of the price mechanism will never be sufficient, and are subject to all of the possible problems we discussed before. To realise real and democratic change, a deliberate and rapid reorganisation of major social infrastructures and institutions will be needed. Still, incentives via the tax regime can, under certain conditions, provide an additional stimulus to move in the right direction. It is important to study and judge all such proposals on the basis of their concrete social, political and ecological merits and effects.

Green economy at what cost?

There is no doubt that individual entrepreneurs can make far-reaching steps in the direction of 'green' forms of production. Early capitalists in the Netherlands made profits with windmills in the seventeenth century, and they can do so again. The real question is whether a green capitalist economy is also possible at the macrolevel. Can the world economy remain based on capital accumulation while maintaining biodiversity, stopping desertification and deforestation and reducing emissions of CO_2 and other pollutants to a minimum?

This is a very complex question, to which a precise answer may not be possible. What we can say with certainty is that there are at least some very difficult obstacles on the way to a really green capitalist economy. The first is that of growth. 'Growth is not negotiable,' states Thomas Friedman, referring especially to developing countries (Friedman 2008, 55). 'To tell people they can't grow is to tell them they have to remain poor forever.' Therefore Friedman argues for a different, greener growth: the growth of renewable energy and 'clean' products. Obviously, we need growth in these and similar sectors, such as manufacturing of wind turbines or solar panels. Moreover, it is clear that several developing countries should realise a certain amount of overall growth in order to raise living conditions to a decent and sustainable level.

But the reference to developing needs in the global South should not be abused, as is sometimes done by proponents of the green economy. Furthermore, the conclusion of the previous chapter is unavoidable: there is no growth in capitalism without additional environmental impact, an impact which is often felt first and foremost by people in the global South. Finally, a key problem is that radically transforming the energy system will in itself require a massive input of energy. Paradoxically, as a journalist from the *Financial Times* states, 'the Green Economy relies very heavily on the brown economy (e.g. steel production) as wind turbines cannot be grown naturally' (McCormack 2012). We will need to use our remaining 'carbon budget' very wisely, therefore. This implies choosing political priorities: emit more in certain sectors which need further development while dismantling others which serve less important social needs.

Second, the transition to a green capitalist economy not only runs into the problem of growth, but above all risks enlarging the already very uneven social relations typical of capitalism (Böhm, Misoczky and Moog 2012, 1620). Indeed, one of the crucial questions is what impact a green capitalist economy will have on the distribution of income, and on the power relations between labour and capital. For 30 years, almost everywhere in the world the share of wages in national income has been falling, increasing social inequality. Can a green capitalist economy reverse that trend, or will it rather reinforce it?

According to the French economist Michel Husson, a greener capitalism is theoretically not impossible (Husson 2009). But there are two conditions attached. First, this kind of capitalism presupposes a global authority that imposes standards that go against the 'spontaneous' functioning of the market. However, it is not obvious what such a global body should look like, and how it could be strong enough to go against the power of large corporations. Second, a carbon price should be introduced, for example on the basis of an eco-tax which is so high that the profitability of many companies will be affected, and which thus, as we argued earlier, could lead to economic turbulence and even crisis.

The biggest problem of the transition to a green variant of capitalism is that there is inevitably a time lag between when such a carbon price is introduced (which immediately puts pressure on profits and/or wages) and when the system again finds a balance after a period of turmoil and crisis. Therefore, a scenario for a truly green capitalism threatens to imply a period full of tensions and crises: the chances are great that (green) entrepreneurs will try to compensate for pressure on profits by further wage moderation. This threatens to reduce the support for climate change measures amongst large sectors of the population.

The possible increase in the prices of some basic commodities, due to the consequences of climate change on agriculture, will not make it easier. The costs of energy, food, land and housing are likely to increase as a result of climate change, or when a carbon price is introduced (and companies pass it on to consumers). Furthermore, there is the problem of peak oil, with its looming oil shortages and increasing oil prices (Leggett 2013). That may create an explosive social cocktail.

In such a context, we risk seeing the rise of authoritarian solutions and the call for a 'strong state' that can quash social unrest, stop migration and push through socially unjust climate policies. The nightmare scenario is that this is done in the developed world with the support of an enlightened green middle class that has sufficient purchasing power 'to buy itself a way out of the problems' (as it has the financial capacity to insulate its houses, move to less affected places and take those adaptation measures which protect its members from the main consequences of climate change), and out of a sense of urgency sees such a repressive policy as the only possible solution.

Finally, the greening of capitalism will also generate tensions within the capitalist class itself. 'Enlightened' green business leaders beg for a new climate agreement and a recovery of the carbon market (e.g. Eurelectric 2013). As long as it is not there, it is difficult for them to compete with companies that do not care about the ecosystems. But there are massive companies that are putting the brakes on. In 2014, the Global 500 list of the largest companies in the world – drafted by *Fortune* magazine – contains no less than five oil giants in the top ten (Royal Dutch Shell, ExxonMobil, BP, Sinopec, China National Petroleum, Chevron and ConocoPhillips), in addition to Wal-Mart, State Grid, Glencore, Volkswagen and Toyota.[21] Most of them will simply have to disappear or change profoundly if we are to address climate change. Proponents of the green economy and the leading forces of fossil fuel capitalism have conflicting interests, although green economy discourses often fail to fully acknowledge this.

Notes

1 Due to the failure of the climate summits in Copenhagen, Cancun, Durban and Warsaw, this has become a bit unlikely, but the potential remains for the rapid growth of a global carbon market.

2 See their website on www.bluegreenalliance.org

3 See figures from the Carbon Dioxide Information Analysis Center, http://cdiac.ornl.gov/trends/emis/weu.html

4 A distinction is often made between environmental economics and ecological economics. In this book we criticise mainly the first approach, and we position ourselves broadly in line with the second, especially where it stresses the need to limit the scale of the economy. Unfortunately, many ecological economists also agree with certain policies to 'correctly' price nature and internalise externalities, which we are criticising. On ecological economics, see Daly (2010) and Burkett (2006).

5 We have to stress that a global rise of average temperatures of 2°C is not (only) a scientific, but (especially) a politically determined threshold, in the sense that many people will experience severe consequences of such a development. It is no coincidence that groups of island states and countries from the global South plead for a threshold of 1.5°C. Even to such seemingly scientific figures there is thus a political dimension.

6 See the ETS website of the European Union: ec.europa.eu/clima/policies/ets.index_en.htm, and the UNFCCC website about the Kyoto Protocol: http://unfccc.int/kyoto_protocol/items/2830.php. For a good introduction to the system, see Brunnengräber (2007).

7 Other greenhouse gases are also included in the ETS, such as nitrous oxide (N_2O) and perfluorocarbons (PFCs). In order not to make our analysis overly technical or complex, we will mainly speak about CO_2.

8 See the European website on ETS, http://ec.europa.eu/clima/policies/ets/cap/auctioning/index_en.htm

9 Regarding the evolution of the price of carbon, see: http://www.eex.com/en/
10 By mid-August 2014 there were 7538 registered projects. For the current situation, see: http://cdmpipeline.org/overview.htm
11 For a critique of this, see CDM-Watch, *Why Coal Projects in the CDM Undermine Climate Goals. Policy Brief*, September 2011.
12 Figures by UNEP, see http://cdmpipeline.org/cdm-projects-type.htm
13 A lot of information concerning HFC-23 projects can be found on the website www.sandbag.org.uk
14 A lot of information about CDM projects can be found at: https://cdm.unfccc.int/
15 For an overview, see: ibid., www.sinkswatch.org, www.carbontradewatch.org.
16 See www.carbonfinance.org
17 E.g. www.carbonratingsagency.com
18 See the EU Directive on Energy Efficiency (http://eurlex.europa.eu/LexUriServ/LexUriServ.do?uri=COM:2011:0370:FIN:EN:PDF). In one passage, it is suggested that fewer emission allowances must be placed on the market when the directive comes into force. The big question is how all this will be calculated and organised.
19 Similar systems exist elsewhere as well, for example in Germany. Cf. Rogers 2010, 88.
20 According to research by Eurima, the European Insulation Manufacturers Association (www.Eurima.org).
21 See the list on http://money.cnn.com/magazines/fortune/global500/2012/full_list/

References

Alberini, Anna, and James R. Kahn. 2006. *Handbook on Contingent Valuation*. Cheltenham: Edward Elgar.

Altvater, Elmar, and Achim Brunnengräber. 2008. *Ablasshandel gegen Klimawandel. Marktbasierte Instrumente in der globalen Klimapolitik und ihre Alternativen, Reader des Wissenschaftlichen Beirats von Attac.* [Trading Indulgences against Climate Change. Market-based Instruments in Global Climate Politics and Their Alternatives. Reader of the Scientific Advisory Council of Attac.] Hamburg: VSA.

Attac. 2012. *La nature n'a pas de prix. Les méprises de l'économie verte*. Paris: Editions Les liens qui libèrent.

Belga. 2014. "Meer dan 800 miljoen euro in CO_2-quota voor ArcelorMittal." *De Standaard*, 14 January.

Bernier, Aurélien. 2008. *Le climat otage de la finance. Ou coment le marché boursicote avec les 'droits de polluer'*. Paris: Mille et Une Nuits.

Böhm, Steffen, and Siddhartha Dabhi, eds. 2009. *Upsetting the Offset: The Political Economy of Carbon Markets*. London: MayFlyBooks.

Böhm, Steffen, Maria Ceci Misoczky, and Sandra Moog. 2012. "Greening Capitalism? A Marxist Critique of Carbon Markets." *Organization Studies* 33 (11):1617–1638.

Bond, Patrick. 2012. *Politics of Climate Justice. Paralysis Above, Movement Below*. Scottsville, South Africa: University of KwaZulu-Natal Press.

Boyer, Robert, and Yves Saillard, eds. 2002. *Regulation Theory. The State of the Art*. London: Routledge.

Brunnengräber, Achim. 2007. "The Political Economy of the Kyoto Protocol." *The Socialist Register 2007*:213–230.

Burkett, Paul. 2006. *Marxism and Ecological Economics. Towards a Red and Green Political Economy*. Leiden: Brill.

Callinicos, Alex. 2010. *Bonfire of Illusions. The Twin Crises of the Liberal World*. Cambridge: Polity.

Carbon Trade Watch. 2007. *The Carbon Neutrality Myth. Offset Indulgences for Your Climate Sins.* Amsterdam: Transnational Institute.

Chaffin, Joshua. 2011. "Into Thin Air." *Financial Times*, 15 February.

Cheam, Jessica. 2010. "Ministers Expected to Speed UN Climate Talks, Forest Deal Could Be Delayed." *Ecobusiness.com*, 7 December.

Daly, Herman. 2010. *Ecological Economics. Principles and Applications.* Washington, DC: Island Press.

De Angelis, Massimo. 2007. *The Beginning of History. Value Struggles and Global Capital.* London: Pluto Press.

Descheneau, Philippe. 2012. "The Currencies of Carbon: Carbon Money and Its Social Meaning." *Environmental Politics* 21 (4):604–620.

Dietz, Simon, and Nicholas Stern. 2014. *Endogenous Growth, Convexity of Damages and Climate Risk: How Nordhaus' Framework Supports Deep Cuts in Carbon Emissions.* Working paper. Centre for Climate Change Economics and Policy/Grantham Research Institute on Climate Change and the Environment.

Energy Business Reports. 2012. *GHG Emissions Credit Trading Report.* http://www.energybusinessreports.com/GHG-Emissions-Credit-Trading.html?v=1 (accessed 3 December 2014).

ETC-Group. 2011. "Who Will Control the Green Economy?" *ETC Group Communiqué* 107. http://www.etcgroup.org/sites/www.etcgroup.org/files/publication/pdf_file/ETC_wwctge_4web_Dec2011.pdf (accessed 3 December 2014).

ETC-Group and Heinrich Böll Foundation. 2013. "La lutte des biomassters pour le contrôle de la Green Economy." *Alternatives Sud* 20 (1):145–172.

EurActiv. 2012. *Yvo de Boer: Put €150 per Tonne Price on Carbon.* http://www.euractiv.com/climate-environment/yvo-de-boer-put-150-tonne-price-news-516383 (accessed 22 September 2014).

Eurelectric. 2013. *Eurelectric Adopts Position on ETS Structural Reform.* www.eurelectric.org/news/2013/eurelectric-adopts-position-on-ets-structural-reforms/ (accessed 17 September 2014).

Fawcett, Tina. 2010. "Personal Carbon Trading in Different National Contexts." *Climate Policy* 10 (4):339–352.

Fawcett, Tina, and Yael Parag. 2010. "An Introduction to Personal Carbon Trading." *Climate Policy* 10 (4):329–338.

Foster, John Bellamy, and Fred Magdoff. 2009. *The Great Financial Crisis: Causes and Consequences.* New York: Monthly Review Press.

Foster, John Bellamy, Brett Clark and Richard York. 2010. *The Metabolic Rift: Capitalism's War on the Earth.* New York: Monthly Review Press.

Friedman, Thomas. 2008. *Hot, Flat, and Crowded: Why We Need a Green Revolution – and How It Can Renew America.* New York: Farrar, Straus and Giroux.

Gilbertson, Tamra, and Oscar Reyes. 2009. "Carbon Trading. How It Works and Why It Fails." *Critical Currents* 7 issue.

Groen. 2009. *Europese Groenen lanceren transnationale verkiezingscampagne.* http://www.groen.be/actualiteit/Persbericht-europese-groenen-lanceren-transnationale-verkiezingscampagne_969.aspx?searchtext=green new deal (accessed 15 July 2012).

Green New Deal Group. 2008. *A Green New Deal. Joined-up Policies to Solve the Triple Crunch of the Credit Crisis, Climate Change and High Oil Prices.* London.

Hansen, James. 2009. *Carbon Tax & 100% Dividend vs. Tax & Trade.* Testimony of James E. Hansen to Committee on Ways and Means. http://www.columbia.edu/~jeh1/2009/WaysAndMeans_20090225.pdf (accessed 3 December 2014).

Hardin, Garrett. 1968. "The Tragedy of the Commons." *Science* 162:1243–1248.

Hardin, Garrett. 1998. "The Tragedy of the Commons." In *Managing the Commons*, edited by John A. Baden and Douglas S. Noonan, 3–16. Bloomington: Indiana University Press.

Harvey, David. 2005. *The New Imperialism*. Oxford: Oxford University Press.

Harvey, David. 2012. *Rebel Cities. From the Right to the City to the Urban Revolution*. London: Verso.

Harvey, Fiona. 2008. "Trade Off." *Financial Times*, 15 September.

Husson, Michel. 1999. "After the Golden Age. On Late Capitalism." In *The Legacy of Ernest Mandel*, edited by Gilbert Achcar, 75–103. London: Verso.

Husson, Michel. 2009. "Un capitalisme vert est-il possible?" *Contretemps* 1. http://www.contretemps.eu/archives/capitalisme-vert-est-il-possible%C2%A0 (accessed 3 December 2014).

Joshua, Isaac. 2009. *La grande crise du XXIe siècle. Une analyse marxiste*. Paris: La Découverte.

Kasibhatla, Prasad, and William Chameides. 2007. *G8 Leadership Is Critical to Curbing Energy-Related CO_2 Emissions*. Nicholas Institute for Environmental Policy Solutions, Duke University.

Kassenaar, Lisa. 2009. *Carbon Capitalists Warming to Climate Market Using Derivatives*. Bloomberg, http://www.bloomberg.com/apps/news?pid=newsarchive&sid=aXRBOxU5KT5M (accessed 15 August 2014).

Keucheyan, Razmig. 2014. *La nature est un champ de bataille. Essai d'écologie politique*, Zones. Paris: La Découverte.

Kwong, Robin. 2008. "New Products and Players in Carbon Credit Market." *Financial Times*, April 27.

Leggett, Jeremy. 2013. *The Energy of Nations: Risk Blindness and the Road to Renaissance*. New York: Routledge.

Lohmann, Larry. 2006. "Carbon Trading. A Critical Conversation on Climate Change, Privatisation and Power." *Development Dialogue* 48 issue.

Lohmann, Larry. 2010. *Regulation vs. Corruption or Regulation as Corruption? The Case of Carbon Offsets*. The Corner House. http://www.thecornerhouse.org.uk/sites/thecornerhouse.org.uk/files/ATHENS%2010.pdf (accessed 3 December 2014).

MacKay, David J. C. (2008). *Sustainable Energy – Without the Hot Air*. Cambridge: UIT Cambridge Ltd.

Marx, Karl. 1982. *Capital. A Critique of Political Economy. Volume 1*. Harmondsworth: Penguin Books.

McCormack, Ade. 2012. "Mission Growth." *Financial Times*, June 6.

Monbiot, George. 2007. *Hurray! We're Going Backwards!* http://www.monbiot.com/2007/12/17/hurray-were-going-backwards (accessed 17 September 2014).

Morrissey, Laura Fano. 2012. "Neo-liberal Conservation and the Cementing of Inequality: Interview with Bram Büscher." *Development* 55 (1):13–16.

Mueller, Tadzio, and Nicola Bullard. 2011. "Beyond the 'Green Economy': System Change, Not Climate Change? Global Movements for Climate Justice in a Fracturing World." UN Research Institute for Social Development conference, Geneva, 10–11 October.

Mueller, Tadzio, and Alexis Passadakis. 2010. "Another Capitalism Is Possible? From World Economic Crisis to Green Capitalism." In *Sparking a Worldwide Energy Revolution. Social Struggles in the Transition to a Post-Petrol World*, edited by Kolya Abramsky, 554–563. Oakland, CA: AK Press.

Musk, Jayson L., Mustafa Jamal, Lauren Kurlander, Maud Roucan, and Lesley Taulman. 2005. "A Meta-Analysis of Genetically Modified Food Valuation Studies." *Journal of Agricultural and Resource Economics* 30 (1):28–44.

Negri, Antonio. 1988. *Revolution Retrieved. Writings on Marx, Keynes and Capitalist Crises and New Social Subjects (1967–1983).* London: Red Notes.

Negri, Antonio. 2005. *Books for Burning. Between Civil War and Democracy in 1970s Italy.* London: Verso.

Neslen, Arthur. 2012a. "Polish 'Ghost' Coal Plants Ignite Emissions Trading Outrage." *The Guardian*, 11 July.

Neslen, Arthur. 2012b. "Tory MP Calls for Personal Carbon-Trading Scheme." *EurActiv*, 6 July.

Neuteleers, Stijn, and Bart Engelen. 2014. "Talking Money: How Market-Based Valuation Can Undermine Environmental Protection." *Ecological Economics*. Available online 19 July 2014. http://www.sciencedirect.com/science/article/pii/S092180091400202X (Accessed 4 February 2015).

OECD. 2011. *Towards Green Growth.* http://www.oecd.org/greengrowth/towardsgreen-growth.htm (accessed 22 September 2014).

Open Europe. 2006. *The High Price of Hot Air. Why the EU Emissions Trading Scheme Is an Environmental and Economic Failure.* London: Open Europe.

Ostrom, Elinor. 1990. *Governing the Commons. The Evolution of Institutions for Collective Action.* Cambridge: Cambridge University Press.

Ostrom, Elinor. 2010. "Beyond Markets and States: Polycentric Governance of Complex Economic Systems." *American Economic Review* 100 (3):641–672.

PointCarbon. 2008. *EU ETS Phase II – the Potential and Scale of Windfall Profits in the Power Sector.* WWF. http://www.wwf.eu/what_we_do/climate/climate_energy_publications. cfm?136901/EU-ETS-phase-II-the-potential-and-scale-of-windfall-profits-in-the-power-sector (accessed 3 December 2014).

Polanyi, Karl. 2001. *The Great Transformation. The Political and Economic Origins of Our Time.* Boston: Beacon Press.

PVDA [Workers Party of Belgium]. 2011. "Jaarlijkse prijsstijging elektriciteitsfac-tuur door zonnepanelen: Info per gemeente." http://www.pvda.be/nieuws/artikel/ jaarlijkse-prijsstijging-elektriciteitsfactuur-door-zonnepanelen-info-per-gemeente. html (accessed 12 August 2012).

Reuters. 2014. "Brazil Sets Final Rules for Forest Use, Allows Tradable Credits." 6 May.

Rogers, Heather. 2010. *Green Gone Wrong. How Our Economy Is Undermining the Environ-mental Revolution.* London: Verso.

Sharife, Khadija, and Patrick Bond. 2013. "Payment for Ecosystem Services versus Eco-logical Reparations: The 'Green Economy', Litigation and a Redistributive Eco-Debt Grant." *South African Journal on Human Rights* 29 (1):144–169.

Simms, Andrew. 2005. *Ecological Debt. The Health of the Planet and the Wealth of Nations.* London: Pluto Press.

Smith, Neil. 2006. "Nature as Accumulation Strategy." In *Socialist Register 2007. Com-ing to Terms with Nature*, edited by Leo Panitch and Colin Leys, 16–36. London: The Merlin Press.

Stern, Nicholas. 2006. *Stern Review on the Economics of Climate Change.* London: HM Treasury.

Stern, Nicholas. 2009. *A Blueprint for a Safer Planet.* London: The Bodley Head.

Sterner, Thomas. 2007. "Fuel Taxes: An Important Instrument for Climate Policy." *Energy Policy* 35:3194–3202.

Stewart, Heather, and Larry Elliott. 2013. "Nicholas Stern: 'I Got It Wrong on Climate Change – It's Far, Far Worse'." *The Observer*, 26 January.

Tanuro, Daniel. 2006. *Qui va payer l'échec sans précédent du marché?* http://www.europe-solidaire.org/spip.php?article4452 (accessed 15 August 2014).

Tanuro, Daniel. 2010. *L'impossible capitalisme vert*. Paris: La Découverte.

Teather, David 2008. "The Woman Who Built Financial 'Weapon of Mass Destruction.'" *The Guardian*, 20 September.

The Economist. 2010. "Worth a Go." 17 June.

Tickell, Olivier. 2010. "Don't Let the Carbon Market Die." *The Guardian*, 25 January.

UN. 2011. *The Great Green Technological Transformation*. New York: United Nations Economic and Social Affairs.

UN News Centre. 2008. *Secretary-General Calls for 'Green New Deal' at UN Climate Change Talks*. http://www.un.org/apps/news/story.asp?NewsID=29264 (accessed 15 August 2014).

UNEP. 2009. *Global Green New Deal*. Policy Brief. Geneva: UNEP.

UNEP. 2011. *Towards a Green Economy: Pathways to Sustainable Development and Poverty Eradication*. www.unep.org/greeneconomy (accessed 3 December 2014).

Unmüßig, Barbara. 2012. *The Green Economy – The New Magic Bullet? Expectations from the Rio+20 Conference*. Washington, DC: Heinrich Böll Stiftung.

Van Cauwelaert, Rik. 2010. "De grote emissieroof." *Knack*, 7 April.

Vandaele, John. 2009. "Tijd voor een Green New Deal XXL." MO*, 24 March.

Verbruggen, Aviel. 2008. *De ware energiefactuur*. Antwerp: Hautekiet.

Vlachou, Andriana. 2014. "The European Union's Emissions Trading System." *Cambridge Journal of Economics* 38:127–152.

Wall, Derek. 2014. *The Commons in History. Culture, Conflict, and Ecology*. Cambridge, MA: MIT Press.

Wara, Michael. 2007. "Is the Global Carbon Market Working?" *Nature* (445):595–596.

Whittington, Dale, and Stefano Pagiola. 2012. "Using Contingent Valuation in the Design of Payments for Environmental Services Mechanisms: A Review and Assessment." *The World Bank Research Observer* 27 (2):261–287.

World Bank. 2012a. *Inclusive Green Growth. The Pathway to Sustainable Development*. Washington, DC: International Bank for Reconstruction and Development/International Development Association or the World Bank. http://siteresources.worldbank.org/EXTSDNET/Resources/Inclusive_Green_Growth_May_2012.pdf (accessed 22 September 2014).

World Bank. 2012b. *State and Trends of the Carbon Market 2012*. Washington, DC: Carbon Finance at the World Bank.

World Bank. 2014. *State and Trends of Carbon Pricing 2014*. Washington, DC: World Bank Group/Ecofys.

WWF. 2012. *A Call from WWF to Measure What We Treasure*. http://wwf.panda.org/?205080/A-call-from-WWF-to-measure-what-we-treasure (accessed 7 September 2014).

5 Change within limits

'*Human activities* threaten to surpass the limits of the Earth's capacity as a source and sink,' it is stated in a report of the UN Department of Economic and Social Affairs (UN 2011, vi). 'The objective of the green economy is to ensure that those limits are not crossed.' In order to realise that objective, three options are suggested: reduction of income growth, reduction of population growth, and technological change. The report particularly focuses on the last option, as do many other approaches to the green economy.

This statement is significant because of the conceptual framework which underpins it and which typifies green economy discourse. It is the long-standing idea that environmental impact is the resultant of three factors, namely population growth, affluence and technology, expressed in the famous I = PAT formula (Ehrlich and Holdren 1971). Bluntly put, this equation states that total environmental impact (Impact) is equal to the number of people (Population) multiplied by the wealth per person (Affluence) – which is usually equated with the average consumption per person – multiplied by a technology factor (Technology).

A mathematical formula always appears to be the pinnacle of science and it is therefore no surprise that one can find the IPAT equation quoted in numerous academic texts. This equation appears to 'prove' that individual consumption, population growth and technology constitute the root causes of the ecological crisis. Three possible policy conclusions emerge from the logic of the formula: reduce the number of people who inhabit the Earth, make sure they all consume less and/or make technological changes. The equation is perfectly tailored to advocates of the green economy. It advocates change without really changing basic parameters of our society: the growth impetus inherent to the market economy, global trade, social inequality, the car culture . . . all remain unaffected. Typically, the IPAT equation leads away from the critical questions we ought to ask about the fundamental structures and institutions of our current society. More precisely, it epitomises a reductive vision of society, which would only consist of the sum of individuals, their lifestyles and technologies. To the extent that it remains blind for social structures and institutions, it threatens not to ask the simple but crucial political question: how is society currently organised, and how should we collectively reorganise it? In other words, it is a typical example of what Erik Swyngedouw calls the 'techno-managerial eco-consensus' which limits change 'within the contours of the existing state of the situation . . . so that nothing really has to change' (Swyngedouw 2011, 264). The formula tends to lead to a managerial approach to environmental politics, focused on controlling population, steering consumer behaviour, or stimulating technological innovation. The post-political effect of the equation is reinforced by its apparently scientific nature, as it portrays a deeply contentious question (what are the human and social root causes of ecological destruction?) in seemingly neutral terms.

In a very critical piece on the IPAT equation, Donella Meadows, one of the co-authors of *The Limits to Growth*, the influential report written in 1972 for the Club of Rome, writes:

> It counts what is countable. It makes rational sense. But it ignores the manipulation, the oppression, the profits. It ignores a factor that scientists have a hard time quantifying and therefore don't like to talk about: economic and political POWER. IPAT may be physically indisputable. But it is politically naïve.
>
> (Meadows 1995, cited in Angus and Butler 2011)

Indeed, if one looks slightly closer at the equation, then cracks are appearing all over the place (Angus and Butler 2011, 215). The population can be calculated more or less exactly. But how can one put a number on something like affluence or technology? Very often, a circular argument sneaks in. The formula gives the impression that one can calculate the total environmental impact by multiplying the population times individual consumptions times a technology factor. However, the only way to get an idea of affluence (understood in terms of individual consumption level) is by taking the total amount of goods and services in the economy and dividing it by the population. The result is a fictional construct, the average consumption per individual, or the average consumer, which of course does not exist.

But the problem with the formula is even more fundamental than that: because one first has to calculate constructs such as affluence and technology on the basis of the total impact (I), P, A and T are not independent variables, but constructions, which, moreover, interact with each other. As Blake Alcott writes, 'the I = PAT equation is transitive: all right-side factors influence each other, leaving impact the same or higher.' In other words, one cannot simply multiply P, A and T as if these would be independent magnitudes. Angus and Butler state that the IPAT equation is not 'a formula at all – it is what accountants call an identity, an expression that is always true by definition' (Angus and Butler 2011, 47). It does not prove that population and individual consumption are key factors, but rather postulates this. Evidently, the choice of assumptions or definitions is never neutral, but expresses a scholar's fundamental ideological viewpoint, whether that is acknowledged or not.

With a little generosity, one could argue that the IPAT equation is an attempt to break down the overall impact into its contributing factors. But this could be done in other ways, which would offer more insight into the real causes of ecological destruction. Donella Meadows suggests such an alternative: 'Impact equals Military plus Large Business plus Small Business plus Government plus Luxury Consumption plus Subsistence Consumption' (Meadows 1995). According to us, putting possible root causes of ecological destruction in a mathematical formula can never yield enough social and political insight, but at least Meadows' proposal reveals the social structures and power mechanisms which are at play. It sheds light on the starting points for political, transformative action.

In this chapter, we will address a series of issues which are highly relevant for the green economy debate, and which relate to the IPAT formula: the extent to which population can be considered a driving force behind ecological destruction, the role of individual consumption (and the role companies play in changing individual consumer behaviour), and the way technology is presented as a key factor. As we argued in Chapter 1, next to the focus on market solutions, these issues are amongst the key elements of the green economy discourse. Their significance resides in the fact that they lead to conceptions of change which refrain from transforming or even questioning fundamental parameters of our current society.

On population

On 3 December 2009, just days before the Copenhagen summit, the British non-governmental organization (NGO) Optimum Population Trust (which has in the meantime changed its name to Population Matters) launched the Pop-Offsets project.[1] The idea behind it is simple: if you want to reduce your CO_2 emissions, you can give money to this NGO, which invests it in projects that will help women to have fewer children. In other words, a new type of offsets can be bought to compensate for CO_2 emissions. The NGO started with one pilot project in Madagascar and a second targeting teenage pregnancies in the UK. The project website states:

> Research indicates that investing in family planning is a highly cost-effective and long acting way of reducing carbon dioxide emissions and thus limiting climate change, comparing favourably with other technological 'fixes'. It has many environmental benefits and no negative side-effects.[2]

Population Matters claims to rely on scientific data. According to a report by the London School of Economics entitled *Fewer Emitters, Lower Emissions, Less Cost*, an investment of $7 in family planning would be enough to prevent a tonne of CO_2 emissions, whilst $32 is needed to get the same effect through technological innovation (Wire 2009). Population Matters is not a small, marginal NGO. The organisation is supported by a number of scientists and well-known figures, including, for example, Jane Goodall and James Lovelock. The most famous amongst them is probably Paul Ehrlich, author of the book *The Population Bomb*, which was published in 1968 and played a key role in the revival of the population debate at that moment.

Some propose to go even further in the marketisation of what is called the 'population problem'. A number of scholars have developed schemes to set up a global market of tradable reproductive rights (De La Croix and Gosseries 2009). The British economist Kenneth Boulding had first suggested such a system back in 1964:

> 'I have only one positive suggestion to make, a proposal which now seems so far-fetched that I find it creates only amusement when I propose it. I think in all seriousness, however, that a system of marketable licenses to have children is the only one which will combine the minimum of social control necessary to the solution to this problem with a maximum of individual liberty and ethical choice' (quoted in De La Croix and Gosseries 2009).

Every woman would have the right to have 2.2 children. 'We would then set up a market in these units in which the rich and the philoprogenitive would purchase them from the poor, the nuns, the maiden aunts, and so on.' This would establish a market logic in a key area of human life.

The last decade witnessed the umpteenth return of the overpopulation discourse, this time often linked to an economic argument: 'Filling the family planning gap may be the most urgent item on the global agenda,' states Lester Brown, president of the Earth Policy Institute (Brown 2009, 184). Adding a typical market argument: '[t]he costs to society of not doing so may be greater than we can afford.' The United Nations Environment Programme (UNEP) states in its green economy report: '[t]he link between population dynamics and sustainable development is strong and inseparable' (UNEP 2011, 15).

Interestingly, however, another focus is adopted here: '[a] transition to a green economy can assist in overcoming the contribution that population growth makes to the depletion of scarce natural resources.' Similarly, the World Bank and the Organisation for Economic Co-operation and Development (OECD) refer to population growth as an argument why (green) growth is necessary (OECD 2011, 18, World Bank 2012, 6). In other words, population growth is presented as a root cause of ecological destruction, or at least as a challenge to be taken into account. Green growth or the green economy are *justified* by referring to the population problem, though no specific population policies are proposed.

Although 'population control' is thus not a major issue in most green economy or green growth initiatives, the analysis that population growth is a key factor behind ecological destruction pops up in each of the most important reports. It is worthwhile, therefore, to add a few caveats to this analysis.

Common sense?

At first sight, it seems to be common sense: more people means more raw materials and energy are used and more waste created, placing the planet under greater pressure. The figures are overwhelming. For many thousands of years the population grew only minimally. At the beginning of the common era the global population was probably about 200 million – 1,650 years later this had more than doubled to half a billion. In 1800 there were about a billion people worldwide; that number was doubled again by 1930 (Kunzig 2011). Since then, population growth has accelerated further. In the space of a lifetime the world population tripled: in 1960 there were three billion people on the planet, by 1974 four billion, in 1987 five billion, in 1999 six billion, and seven billion in late 2011.

Although the population continues to grow, the rate at which it is growing has been slowing down since reaching a peak in the 1960s. The UN predicts that population growth will continue to slow and come to a halt around 2045. At that time we will have a global population of approximately nine billion. This is a staggering prospect for many people. There are currently more than one billion people suffering from hunger. What will happen if two billion more people have to be fed and are in need of housing and energy? And above all, some worry, what if they want a better life, like the one enjoyed in the rich parts of the world?

The argument that population growth is a huge problem seems to be a substantial one. Yet the reality is not as straightforward as it may seem. It is impossible to deny that a population of nine billion people brings huge ecological challenges with it. However, it seems to us that considering population growth as one of the root causes of ecological destruction, let alone considering it as a priority in the struggle against climate change and other major ecological crises, is a step in the wrong direction. Moreover, promoting growth (green or otherwise) as an answer to population growth, as is done in a number of green economy reports, is not as evident as it may seem. In what follows, we will develop a couple of arguments to substantiate these claims.

Z-factor

Crucially, the link between population growth and ecological destruction is not so obvious as it might appear. It is true that there is a correlation between population growth and greenhouse gas emissions *at the global level*. Over the past two decades, both rose sharply. However, if we look at *specific regions*, the correlation falls away. Between 1980 and 2005, sub-Saharan Africa accounted for 18.5% of the global population growth, but only 2.4% of the growth in emissions. The proportion of the US in global population growth in that period was 3.4%, whilst the US contributed 12.6% to the increase in greenhouse gas emissions (Angus and Butler 2011, 40). From the moment one leaves behind the homogenising viewpoint of a global perspective, the correlation between population growth and greenhouse gas emissions therefore does not seem to be so clear at all. As Joni Seager states, '[t]here is only the loosest correlation between numbers of people and environmental stress,' and she concludes that an 'environmental analysis that focuses on population numbers is largely diversionary' (Seager 2000, 1712).

Furthermore, as every scholar knows, a *correlation* does not mean by definition that there is also *a causal relation*. In other words, the observation that there is a correlation between population growth and greenhouse gas emissions at the global level does not warrant the conclusion that population growth *leads to* a rise in greenhouse gas emissions. There is also a correlation between eating ice cream and melting asphalt, but this does of course not mean that a causal relationship exists between the two. The common explanatory factor (the so-called Z-factor) is the warm temperature on a beautiful summer's day. In the current case, we could diagnose the Z-factor as the global socio-economic system.

Indeed, as John Bellamy Foster argues, the way our current global society is organised leads both to an increase in greenhouse gases and, because of the 'demographic trap' in which several developing countries are caught, to population growth in the global South (Foster 1999, 16). Foster refers here to the work of Barry Commoner, who speaks about a kind of 'demographic parasitism' in this regard. According to Commoner, '[c]olonialism has determined the distribution of both the world's wealth and of its human population, accumulating most of the wealth north of the equator and most of the people below it' (Commoner 1992, 160).

Crucially, even if world population would stabilise, the ecological crisis would not end tomorrow as long as the economic machine continues its inexorable 'progress', which is something many overpopulation discourses rarely take into consideration. Stating that we need more (green) economic growth as an answer to 'the contribution that population growth makes to the depletion of scarce natural resources' (UNEP 2011, 15) is thus putting the problem on its head. But more problematically, a focus on population as a root cause for ecological destruction tends to shift responsibility for our current predicament from the global North to the global South.[3] Cynically, those countries that contributed least to greenhouse gas emissions (surely if one calculates these emissions per capita) suddenly become the object of ecological blame.

'We acknowledge that the carbon emission per capita in less-developed countries is relatively low in comparison to that of the industrialised nations,' Population Matters states on its website. 'People in the developing world will not continue to live in relative poverty indefinitely, however, and their growing economies will, inevitably, lead to greater emission per capita' (PopOffsets 2014). Ironically, poor people are seen as a problem because they want to be rich. Such ecological footprint analyses, moreover, entail a shift from a strict focus on 'the number of people' to a focus on 'the number of consumers' (Foster, Clark and York 2010, 378). In other words, a second factor is added to the equation: affluence.

Before moving to the consumption question, we want to underscore that we do not deny that 'the number of people' matters from an ecological point of view. From a materialist perspective, it would be absurd to argue otherwise. As we argued in Chapter 2, everything, and therefore also everyone, has by definition an ecological impact. But we also argued that social-ecological change entails more than summing up different factors which are relevant and which can be acted upon. If we want to tackle ecological destruction, we have to understand its root causes, and make strategic choices. In this context, it does not make much sense to consider ecosystems and human beings in an abstract way without examining the social structures that stand between the two. Such an approach makes it impossible to analyse political fault lines and to discover the leverage needed to realise political change. Furthermore, as Sherilyn MacGregor argues, the question 'are we too many' 'is neither a straightforwardly scientific nor politically innocent question. It is loaded with assumptions and value judgements and is part of a discourse that does a very particular job of ideological work' (MacGregor 2009, 4). It is of crucial importance to be conscious of these ideological underpinnings if we want to embark on a pathway towards just, democratic and effective forms of social-ecological change.

Sustainable consumption

Many people are genuinely concerned about climate change and other ecological problems and want to do something. The first thing they often think about is reducing their own ecological footprint by making different consumption choices: buying organic food, sustainable cleaning products, electricity-saving household appliances or even a hybrid or electric car. They thus act as many companies, policymakers and NGOs like them to: as individuals and as consumers. Many campaigns aim at influencing individual consumer behaviour. One of the most famous examples is the global 10:10 campaign which 'inspires and supports people and organisations to cut their carbon emissions by 10% in a year'.[4] Many documentaries and movies about climate change also urge people to change their individual (consumer) behaviour. The most well-known example is probably Al Gore's film *An Inconvenient Truth*, which ends with a long list of tips for sustainable behaviour choices: use energy efficient light bulbs, recycle, drive less, use less hot water, turn off electrical appliances instead of leaving them on standby and so on, all remarkably formulated in an imperative mood.

The last decade saw a steady growth of policy reports investigating the factors behind what is called pro-environmental behaviour. Examples are Tim Jackson's *Motivating Sustainable Consumption: A Review of Evidence on Consumer Behaviour and Behavioural Change* (Jackson 2005), Greg Stevenson and Beth Keehn's *I Will If You Will. Towards Sustainable Consumption* (Stevenson and Keehn 2006) and the UK Department for Environment, Food and Rural Affair's *A Framework for Pro-Environmental Behaviours* (DEFRA 2008). On the basis of social and psychological research, these reports try to find an answer to the question of how individual behaviour can be 'steered' in a pro-environmental direction. Solving this question is considered a key step towards a more sustainable society. As Jackson argues, sustainable consumption is fast becoming a kind of 'holy grail' for sustainable development policies (Jackson 2005, xi).

The goal of such policies is to 'encourage, motivate and facilitate more sustainable attitudes, behaviours and lifestyles' (Jackson 2005, iii). These attitudes, behaviours and lifestyles involve 'more sustainable patterns of consumption, covering the purchase, use and disposal of goods and services' (p. 13). A broad spectrum of measures is developed to reach this goal: from awareness raising campaigns, via education, to economic rewards. Through a whole range of incentives, policymakers aim to find ways to steer individual consumers' behaviour in the desired 'green' direction.

This focus on changing individual (consumer) behaviour has its counter-part in the academic literature. Several hundreds of studies have been undertaken to gain a better understanding of why and when people behave in pro-environmental ways (Bamberg and Möser 2007, Heimlich and Ardoin 2008, Kollmuss and Agyeman 2002, Rickinson 2001). In particular, a lot of studies have been concerned with the so-called knowledge-action gap (Kollmuss and Agyeman 2002). This research literature deals with the question of why people who are aware of ecological issues often do not change their behaviour, despite the knowledge they have. The goal is to explain, predict, or even influence the performance of 'pro-environmental behaviour'. It is remarkable that also in this literature, 'pro-environmental behaviour' is almost always framed as individual (consumer) behaviour. Anja Kollmuss and Julian Agyeman, for example, argue: 'By "pro-environmental behaviour" we simply mean behaviour that consciously seeks to minimise the negative impact of one's actions on the natural and built world (e.g., minimise resource and energy consumption, use of non-toxic substances, reduce waste production)' (Kollmuss and Agyeman 2002, 240).

Green economy discourses are also starting to integrate such approaches. In its *Inclusive Green Growth* report, for instance, the World Bank presents sustainable consumption as one of the key ingredients of the transition to a green economy. The World Bank argues: 'the current model is not just unsustainable, it is inefficient. Improving it is good economics, so let's fix market failures, internalise externalities, assign property rights, improve governance, and *influence behaviours*' (our italics). It proposes a whole range of tools to change and even steer individuals' behaviour:

> Incentivising, informing and nudging, or imposing – some combination of the three is likely to be needed. Determining the best mix requires a solid understanding of how individual decisions are made and framed. Behavioural economics and social psychology thus provide indispensable insights into how to green growth. Economists will ignore them at their peril.
>
> (World Bank 2012, 47)

At first sight it seems evident: if every individual makes an effort, then the sum of these must have a significant impact. Do lots of small actions not add up to make a big difference? Is it not the case that if enough consumers use their purchasing power as leverage, companies will have to follow? By playing the rules of the market, people can maybe help to make it more sustainable. NGOs and governments could play a key role by informing consumers and encouraging them to make sustainable choices.

Sustainable consumption and other efforts to reduce one's own ecological footprint are without any doubt important. But as a key strategy for change, this approach triggers a number of critical questions. What vision of society underpins policies and campaigns which aim to change individual (consumer) behaviour? Are market changes indeed driven by consumer choices? What can 'influencing behaviour' mean?

The power of the consumer?

It is not an innocent choice to opt for sustainable consumption as a means to involve citizens in the transition to a green economy. Neither is it neutral to define pro-environmental behaviour as individual (consumer) behaviour, as is done in many policy documents and a lot of academic literature. With such an approach, one tends to ignore a whole range of 'actions that often go beyond simply consciously seek(ing) to minimise the negative impact of one's actions on the natural and built world by demanding profound structural and policy change', as Darlene Clover argues (Clover 2002, 316).

In the literature, the distinction between changing individual (consumer) behaviour and this latter type of action is often referred to as the distinction between 'direct' and 'indirect' environmental action. Kollmuss and Agyeman, who generally tend to downplay indirect action, describe both categories as follows: 'Indirect environmental actions include donating money, political activities, educational outreach, environmental writing, etc. Direct environmental actions include recycling, driving less, buying organic food, etc.' (Kollmuss and Agyeman 2002, 258). The evident difference between both is that indirect actions, unlike direct actions, do not immediately reduce the impact on the environment.

A number of criticisms can be formulated against this distinction. The most important is that by calling certain actions 'indirect' (and especially by not even mentioning them), they are devalued and marginalised in a large part of the literature (Clover 2002). By reducing pro-environmental behaviour to direct environmental actions, important dimensions of what action can consist of are lost from sight.

Furthermore, by defining action as 'individual' behavioural change, the result is a tendency towards the privatisation of the solutions for ecological problems (Courtenay-Hall and Rogers 2002). Not only 'indirect' action, but also 'collective' action is thereby downplayed. As Catriona Sandilands puts it succinctly:

> [it] shifts the burden of responsibility onto individuals and households, and away from states, corporations, and global political arrangements. [It] undermines both collective and individual resistance; it turns [environmental] politics into actions such as squashing tin cans, [environmental] morality into not buying overpackaged muffins, and environmentalism into taking your own cloth bag to the grocery store. None of these actions . . . makes public or collective or cooperative the act of environmental restoration; none of these actions provokes a serious examination of the social relations and structures that have brought about our current crisis.
>
> (Sandilands 1993, 46, quoted in Courtenay-Hall and Rogers 2002, 290)

However, the main problem is that the conceptualisation of pro-environmental behaviour as sustainable consumption threatens to downplay the complexity of current ecological crises. Indeed, it starts from 'the assumption that today's complex environmental problems can be tackled through unambiguous means' (Jensen 2002, 328). As we argued at length in this book, the ecological crises we are confronted with are structurally anchored in the way our society is organised. This has implications for the extent to which people can contribute to tackling climate change and other ecological crises *in their role as consumers*. To give a very simple example: the high real-estate prices in big cities are unaffordable for many people, who consequently have no other choice but to buy a house in the countryside, even though that means they have to commute each day, with all the social-ecological problems resulting from that.

These examples not only reveal the limits of addressing people as mere individuals or consumers. They also show that it is absolutely not evident to look in the first instance to the individual level in order to explain the observed gap between environmental knowledge and pro-environmental behaviour we described above. Even if we want to give a crucial role to individual action, it is in the first place on the structural level that the problem of this gap has to be addressed. To give the example of the problem of waste: numerous campaigns aim to encourage people to minimise the amount of household waste they produce. However, the bulk of waste comes from the production, distribution and trade of goods and services, and not from the individual consumption of the final product. According to the European Commission, 6 tonnes of waste per person are currently produced each year in the EU.[5] But looking only at household waste, the figure is much lower, albeit still substantial: half a tonne per person on average. Really tackling the waste problem therefore requires a completely different kind of action. If we want the mass of the people to contribute to solving the waste problem, they will have to be mobilised beyond their role as consumers. They will first and foremost have to be addressed as *citizens*, in order to create the political counterforce needed to get waste production under control. The conclusion seems simple, but could have a big impact on the research concerning pro-environmental behaviour and on the strategies of environmental policymakers and movements.

Is it not possible that, exactly because of the structural character of many environmental problems, actions that are now marginalised as 'indirect' should have a central role? If this is the case, should the goal not be to *empower* people to act not only on the personal, but also on the collective level? As Louise Chawla and Debra Cushing put it: 'the most effective actions are collective, when people organise to pressure government and industry to act for the common good' (Chawla and Cushing 2007, 438). This is not as far-fetched as it might seem: many neighbourhood committees or civic groups have already sprung up to oppose incinerators or other polluting industries.

Action

Such a broader concept of action requires a more sophisticated vision of the actor of change. The question has to be asked whether many campaigns and policies to promote sustainable consumption do not see people as the objects rather than as subjects of change.

Most prominent amongst these policies are, of course, economic incentives (Berglund and Matti 2006, World Bank 2012). As Andrew Dobson and Derek Bell argue, the predominant idea is that '[i]f the sticks and carrots are appropriately

placed and priced, self-interested rational actors [. . .] will be induced to push
their own appropriate behavioural buttons without further government intervention' (Dobson and Bell 2006). They conclude that '[i]t is this last aspect of the
scheme that makes it so enticing for liberal-capitalist governments.' Others opt
to try to steer people's consumer behaviour by non-rational means (Heimlich
and Ardoin 2008, Jackson 2005, McKenzie-Mohr and Smith 1999). Indeed, from
the observed knowledge-action gap, they draw the conclusion that people do
not behave 'rationally' and that their behaviour should therefore be influenced
through other means, such as role models, social pressure or connecting the
desired behaviour to positive feelings of freedom, friendship or sex, as is done in
the advertisement industry. Jackson underlines, for example, 'the need for policy
to [. . .] attempt to affect individual behaviours (and behavioural antecedents)
directly' (Jackson 2005, vi). In this way, one no longer has to bother about rationally convincing people and enabling them to draw their own conclusions and to
decide about the desired change by themselves. Instead, their behaviour can be
steered in a 'direct' way.

In order to gain a better understanding into what exactly is at stake here, it is
interesting to draw a distinction between 'behaviour' (as present in the idea of
changing people's individual consumer behaviour) on the one hand and 'action'
on the other (Jensen 2002). Too often, these terms are used as synonyms, although
their meanings subtly but significantly differ. The central difference is that action
includes a moment of conscious decision making, which is not necessarily the
case with behaviour change, which can also be reached through social pressure,
for example. Actions can therefore consist of the same acts as behaviours, but
differ from them because they are intentional. This means that actions have to
be explained in terms of conscious motivations and reasons, rather than in terms
of mechanisms and causes. This is not a superficial semantic discussion. What
is at stake is a crucial difference in the way people are approached, as subjects
or merely as objects of change, as citizens or as parts of a mass that needs to be
steered.

What Jon Hellesnes states about conditioned-socialisation is very clarifying in
this context: 'Conditioned-socialisation reduces humans to objects for political
processes which they do not recognise as political; a conditioned human being is
thus more an object for direction and control than a thinking and acting subject'
(Hellesnes 1976, 18, quoted in Jensen and Schnack 2006, 474). In other words,
the sustainable consumption approach often starts from a kind of behaviourism
which does not consider people as conscious citizens. At best, they are viewed as
conscious consumers, but even that is very often not the case (see also Kenis and
Mathijs 2012).

Biopower

There is thus something very ambiguous about the discourse on sustainable consumption: on the one hand, it is a liberal form of environmental politics *par
excellence*, in which the individual consumer and her own freedom of choice are
central. But on the other hand, this individual must be influenced to make the

'correct', 'ethical' choices. On the one hand, the consumer is sovereign, on the other hand, she should be closely guided. Moreover, this 'guidance' seems to take on steadily more problematic forms, including social marketing campaigns making use of advertisement techniques. Take the campaigns of PETA, the American animal rights organisation which uses pin-ups to make eating meat and wearing fur unappealing. It is the oldest trick in the box: sex sells. Such campaigns epitomise the tendency in behaviour change literature hinted at above: rather than giving arguments or information, one increasingly uses the tools of mainstream advertisement campaigns.

It is a curious paradox: apparently consumers should be steered and governed (even in unconscious ways) in order to make sure they freely and ethically choose for the sustainable alternative. Michel Foucault pays a lot of attention to the subtle ways in which people's behaviour is governed, particularly in liberal societies, and his analyses could therefore also help towards a better understanding of what is happening in current sustainable consumption discourses (Foucault 2004). According to Foucault, liberal, individual freedom does not precede and oppose the state, but is a *product* of governmental strategies. It is, in other words, a product of power: the individual should be governed and steered in such a way as to make her experience herself as a free and responsible subject. Foucault coined the term 'governmentality' to refer to the specific rationalities of governing which aim at producing subjectivity, in this case, for example, the subjectivity of the conscious and responsible, 'free' consumer. He defines governmentality as the 'conduct of conduct': governing an other is to steer the ways the other conducts or governs herself. A liberal type of governing thus implies making sure people govern themselves in an 'ethical' way, as free and responsible individuals. Foucault's aim was to uncover the power mechanisms implied in governing practices in order to generate a space for people to give shape to their own subjectivity, to create themselves. This could become a kind of resistance against existing forms of governmentality.

The ultimate aim of governmental practices is usually not the individual as such, however. As Foucault argues in his lectures on biopower, these practices are rather focused on realising effects at population level. Studying new governmental practices from the eighteenth century onwards, Foucault shows how the population emerged as a new object of the exercise of power. The state became increasingly interested in mortality and birth rates, hygiene and health. It set itself new, statistically determined targets: to decrease the mortality rate by a certain percentage or to boost the birth rate. In order to achieve that goal, it developed a number of power techniques which could help shape people's behaviour and make them act in ways that were more ethical, more hygienic or more responsible. The conduct of conduct, in other words, ultimately serves goals at the population level. The individual therefore ultimately interests the state less than the general health of the population, which could be measured by statistics. Foucault coined the notion of biopower to refer to the power it exercises over the processes of the population (health, birth and death rates, etcetera).

Something very similar is at stake in attempts to influence consumer behaviour: power mechanisms are put in place to change individual behaviour, to 'conduct their conduct' and to produce subjects who see themselves as free, ethical and responsible. The actual goal, however, is to realise effects at the level of the population as a whole, namely to reduce total greenhouse gas emissions. In the end, therefore, the individual is of no great interest to power, as she is only an object to be influenced or steered in view of this larger goal.

Steering or being steered?

Many sustainable consumption campaigns are implicitly based on a dichotomy between those who decide what has to be done and those who have to perform this activity (Clover 2002, Courtenay-Hall and Rogers 2002). The campaigner in an NGO, the government official or the marketer then determines the strategy for change, which everyone else must carry out through their behaviour, whether they are aware of this or not. In this sense, the very discourse about 'shaping behaviour' is significant in itself (Courtenay-Hall and Rogers 2002, 285).

Interestingly, many policymakers and environmental campaigners (and academics!) often do not apply their own models to themselves (Gough 2002). Indeed, the environmental actions they perform are typical examples of *indirect environmental actions*, which many scholars and policymakers ignore in their behaviour change models. Think, for example, about the writing of reports, giving lectures or making documentaries: these are all actions which may increase the impact on the ecosystems in the short term, for instance by taking the plane to international meetings and conferences. But they could possibly contribute in an 'indirect way' to the transition to a more sustainable society on a longer term (depending, of course, on the exact content these actions get).

Two points are relevant here. First, by making abstraction from *indirect environmental actions*, the type of actions they are engaged in themselves disappears from the policy and research field. Second, the actions these policymakers, campaigners or academics consider as suitable for themselves are of a completely different nature than those they deem fit for others. This leads to an elitist relation between those 'who steer' the transition to a green economy and those 'who have to be steered', between the Al Gores of the green economy project and the rest.

We do not want to suggest that politicians, policymakers or campaigners should be primarily occupied with reducing their ecological footprint (although paying more attention to it would certainly not be bad). To use the words of Darlene Clover, we especially want to question the fact that this approach 'dismisses or ignores people's knowledge and reinforces the idea that we can attribute different levels of status to knowledge, based on the rationale that, say, professionals "know" and "others" do not' (Clover 2002, 317).

Strategy scepticism

What is fundamentally at stake in this discussion of sustainable consumption is again our relation to the political. If the aim is merely to achieve changes in behaviour, then adopting advertising techniques, economic incentives or social pressure might be an appropriate strategy. But if we want to build a movement for social change, and create political spaces where ideas about such change can confront each other, a more politicised strategy will be necessary. The fundamental question is which political strategy has the best chance to lead to a more sustainable social-ecological future.

It is not surprising that many people demonstrate a certain scepticism about changing individual (consumer) behaviour as an appropriate strategy towards change. Remarkably, this scepticism can be observed not only amongst people *who do not* actively engage in sustainable consumption, but also amongst those *who do* (Kenis and Mathijs 2012). At first instance, this appears paradoxical: people change their individual (consumer) behaviour, even though they do not believe that this really changes anything fundamentally. They buy organic food, take the train instead of the plane, try to lower their energy consumption, opt for sustainable cleaning products, and still they think that basically, this does not make a difference. If one tries to grasp this paradox, it turns out that people especially have moral reasons for engaging in a practice they actually do not really believe in. It is a matter of 'not having a bad conscience', or 'earning a place in heaven'. One possible explanation is that people do not see many opportunities to bring about any 'real' change, and therefore try to make sure they at least do not do anything wrong. That is obviously very honourable, but again, we see a kind of depoliticisation at work here. In this way, climate action becomes a question of mere individual morality, and this morality is especially a matter of 'not feeling guilty oneself', of not being 'part of the problem'. Politically speaking, however, what is at stake is to become 'part of the solution'.

That is undoubtedly also what many people would like to be. However, the problem is that our current form of society appears to be so insurmountable that many people hardly see opportunities to bring about profound social-ecological change. They see no alternative, do not dare to hope for it or are fearful about engaging in political or social conflict. Sustainable consumption fills the remaining gap.

A hypothesis that can explain why rather few people engage in individual behaviour change, is that a kind of 'strategy scepticism' is at play (Kenis and Mathijs 2012). Compared with climate scepticism, whose impact is dwindling (certainly in Western Europe), strategy scepticism is maybe a much more important factor explaining the relatively limited efforts to consume sustainably by people who are actually concerned about climate change and its consequences. Strategy scepticism refers to the sheer disbelief that sustainable consumption is a relevant or credible strategy.

Interestingly, the influential DEFRA report on sustainable consumption makes a similar observation, even though it does not draw the same conclusions (DEFRA 2008). Amongst the main obstacles to pro-environmental behaviour, it mentions the following elements:

(1) Scepticism around the climate change debate and distrust of both government and industry. For example, about a quarter don't believe their behaviour contributes to climate change. (2) Disempowerment, as there is

a disconnect between the size of the problem (Global Climate Change) and the individual's contribution (e.g. turning off lights) and a sense that individuals cannot make a difference. [. . .] More than half claimed if government did more, they would too.

(DEFRA 2008, 35)

Remarkably, however, DEFRA frames these obstacles as 'psychological barriers' to be overcome. The authors suggest that what is at stake is a 'feeling' that the individual cannot make a difference, and that only powerful others can realise real change. In our view, however, the experience of powerlessness cannot be reduced to a 'psychological experience'. Scepticism concerning individual (consumer) behaviour strategies can perfectly be based on a rational and profound analysis of the challenges we are confronted with. As Michael Redclift and Ted Benton put it:

One of the most important insights which the social scientist can offer in the environmental debate is that the eminently rational appeals on the part of environmentalists for 'us' to change our attitudes or lifestyles, so as to advance a general 'human interest' are liable to be ineffective. This is not because (. . .) 'we' are irrational, but because the power to make a significant difference, one way or the other, to global or even local environmental change is immensely unevenly distributed.

(Redclift and Benton 1994, 7–8, quoted in Blake 1999, 265)

This analysis can also shed a new light on what remains of climate scepticism. If people do not take climate change seriously, this might be related to a strategic estimation: if international institutions, governments and NGOs suggest individual (consumer) behaviour is the solution, this can only mean that the problem of climate change cannot be so serious after all. If the ecological crisis were really so grave, then it is reasonable to expect that more would be done about it. Would the government then not take more decisive action? Such reactions especially pop up to the extent that campaigns focus on marginal changes. In Flanders (Belgium), a yearly 'wear a thick jumper day' was set up to highlight the Kyoto commitments. People are encouraged to wear an extra jumper that day, which makes it possible to set the thermostat slightly lower. Without a doubt this is a nice action, which also has a fairly wide reach. But the underlying suggestion is problematic. Who takes the problem seriously if it is suggested that such campaigns can really change anything?

Class bias

The privatisation of environmental morality is even more outspoken to the extent that the focus is on individual 'consumer' behaviour. Taking action is then made conditional upon having enough purchasing power. In the literature, it is suggested that this reveals the 'class bias' of the sustainable consumption strategy (Courtenay-Hall and Rogers 2002, 289): those who have the capacity to buy organic food, for instance, can contribute to the transition to a green economy, others cannot.

This also leads to a new cleavage between the 'haves' and 'have nots' (Seager 1993). To turn back to the example of organic food: those who can afford to buy organic food have a kind of ecological privilege, as they can avoid the harmful substances that conventionally cultivated food sometimes contains. Instead of ensuring that the use of harmful substances is simply no longer allowed, specific groups have the capacity to protect themselves, thanks to their purchasing power, by buying green.

This class bias also manifests itself in the relationship between the global North and the global South. As Vandana Shiva shows, the demand from Western consumers for organic food has led to the development of large-scale organic agro-industries in the global South (Shiva 2006). Apart from the fact that much of this 'organic' food is not cultivated in a very ecological and socially just way, the main problem is that these healthier organic crops are exported to the rich global North, whereas local people are left with less healthy, conventionally cultivated ones. In this way, (neo)colonial relationships are reproduced. Furthermore, most people in the global South do not dispose of the income needed to assert their power as consumers. The law of supply and demand offers them few opportunities for 'pro-environmental behaviour' in this regard. Therefore, the ecological struggle in the global South will have to make use of other strategies than changing individual consumer behaviour, and the same also goes for many people and places in the global North.

But there is an even more fundamental, strategic issue related to this point: if one starts from the perspective of purchasing power, solving the ecological crisis requires getting the richest consumers on board. This is a strategic choice which often remains implicit in green economy discourses, but is of great political importance: it is a choice to primarily engage with economically powerful actors, those who have capital or purchasing power, and turn them into the protagonists of a sustainability transition.

'Packages don't litter, people do'

The individualisation and depoliticisation of environmental action has not happened naturally or spontaneously. At least to a certain extent, it is the result of a subtle struggle for hegemony, whereby powerful economic actors have been quite successful in framing the ecological question in a very particular way. When the environmental movement got off the ground in the 1960s and '70s, the predominant reaction was to organise and protest against polluting practices. When, partly as a result of this, the first environmental legislation emerged, many companies realised that they could no longer deny that pollution was a fact (Williams 2010, 132). Neither could they remain blind to the actors who were putting the topic on the agenda. They would have to adjust or come up with their own answers. Concerned about an increase of government regulations, a number of them started to develop alternative environmental strategies.

The treatment of waste is a good example. Over the last decades, companies have developed strategies intended to prevent government intervention, and to make individuals rather than companies responsible for the problem. A story by Heather Rogers is illuminating in this regard (Rogers 2007, 231). She reconstructs how in the 1950s, the US government wanted to regulate and even ban disposable bottles. In response to this, and with the support of the packaging industry, the non-profit Keep America Beautiful was set up. Keep America Beautiful was actually the first major campaign of greenwashing (projecting a green image without actually being sustainable) launched by the industry. But there was more at stake than greenwashing. The campaign had huge ideological and political stakes, far beyond companies' attempt to present themselves as concerned about environmental issues.

The campaign's core message was that waste was not the problem, but the fact that people were dropping it on the street instead of putting it in the bin. 'Packages don't litter, people do' was one of its slogans. The problem was neither the product nor the manufacturer, but the consumer. In this way, the industry tried to change the tone of the environmental debate, pointing to individual consumers as the main culprits, and engaging in a huge operation towards reconstructing the perceptions of the root causes of ecological destruction. According to Heather Rogers, this 'key tactic of blaming individuals [. . .] obfuscated the real causes of mounting waste' (Rogers 2007, 234).

The campaign set the tone for many subsequent environmental initiatives, not only by industries, but more and more also by environmental movements. It is pointed out to individuals that they have their own responsibility, while fundamental questions about how society functions are ignored. Instead of avoiding waste, the issue was reduced to teaching people how to throw things in the right bin, which is the weakest form of environmentalism imaginable, as waste is not even reduced, but at best recycled.

The slogan was later to be reused by the US gun lobby, which transformed it into 'Guns don't kill people, people do'. Again, the message was that government intervention or any other form of structural change is not necessary, as individual responsibility should suffice. Similar ideologies and practices have since also found acceptance in Western Europe. Individual behaviour, such as keeping the streets clean and sorting your waste, increasingly became a moral deed. The environmental problem was not only privatised, but also moralised (Sandilands 1993). Ironically enough, such campaigns were successful in giving businesses a green image and convincing governments that regulation was no longer needed (Rogers 2007).

Rogers also shows how similar mechanisms are operational today. Think about the messages that can be found on packaging and that call on the consumer to recycle or not to drop litter on the street. This effectively kills two birds with one stone. On the one hand, it gives an ecological touch to a company's brand without really making fundamental changes. On the other hand, it reinforces the ideology that environmental problems are actually primarily a matter of individual consumer choices.

Of course, this is not to suggest that sorting and recycling waste is not important. Neither do we wish to downplay other attempts to change one's individual (consumer) behaviour. Quite the contrary: it seems more than logical that people try to reduce their ecological footprint where possible. But we have to be conscious about the broader frame. What we want to stress is that under the surface, a hegemonic struggle is playing out: a battle for how ecological problems are framed and how and by whom they should be addressed. Do we make sure that there is less waste, or do we simply recycle it? Do we set up campaigns to make sure people cycle, or do we invest in bicycle-friendly cities? Do we want the government to impose quality norms on producers, or do we prefer to let individual consumers take their own responsibility? Of course, in principle, these options do not exclude each other. However, the question is where the focus is put.

Moreover, the issue is not only whether sustainable consumption can ever develop enough leverage to realise substantial change. Crucial is the question of what kind of awareness is created by such approaches. The implicit message of many behaviour change campaigns is that the ecological crisis results from the sum of 'our' environmentally unfriendly (consumption) choices. This is the linchpin of a liberal vision of society, making abstraction from social, political and economic structures.

In this context, it is important to draw a distinction between actual behaviour and its representation. The point is not only whether a specific act is desirable in itself or not, but also how it is portrayed. Individual behaviour change is not good or wrong in itself: a lot depends on how it is framed, which meaning is given to it, and within which strategic framework it fits. From a social and political perspective, there is a huge difference between someone thinking her behaviour choices contribute to companies changing their business strategies and someone who changes her individual behaviour because she wants to become more autonomous from the market, even though from a strictly economic or ecological point of view, both can have similar effects.

From this perspective, proposing sustainable consumption as a real strategy for change is creating an illusion. Framing consumption as a moral act threatens to create a culture of blame and guilt that distracts from the necessity of political action. Thinking that consumers have the power to really influence companies threatens to lead up a blind alley. Trying to control and steer consumer behaviour using all kinds of subtle influence could well encounter resistance from emancipated citizens.

The post-politics of private governance

As explained in the previous part, the focus on sustainable consumption has a counterpart in the attempt to develop green business practices. From selling sustainable products or services and setting up labelling systems for such products, to adding environmental messages on product packages and engaging in initiatives for sectorial self-regulation: there is a broad range of voluntary actions undertaken by companies, which are often brought together under the heading of 'corporate social responsibility' (CSR).

As UNEP argues, CSR can yield a number of benefits, such as 'cost savings, greater access to capital, enhanced productivity, enhanced product quality (through enhanced employee morale and better working conditions), attraction and retention of human resources, enhanced reputation and brand, and reduced legal liability' (UNEP 2011, 566). Although high profits can still be made in the fossil fuel economy, there are market niches for green products that are slightly more expensive and enable profitable investments. The global market for organic food and drinks is expected to be worth more than $200 billion by 2020 (Grand View Research 2014). Climate change offers opportunities for manufacturers of wind turbines, solar panels, zero-energy houses, electric cars and many other green products. Intelligent business owners attempt to create a competitive advantage so they can be the first to profit as opportunities arise through a sharpening ecological crisis.

In any case, it is clear that a green image sells (Dale 2008). A significant proportion of consumers appear willing to pay at least 10% more for green products. Moreover, marketing literature predicts that this 'green trend' is set to increase (Iannuzzi 2012). However, there are also limits to this trend. The boundary between green business and greenwashing is often very thin (Tokar 1997). Making small changes in business operations is often an attractive option for businesses, since they can yield large differences in turnover without having to make fundamental changes (Rogers 2007). As it is difficult for consumers to assess whether there is actually a genuinely green practice behind the green image, many corporations opt for superficial changes like sponsoring environmental organisations or making marginal changes in production processes. Well-known examples are IKEA and BP. IKEA was able to adopt a green image through cooperation with the World Wildlife Fund and the investment in renewable energy, while its core business, the production of furniture with a short lifespan, remained unaffected. A small investment in renewable energy was apparently sufficient to change the branding of BP to 'Beyond Petroleum'.

Of course, there are also more genuine corporate initiatives to engage with ecological challenges. In the framework of this chapter, we cannot discuss the whole range of voluntary sustainability initiatives by companies in detail. We will limit ourselves to an issue which is closely related to the discussion on sustainable consumption and is very relevant for our analysis of post-politics, namely product labelling. In its green economy report, UNEP refers to '[c]onsumer-driven accreditation and certification schemes that create an opportunity for consumers to identify products that have been produced sustainably and pay a premium for access to them' as one of the key 'market-based instruments that can be harnessed to foster a green economy' (UNEP 2011, 138).

Many different labelling systems exist (Marx 2014). The most effective and legitimate systems include three parties: an organisation that sets the standards, a company that aims to get the label for its products, and an audit company that verifies whether the standards have been respected (Marx 2013). A typical example is the Forest Stewardship Council (FSC), a certification system for forest products (mainly wood and paper) which respects certain environmental and social standards. FSC itself is a private association composed of forest owners, timber industries and social and environmental NGOs. Its label can be attached to paper or wood products that respect its standards, and are monitored by a private audit company.

Although FSC is recognised as one of the better labelling systems for forest products, and is also included as an example in UNEP's green economy report (UNEP 2011, 139), it exhibits a tension typical for many similar initiatives. A key problem is that the company that wants to have the label has to pay the audit firm, and thus becomes its client. This means the audit firm is given an incentive not to be too tough with its clients, in order to prevent the latter from going to a competing audit company that is less strict. The way the system works thus threatens to exert a downward pressure on the criteria used to assign labels. Carrying out more stringent checks means higher costs for audit firms, again creating perverse incentives.

A further problem is that such private governance schemes are typical examples of a type of governing that can hardly be called democratic (Lievens forthcoming). Economic regulation is a deeply political affair, in the sense that it entails choices relating to fundamental social institutions. From a democratic point of view, such choices should be contestable and debatable, and this requires that they are visible for citizens. Admittedly, many private governance schemes, including FSC, are relatively transparent, in the sense that a lot of information about their mode of operation, membership or decision-making procedures is publicly available, e.g. via the Internet. Democratic visibility is something else, however: it means that citizens can see and interpret what is at stake in decision making (Lievens et al. forthcoming). Though many citizens have good reasons to be critical about how 'political' institutions such as the parliament work today, the conflictual setting of a parliament, namely the play of majority and opposition, has the merit that it makes citizens sharply aware of what is politically at stake. In that sense, it is the ideal type of democratic visibility. A similar visibility is completely lacking in private governance schemes, which, moreover, are often represented in consensual and managerial terms. The point is that if the world market is governed by a patchwork of similar sector-based governance initiatives, this fundamentally threatens the democratic quality of economic regulation. If democratically elected politicians adopt laws regulating economic practices, this happens through a public and visible process which stimulates broader involvement, participation and contestation by citizens and civil society actors. If regulations are adopted by a panoply of private initiatives, most of which are completely unknown to citizens, this undermines democratic visibility.

Technology is a political choice

'Give me abundant, clean, reliable, and cheap electrons, and I will give you a world that can continue to grow without triggering unmanageable climate change,' Thomas Friedman states (Friedman 2008, 186–187). He hopes for a Bill Gates scenario: innovative people experimenting with new ideas in their garage, developing new technologies that can eventually conquer the world. In order to make that possible, the economic context should, of course, be right, by pricing carbon and stimulating venture capitalists to invest in risky new projects.

Technology and its role in the transition to a green economy is a broad topic of discussion, ranging from smart grids to clean tech, from renewable energy to battery technology. In the framework of this book, it is not our intention to discuss all possible (supposedly) green technologies in detail. Our aim is rather to critically question the strong focus on technological solutions which is present in many green economy documents and the way this focus is framed. Of course, technology is an inevitable ingredient of every sustainability project. However, it is important to distinguish two issues. One question is which technologies are chosen and developed in view of greening the economy, and why. Another, albeit related, question concerns the technical way of thinking in which sustainability issues are often approached, which is underpinned by specific representations of society and technology. We refer here to the idea that technological solutions can be found for every social and ecological problem, as if this would make it possible to evade more profound changes.

As Amanda Machin argues, '[t]his corresponds to the call today for a "technological revolution" in response to climate change. For if we can develop and implement the right technology, then surely we can sustain the existence of our cake while we continue to eat it' (Machin 2013, 12). The term 'revolution' seems to have won a new credibility in the perspective of the pending ecological catastrophes. From NGOs such as Greenpeace to international institutions such as the International Energy Agency, a number of actors calls for 'revolution' (Teske 2008). Thomas Friedman states it even explicitly in the subtitle of his book *Hot, Flat, and Crowded: Why We Need a Green Revolution* (Friedman 2008). Remarkably, however, they are all referring to 'technological' revolutions, suggesting that technological change can facilitate the profound transformation that we need. Not only does this idea circumvent the social and political root causes of climate change and other ecological crises, but underpinning such a conception is often also the idea that technology could be socially or politically neutral.

Interestingly, an analysis of how technology and especially technological thinking can lead to the loss of the political was already present in the work of Carl Schmitt, who, as we argued, is one of the pioneers of contemporary theories of the (post-)political. He speaks about the 'spirit of technicity' to refer to a specific way of thinking about – or representing – technology, but also about society at large. It entails 'the belief in unlimited power and the domination of man over nature' (Schmitt 2007, 94). It is based on a specific notion of technological progress, which disregards other ways of looking at society. Fundamentally, he argues, such a technical way of thinking has a depoliticising effect. The point of the matter is that using and developing technologies needed for a sustainable future is something other than to believe that there are technological solutions for what are basically problems of society, such as climate change. As Amanda Machin argues:

> This approach fits within the dominant understanding of climate change, in which technological solutions are expected to appear inevitably if and when the heating of the atmosphere through human activity becomes desperate.

The right technology, this story suggests, will allow us to live the lifestyles that some have become accustomed to and to which others aspire. (Machin 2013, 13)

The belief in technological progress as the ultimate solution for current global ecological crises is highly problematic, precisely because it circumvents more fundamental questions concerning how society is organised.

Over the past two centuries, capitalism has been the engine behind a series of impressive technological changes. This is also one of the main arguments made to justify capitalism: there appears to be no problem for which the market and its engineers fail to develop a solution. But it is naive to believe that technology will solve everything in the end, as if there would be no limits to what human beings can realise.

Furthermore, it is important to underline that the development of technologies is the result of choices and decisions, not of a rational, automatic or neutral progression. One of the crucial questions is, therefore, which choices are made, and how these are framed or represented. Technological choices can challenge the way society is organised, or they can reproduce it, and in this sense, they have a fundamentally political thrust. We often observe how those technologies are chosen which are perfectly compatible with the way society is currently organised, as they merely provide a substitute for existing technologies: the electric car instead of a conventional car, biofuels instead of gasoline, large-scale and centralised solar energy systems, huge hydroelectric dams or even nuclear energy instead of power plants using coal, oil or gas. Each time, basic patterns of social organisation are left untouched. As a result, the change realised risks not to go far enough, and often even has detrimental social or ecological side effects.

In this sense, a longer history of technological choices is being continued. The history of how fossil fuels became the key source of energy for capitalism is illuminating in this regard. Wind and solar power and other forms of renewable energy are the technologies of the future. But who remembers that they are also the technologies of the past? When Holland was at the peak of its trading power in the seventeenth century, the country was full of windmills. The photovoltaic effect, on which solar panels are based, was discovered as early as 1839.[6] That is before commercial oil drilling took place. The first commercial oil well, it is often argued, was drilled in 1859 in Pennsylvania (Cox 2011, 25). In 1877, the first solar cell was constructed using selenium. In 1921, Einstein received the Nobel Prize for his explanation of the photovoltaic effect. However, its practical application only got wind in its sails with the growth of space travel, in particular under the influence of the US space agency, NASA.

Already in the nineteenth century, however, fossil fuels became the fuel of choice. This is no coincidence: fossil fuels have some fundamental advantages from a capitalist point of view. First, they can provide constant, high-intensity energy 24 hours a day, 365 days a year. This makes round-the-clock production possible, regardless of the climate, the weather conditions or the availability of local energy sources. Fossil fuels facilitate transportation and decrease companies' dependence on local ecosystems. Raw materials or energy do not need to be present on the spot, but can all be imported, thanks to cheap transport. It is worth noting how strikingly similar the characteristics of fossil fuels and money are. Both are very mobile and easy to transport. Both make it possible to make abstraction from local ecologies. Both lubricate the global economy.

Fossil fuels also make it possible to constantly speed up production. It takes many years for a tree to grow, but fossil fuels allow the economic system to disregard nature's slow life-cycles, at least as long as they remain plentiful and easily exploitable. In a few decades and centuries, we are burning supplies of fossil fuels which took millions of years to form. The gap between the slow cycle of nature and the ever accelerating cycle of the economy could hardly be any bigger. We see this gap recurring in many areas: forests are being cut down faster than trees can grow, greenhouse gases are emitted faster than ecosystems can absorb them, underground aquifers are drained faster than they can be replenished. NASA satellites have found that this rapid depletion of aquifers even has an effect on the gravitational field of the Earth (*The Economist* 2010).

The history of technology, including that of the energy system, is a history in which choices have been made which could have been different. In principle, we could have opted for solar and wind power much earlier, rather than waiting until we will be forced to. The choice of fossil fuels is a choice for a particular model of society: a model of non-stop production and maximum profit. The introduction of the 24-hour economy might have proved much more difficult with renewable energy. Moreover, the ability to make huge profits would have been greatly reduced. Once the world is full of windmills and solar panels, there is not much to be earned any more. Fossil fuels, on the other hand, have to be bought continuously. They can be owned privately, which is not the case with wind and the sun. Moreover, fossil fuels make centralised control over the energy system possible, just as nuclear power does. This is a political asset which is often absent from renewable energy systems, which lend themselves better to a decentralised structure.

Technologies have thus been chosen because of their compatibility with a capitalist way of organising the economy. When we look at many technological choices advocated in the framework of the green economy debate, this logic is still prevalent. We will illustrate this with the example of some key technologies, such as biofuels, carbon capture and storage and nuclear energy.

Biofuels feature quite centrally in many green economy scenarios (e.g. UNEP 2009, European Commission 2011), although its ecological credentials are quite dubious. A number of large companies have bet on biofuels, such as Virgin, BP, McDonald's, Tesco, Volvo and Volkswagen (Dale 2008). Governments have provided support through subsidies and regulations. In the beginning of 2014, more than 60 countries had regulations promoting the use of biofuels for transport (REN21 2014, 14). In 2006, the then president of the US George Bush decided that biofuel production should replace 75% of oil imports by 2025 in the US, which is striking, as Bush's legacy on the environmental front is otherwise extremely negative. An EU directive from 2009 put forward the objective of sourcing 10% of transport fuel (excluding air-traffic) from biofuels by 2020.[7] However, as the

World Bank admits in its *Inclusive Green Growth* report, 'the biofuel policies of Europe and the United States can be considered examples of green industrial policies that failed to generate even an environmental benefit, as they are generally considered to have harmed the environment' (World Bank 2012, 80).

The problems with biofuels are manifold: huge amounts of plants are needed to produce limited quantities of fuel, the energy return on energy invested is very low, and the production of biofuels often happens at the expense of the production of food crops, pushing up prices for basic food. That a choice for biofuels is nevertheless made is significant. From the perspective of our analysis, a key point is again that biofuels make it possible to avoid any structural transformation: nothing has to change but the type of fuel that is put in the fuel tanks of cars (Tanuro 2010, 129, 181, Williams 2010, 146). Biofuels thus appear to be entirely neutral with regard to current ways of life, private car transport, urban development, spatial planning, etcetera. They are attractive precisely because they are perfectly compatible with existing transport and distribution systems, as a result of which more difficult (but necessary) debates and conflicts can be evaded.

Moreover, they allow governments and companies to adopt a green image, even though the green credentials of biofuels are increasingly questioned. Unsurprisingly, critical environmental NGOs have strongly contested government policies in favour of biofuels, e.g. in Europe, and have thus repoliticised the debate on the topic, by pointing to the socially and ecologically devastating effects of biofuels.

Carbon capture and storage (CCS) is another example of a technology that is especially attractive because it suggests action is being taken against climate change, while the actual transformation of the energy system is averted or postponed. It is a typical end-of-pipe solution, which cleans up the mess at the end of the production process, rather than transforming the latter. CCS is attributed an important role in different green economy scenarios (IEA 2010, Stern 2006, UNEP 2011, World Bank 2012). It consists of capturing CO_2 released by combustion, for example in power plants or steel mills, and storing it underground, for example in depleted oil and gas reservoirs, where the stored CO_2 can also help to extract the last remaining oil and gas. In this way CCS would be able to transform coal and other fossil fuels into 'clean' energy sources.

This idea has even led the Polish Ministry of Economy to set up an 'International Coal and Climate Summit' during the nineteenth session of the Conference of the Parties (COP 19), the yearly summit of the UN Framework Convention of Climate Change in 2013, in collaboration with the World Coal Association. Strongly contested by a large number of NGOs, the 'Warsaw Communiqué' issued by the organisers calls for the continued use of coal, integrating CCS technology (World Coal Association 2013). For fossil fuel companies, CCS is a potential panacea. According to the World Coal Association, the world club of the coal industry, the proven global coal reserves are good for more than 861 billion tons of coal. This would be sufficient to last until around 2126 at the current production rate (WCA 2014). Coal can be found in many places in the world, but the US, Russia, China, Australia and India in particular have large reserves. There is a lot of pressure to exploit these coal reserves and CCS is supposed to help make 'clean coal' possible. CCS gives coal a lifeline.

A report from the third working group of the Intergovernmental Panel on Climate Change (IPCC), which examines ways to reduce greenhouse gas emissions and therefore publishes on more political (and thus controversial) subjects, states that CCS could reduce the CO_2 emissions of a power plant by 80% to 90% (IPCC 2005). However, CCS comes with important uncertainties and risks. The biggest risk is that of CO_2 leakages, which could result from earthquakes caused by the very injection of significant quantities of CO_2 in the fragile rocks of continental interiors (Zobacka and Gorelick 2012). CCS is thus a typical example of a technology which may temporarily help control the problem, but threatens to basically replace or postpone it, possibly enlarging it in the longer term.

A similar argument could be made concerning nuclear energy, whose dangers are well documented (Sovacool 2011). It is sometimes put forward as a part of the solution in green economy projects. In its G2 scenario, UNEP includes a modest share for nuclear energy, although it primarily focuses on renewables. Some advocates of the green economy suggest nuclear energy could be considered a 'green technology' (Rogner 2012). In its 2007 report, the third IPCC working group states that '[n]uclear energy, already at about 7% of total primary energy, could make an increasing contribution to carbon-free electricity and heat in the future,' providing an apparently scientific foundation for the nuclear option. The main obstacles, says the IPCC, are 'long-term fuel resource constraints without recycling; economics; safety; waste management; security; proliferation, and adverse public opinion' (IPCC 2007). Given all these 'constraints', it is odd that the IPCC still considers nuclear energy as a feasible option. At best, such a bet on nuclear energy is a way to buy time. At worst, it is a way to avoid (or at least postpone) further-reaching transformations, as investing in nuclear energy does not contribute in any way to a transition towards a model of society based on renewable energy. On the contrary, the longer we hold on to nuclear energy, the longer we maintain an energy system that is based on undemocratic forms of centralisation and a sheer lack of transparency.

Energy democracy

Crucially, the choice for a particular technology is a political choice, in the sense that it helps shape the very structure of society. Many renewable energy technologies, for example, lend themselves easily to a decentralised organisation, and allow for levels of transparency and democratic control which are impossible in the murky world of nuclear energy. This is important in view of the challenge we face today. Radically changing the energy system is not just an environmental or economic issue, it is also political. It represents a tremendous opportunity to put in place a form of energy democracy.

We are facing a political choice, and it is important to be conscious of it. The transition to renewable energy systems can take different forms. Systems have been developed for the production of renewable energy which are perfectly compatible with centralised control and concentrated ownership. Desertec, which some have called 'the green economy in action', is a good example of this (Being Green 2011). Desertec is a consortium of banks and insurance companies that wants to build mega-installations to produce electricity from solar energy in sunny regions, such as the Sahara. It is predicted that by 2050, this project would be able to provide at least 15% of European energy supply (Mackenzie 2011). 'The consistent implementation of the Desertec Concept and, in the future, the substitution of fossil fuels with clean energy from desert and arid regions could reduce global CO_2 emissions by 80%,' it is stated in the Desertec concept note.[8]

It sounds appealing, but it is important to underline the political implications of such a project. Desertec means that a concentration of private economic power would be installed in an area that will be of decisive importance in the future. This project would cause Europe's energy supply to be yet further centralised and privatised, but also threaten to lead to the monopolisation of the North African energy supply. Critical social movements are therefore already speaking about a form of 'solar colonialism'. As a society, we face a huge choice: do we opt for mega-plants in the desert controlled by multinational corporations and banks, or for a decentralised energy network over which citizens and communities have real control?

Transforming and decentralising the energy system is a challenge that cannot be understated. It is not possible to realise such a transformation without asking deeply political questions about the very basic institutions of society. Major revolutions in history were frequently accompanied by a transformation of the energy system, from hunting and gathering to agriculture, from human and animal power to wind and steam energy, from coal to oil and nuclear energy (Abramsky 2010, 8). All these changes had an immense impact on the structure of society. Until now, they always led to an increase in energy consumption and a further concentration of power and property. The current challenge is therefore enormous and unprecedented: for the first time the energy system needs to be changed in a way that reduces power consumption, and at the same time becomes decentralised and democratically accountable. It is difficult to imagine such a change happening within a framework based on continuous economic growth.

Notes

1 http://populationmatters.org/ and http://www.popoffsets.com/
2 http://populationmatters.org/get-involved/other-activities/offset-carbon/ and http://www.popoffsets.com
3 The focus on population shifts the 'blame' for ecological destruction not only from the global North to the global South, but also from men to women and from past and current to future generations.
4 http://www.1010global.org/
5 http://ec.europa.eu/environment/waste/
6 This was the work of the French scientist Edmond Becquerel. Note also that electric and hybrid car technology has existed for more than a hundred years, but that the internal combustion engine was chosen because it was more profitable (Cf. Rogers 2010).

7 See the website of the European Commission on renewable energy: http://ec.europa.eu/energy/renewables/biofuels/biofuels_en.htm

8 See https://dl.dropboxusercontent.com/u/2639069/DESERTEC%20Concept.pdf

References

Abramsky, Kolya, ed. 2010. *Sparking a Worldwide Energy Revolution: Social Struggles in the Transition to a Post-Petrol World.* Oakland, CA: AK Press.

Alcott, Blake (2005) Jevons' Paradox. *Ecological Economics* 54: 9–21.

Angus, Ian, and Simon Butler. 2011. *Too Many People? Population, Immigration, and the Environmental Crisis.* Chicago: Haymarket Books.

Bamberg, Sebastian, and Guido Möser. 2007. "Twenty Years after Hines, Hungerford, and Tomera: A New Meta-Analysis of Psycho-Social Determinants of Pro-Environmental Behaviour." *Journal of Environmental Psychology* 27:14–25.

Being Green. 2011. *A Green Economy in Action: Desertec.* Last Modified 27 June 2011. http://advanceconsultingforeducation.wordpress.com/2011/06/27/a-green-economy-in-action-desertec/ (accessed 22 September 2014).

Berglund, Christer, and Simon Matti. 2006. "Citizen and Consumer: The Dual Role of Individuals in Environmental Policy." *Environmental Politics* 15 (4):550–571.

Blake, James. 1999. "Overcoming the 'Value-Action Gap' in Environmental Policy: Tensions between National Policy and Local Experience." *Local Environment* 4 (3):257–278.

Brown, Lester R. 2009. *PLAN B 4.0. Mobilizing to Save Civilization.* New York: Earth Policy Institute.

Chawla, Louise, and Debra F. Cushing. (2007). "Education for Strategic Environmental Behavior." *Environmental Education Research* 13(4): 437–452.

Clover, Darlene. 2002. "Traversing the Gap: Concientización, Educative-Activism in Environmental Adult Education." *Environmental Education Research* 8 (3):315–323.

Commoner, Barry. 1992. *Making Peace with the Planet.* New York: The Free Press.

Courtenay-Hall, Pamela, and Larson Rogers. 2002. "Gaps in Mind: Problems in Environmental Knowledge-Behaviour Modelling Research." *Environmental Education Research* 8 (3):283–297.

Cox, Roger H. J. 2011. *Revolutie met recht.* Maastricht: Stichting Planet Prosperity Foundation.

Dale, Gareth. 2008. "'Green Shift': An Analysis of Corporate Responses to Climate Change." *International Journal of Management Concepts and Philosophy* 3 (2):134–155.

DEFRA. 2008. *A Framework for Pro-Environmental Behaviours.* London: DEFRA.

De La Croix, David, and Axel Gosseries. 2009. "Population Policy through Tradable Procreation Rights." *International Economic Review* 50 (2):507–542.

Dobson, Andrew, and Derek Bell. 2006. "Introduction." In *Environmental Citizenship*, edited by Dobson and Bell, 1–18. London: MIT Press.

Ehrlich, Paul R., and John P. Holdren. 1971. "Impact of Population Growth." *Science* 171:1212–1217.

European Commission. 2011. *A Roadmap for Moving to a Competitive Low-Carbon Economy in 2050.* http://ec.europa.eu/clima/policies/roadmap/index_en.htm (accessed 22 September 2014).

Foucault, Michel. 2004. *Sécurité, territoire, population. Cours au Collège de France, 1977–1987.* Paris: Gallimard/Seuil.

Foster, John Bellamy. 1999. *The Vulnerable Planet. A Short Economic History of the Environment.* New York: Monthly Review Press.

Foster, John Bellamy, Brett Clark, and Richard York. 2010. *The Ecological Rift. Capitalism's War on the Earth*. New York: Monthly Review Press.

Friedman, Thomas. 2008. *Hot, Flat, and Crowded: Why We Need a Green Revolution – and How It Can Renew America*. New York: Farrar, Straus and Giroux.

Gough, S. 2002. "Whose Gap? Whose Mind? Plural Rationalities and Disappearing Academics." *Environmental Education Research* 8 (3):273–282.

Grand View Research. 2014. *Organic Food and Beverages Market Analysis and Segment Forecasts to 2020*. San Francisco: Grand View Research.

Heimlich, Joe E., and Nicole M. Ardoin. 2008. "Understanding Behavior to Understand Behavior Change: A Literature Review." *Environmental Education Research* 14 (3):215–237.

Hellesnes, Jon. 1976. *Socialisering og Teknokrati* [Socialization and Technocracy]. Copenhagen: Gyldendal.

Iannuzzi, Al. 2012. *Greener Products. The Making and Marketing of Sustainable Brands*. Boca Raton, FL: CRC Press.

IEA. 2010. *Energy Technology Perspectives. Scenarios and Strategies to 2050*. Paris: International Energy Agency.

IPCC. 2005. *IPCC Special Report: Carbon Dioxide Capture and Storage. Summary for Policymakers. A Special Report of Working Group III of the Intergovernmental Panel on Climate Change*. http://www.ipcc-wg3.de/special-reports/special-report-on-carbon dioxide-capture-and-storage (accessed 8 December 2014).

IPCC. 2007. *Climate Change 2007: Working Group III: Mitigation of Climate Change. Executive Summary*. http://www.ipcc.ch/publications_and_data/ar4/wg3/en/ch4s4-es.html (accessed 3 December 2014).

Jackson, Tim. 2005. *Motivating Sustainable Consumption. A Review of Evidence on Consumer Behaviour and Behavioural Change*. Surrey: SDRN.

Jensen, Bjarne Bruun. 2002. "Knowledge, Action and Pro-Environmental Behaviour." *Environmental Education Research* 8 (3):325–334.

Jensen, Bjarne Bruun, and Karsten Schnack. 2006. "The Action Competence Approach in Environmental Education." *Environmental Education Research* 12 (3–4).471–486.

Kenis, Anneleen, and Erik Mathijs. 2012. "Beyond Individual Behaviour Change: The Role of Power, Knowledge and Strategy in Tackling Climate Change." *Environmental Education Research* 18 (1):45–65.

Kollmuss, Anja, and Julian Agyeman. 2002. "Mind the Gap: Why Do People Act Environmentally and What Are the Barriers to Pro-Environmental Behavior?" *Environmental Education Research* 8 (3):239–260.

Kunzig, Robert. 2011. "Population 7 Billion." *National Geographic*, January.

Lievens, Matthias. 2014. "From Government to Governance. A Symbolic Mutation and Its Repercussions for Democracy." *Political Studies*. Article first published online: 28 October 2014, http://onlinelibrary.wiley.com/doi/10.1111/1467-9248.12171/abstract.

Lievens, Matthias, Emilie Bécault, Antoon Braeckman, and Jan Wouters. 2014. "Democratising Global Governance: An Ongoing Conversation." In *Global Governance and Democracy: A Multidiscplinary Analysis*, edited by Jan Wouters, Antoon Braeckman, Matthias Lievens and Emilie Bécault. Cheltenham: Edward Elgar.

Machin, Amanda. 2013. *Negotiating Climate Change. Radical Democracy and the Illusion of Consensus*. London: Zed Books.

MacGregor, Sherilyn. 2009. "Are We Too Many? Some Questions about the Population Question." *In-Spire Journal of Law, Politics and Societies* 4 (1): 4–18.

Mackenzie, Kate. 2011. "EU Talks Up Desertec Plan: Saharan Solar Just Five Years Away." *Financial Times*, 21 June.

Marx, Axel. 2013. "Varieties of Legitimacy: A Configurational Institutional Design Analysis of Eco-labels." *Innovation. The European Journal of Social Sciences* 26 (3): 268–287.

Marx, Axel. 2014. *Competition and Cooperation in the Market of Voluntary Sustainability Standards*. Leuven: Leuven Centre for Global Governance Studies.

McKenzie-Mohr, Doug, and William Smith. 1999. *Fostering Sustainable Behavior: An Introduction to Community-Based Social Marketing*. Gabriola Island, British Columbia: New Society Publishers.

Meadows, Donella. 1995. *Who Causes Environmental Problems?* Sustainability Institute. http://www.donellameadows.org/archives/who-causes-environmental-problems/ (accessed 22 September 2014).

OECD. 2011. *Towards Green Growth*. http://www.oecd.org/greengrowth/towardsgreen growth.htm (accessed 22 September 2014).

PopOffsets. 2014. *What We Do and How It Works*. http://www.popoffsets.com/what_we_do.php (accessed 30 August 2014).

Redclift, Michael, and Ted Benton, eds. 1994. *Social Theory and the Global Environment*. London: Routledge.

REN21. 2014. *Renewables 2014. Global Status Report*. Paris: REN21 Secretariat.

Rickinson, Mark. 2001. "Learners and Learning in Environmental Education: A Critical Review of the Evidence." *Environmental Education Research* 7 (3):208–320.

Rogers, Heather. 2007. "Garbage Capitalism's Green Commerce." *The Socialist Register* 2007 43:231–253.

Rogers, Heather. 2010. *Green Gone Wrong. How Our Economy Is Undermining the Environmental Revolution*. London: Verso.

Rogner, Holger. 2012. *Green Growth and Nuclear Energy*. Munich: CESifo.

Sandilands, C. 1993. "On 'Green' Consumerism: Environmental Privatization and Family Values." *Canadian Women Studies* 13 (3):45–47.

Schmitt, Carl. 2007. "The Age of Neutralizations and Depoliticizations." In *The Concept of the Political*, 80–96. Chicago: University of Chicago Press.

Seager, Joni. 1993. *Earth Follies Feminism, Politics and the Environment*. London: Earthscan.

Seager, Joni. 2000. "Commentary: The 6-Billionth Baby: Designated Green Scapegoat." *Environment and Planning A* 32:1711–1714.

Shiva, Vandana. 2006. *Earth Democracy. Justice, Sustainability and Peace*. London: Zed Books.

Sovacool, Benjamin K. 2011. *Contesting the Future of Nuclear Power: A Critical Global Assessment of Atomic Energy*. Singapore: World Scientific.

Stern, Nicholas. 2006. *Stern Review on the Economics of Climate Change*. London: HM Treasury.

Stevenson, Greg, and Beth Keehn, eds. 2006. *I Will If You Will. Towards Sustainable Consumption*. London: SDC/NCC.

Swyngedouw, Erik. 2011. "Depoliticized Environments: The End of Nature, Climate Change and the Post-Political Condition." *Royal Institute of Philosophy Supplement* 69:253–274.

Tanuro, Daniel. 2010. *L'impossible capitalisme vert*. Paris: La Découverte.

Teske, Sven. 2008. *Energy [R]evolution. A Sustainable Global Energy Outlook*. Greenpeace International, European Renewable Energy Council (EREC).

The Economist. (2010). "The World's Most Valuable Stuff." 22 May.

Tokar, Brian. 1997. *Earth for Sale: Reclaiming Ecology in the Age of Corporate Greenwash*. Boston: South End Press.

UN. 2011. *The Great Green Technological Transformation.* New York: United Nations Economic and Social Affairs.

UNEP. 2009. *Global Green New Deal. Policy Brief.* Geneva: UNEP.

UNEP. 2011. *Towards a Green Economy: Pathways to Sustainable Development and Poverty Eradication.* www.unep.org/greeneconomy (accessed 3 December 2014).

WCA. 2014. "Where Is Coal Found." http://www.worldcoal.org/coal/where-is-coal-found/ (accessed 30 August 2014).

Williams, Chris. 2010. *Ecology and Socialism. Solutions to the Capitalist Ecological Crisis.* Chicago: Haymarket Books.

Wire, Tomas. 2009. *Fewer Emitters, Lower Emissions, Less Cost: Reducing Carbon Emissions by Investing in Family Planning. A Cost/Benefit Analysis.* Operational research. London School of Economics.

World Bank. 2012. *Inclusive Green Growth. The Pathway to Sustainable Development.* Washington, DC: International Bank for Reconstruction and Development / International Development Association or the World Bank. http://siteresources.worldbank.org/EXTSDNET/Resources/Inclusive_Green_Growth_May_2012.pdf (accessed 22 September 2014).

World Coal Association. 2013. *The Warsaw Communiqué.* http://www.worldcoal.org/extract/the-warsaw-communique/ (accessed 22 September 2014).

Zobacka, Mark D., and Steven M. Gorelick. 2012. "Earthquake Triggering and Large-Scale Geologic Storage of Carbon Dioxide." *PNAS* 109 (26):10164–10168.

6   Repoliticising the present

Breaking out of the limits of green economy thinking

In a piece arguing why it is impossible to limit global warming to 2°C through price corrections, Kevin Anderson, professor of energy and climate change at the University of Manchester and Deputy Director of the Tyndall Centre for Climate Change Research, states the following:

> Perhaps at the time of the 1992 Earth Summit, or even at the turn of the millennium, 2°C levels of mitigation could have been achieved through significant *evolutionary changes* **within** *the political and economic hegemony*. But climate change is a cumulative issue! Now, in 2013, we in high-emitting (post-)industrial nations face a very different prospect. Our ongoing and collective carbon profligacy has squandered any opportunity for the 'evolutionary change' afforded by our earlier (and larger) 2°C carbon budget. Today, after two decades of bluff and lies, the remaining 2°C budget demands *revolutionary change* **to** *the political and economic hegemony*.
>
> (Anderson 2013)

Year after year, global CO_2 emissions are increasing, breaking one record after the other. Far from even making modest steps toward climate mitigation, the globe is increasingly on a path to catastrophic climate change. This is not without political consequences: the more time is lost, the more strict the parameters become within which change can happen. The space available for a gradual transition shrinks, demanding more drastic transformations. Furthermore, evidence is growing about how difficult it is to reconcile a market economy based on profit and growth with sustainability demands. The change needed appears so profound that gradual solutions within the parameters of the existing model are increasingly unlikely to suffice.

In March 2012, the Carbon Tracker Initiative published its *Unburnable Carbon* report, causing a stir with its message that the world was using its remaining carbon budget at high speed. More in particular, attention was drawn to its analysis that 'fossil fuel reserves held by the top 100 listed coal companies and the top 100 listed oil and gas companies represent potential emissions of 745 $GtCO_2$' (Leaton 2012), which is much more than the 'carbon budget' which remains available if the world is serious about avoiding runaway climate change. In other words, compared with scenarios whereby we avert catastrophic climate change, fossil fuels are currently severely overvalued, and a large majority of fossil fuel reserves can be considered stranded assets.

In a report analysing the exposure of European financial institutions to fossil fuel firms, the Green European Foundation argues that in a breakthrough scenario which would result in 'a quick and definite transition to a low-carbon economy', 'losses for all EU banks, insurance companies and pension funds combined', caused by the carbon bubble, 'would be €350–400 billion' (Weyzig et al. 2014, 6). In itself, the report argues, this would not necessarily be a source of major systemic risks. However, combined with other risks and tensions, the effect can be unpredictable. In a turbulent world, with increasing social, ecological and geopolitical tensions, even small happenings can suffice to put a chain of events in motion. Moreover, the risks of the carbon bubble can increase if companies continue to invest in high-cost fossil fuels which are in excess of this carbon budget, which is precisely what another report by the Carbon Tracker Initiative is warning against (Leaton 2014).

In a report by Trucost commissioned by The Economics of Ecosystems and Biodiversity (TEEB) for Business Coalition, a calculation is made of the unpriced natural capital costs of major economic sectors in different regions of the world, showing that a large number of them would be unprofitable if so-called natural capital costs would be internalised in prices. Even though the concept of natural capital can be criticised for a variety of reasons, as we have shown, it is fascinating to follow the reasoning developed in the report and the debate it provoked. The report argues:

> Trucost's analysis has estimated the unpriced natural capital costs at US\$7.3 trillion relating to land use, water consumption, [greenhouse gas] emissions, air pollution, land and water pollution, and waste for over 1,000 global primary production and primary processing region-sectors under standard operating practices, excluding unpredictable catastrophic events. This equates to 13% of global economic output in 2009.
>
> (Trucost 2013, 8)

As a conclusion, the report states that '[n]o high impact region-sectors generate sufficient profit to cover their environmental impacts,' suggesting that 'if unpriced natural capital costs are internalised, a large proportion would have to be passed on to consumers' (Trucost 2013, 12). If one takes the principles of natural capital accounting seriously, the conclusions are drastic and overwhelming. Internalising the natural capital costs would mean a large number of the biggest companies and sectors on Earth simply become unprofitable.

It is worth citing in full the conclusion of an article published on the website of the Green Economy Coalition, an alliance of companies, non-governmental organizations (NGOs), research institutions and UN organisations, on the Trucost report:

> Ponder that for a moment: none of the world's top industrial sectors would be profitable if they were paying their full freight. Zero. [. . .] The distance between today's industrial systems and truly sustainable industrial systems – systems that do not spend down stored natural capital but instead integrate into current energy and material flows – is not one of degree, but one of kind. What's needed is not just better accounting but a new global industrial system, a new way of providing for human wellbeing, and fast. That means a revolution.
>
> (Roberts 2013)

One cannot fail to observe the deep tension between this radical conclusion and the optimistic discourse about the possibility to 'green' economies through technology, green growth and price corrections. Would the 'revolution' that is suggested here fit within the mould of ecological modernisation, green markets and green investment strategies? Natural capital accounting seems to lead to conclusions which many advocates of the natural capital concept do not draw, precisely because they remain within a market economic paradigm, holding on to notions of private property, market competition, innovation and prices as the main tools for change.

Sticking to these terms, in other words, does not allow us to fully grasp the chasm which confronts us: a chasm between huge social-ecological challenges and the limited capacity of the market to address these. If we want to break out of the limits of the green economy, a profound repoliticisation of the ecological field will be required, which allows us to put a number of issues into question which have become so hegemonic and commonsensical that it appears as impossible to think beyond them.

This repoliticisation will be inevitable, not only because conventional market approaches might not suffice to turn the tide, but also because of the huge social costs entailed by ecological destruction and the suggested market solutions of the green economy. Bluntly put, greening the economy requires huge investments, and the big question is who will bear the burden of these costs. The Trucost report's conclusion that the internalised natural capital costs will to a great extent be passed on to consumers subtly hints at the major distribution conflicts which are yet to come.

From passive revolution to repoliticisation

In the first chapter, we described the green economy as a project of passive revolution, implying a fundamental restructuration of political, social and especially economic institutions in order to tackle a major (ecological) crisis, but within the fundamental parameters of the existing form of society (Gramsci 1998; see also Lievens 2011). As we explained during the previous chapter, these parameters include the central role of private property, commodification and market mechanisms.

Passive revolution occurs in the context of a conflict which has not been fought until the end, but which is used by powerful actors as the starting point or breeding ground for a renewal of existing political, social and economic structures.

In other words, resistance or opposition feeds into the transformation realised through passive revolution. This means, on the one hand, that ideas, practices or demands of those who oppose the existing state of affairs (in this case, bluntly speaking, green opposition to fossil fuel capitalism) are appropriated, translated and integrated into a transformed version of predominant frameworks (in this case, the green economy). As a consequence, critical notions such as the ecological 'limits' of the planet are translated into, for example, the idea of 'capping' the amount of emission rights that can be traded on the market. The ecological vision that nature is not only a basic condition of human life, but also has intrinsic value (and should therefore be preserved) is translated into the idea that nature is (economically) productive, as if it were an enterprise, and therefore represents economic value. The critique of industrial civilisation is turned into a call for new, innovative technologies.

On the other hand, an important aspect of passive revolution is what Gramsci called 'transformism'. This means that specific groups or 'leaders' of the opponent camp are integrated into the transformed power bloc. While Gramsci referred to social-democratic or trade unionist leaders becoming a part of the state apparatus, in our case the most obvious example are NGOs, which finally see their chance to mainstream their concerns and become part of green economy coalitions, engage in public-private partnerships with public institutions and companies, or start to promote the green economy paradigm. This is not to suggest that this should be considered as betrayal. Taking part in the green economy project is a perfectly legitimate and understandable political choice for many big NGOs. However, the limits of the project imply that new counterforces will have to be built which can address these limits and reinvent a critical ecological discourse. In other words, the transformation of the ecological field which results from the emergence of the green economy discourse will bring a recomposition of the environmental movement. The formation of alliances around the green economy concept will (hopefully) trigger countervailing forms of regroupment around alternative, critical and radical notions, such as environmental or climate justice. The latter notions have already been used as rallying points purporting to unify dispersed forms of opposition against the green economy, and even against capitalism as such, and to repoliticise the ecological debate by re-establishing a clearly recognisable political fault line (Mueller and Bullard 2011).

The strategic terrain thus becomes complex. Fossil fuel capitalism is still predominant, and many states and public institutions remain trapped in policy frameworks which are not capable of exiting or 'greening' the system, but reinforce actually existing 'brown' economies. At the same time, it is increasingly confronted by the project for a 'green economy', in all its variants, and including a broad range of recipes from green Keynesianism, new markets, green global governance and technological innovation to sustainable consumption and entrepreneurship. It is an attractive project, but with a number of serious pitfalls. Specific sectors or companies can go far in 'greening' their practices. But what will the macro picture look like? Can a greened world economy, divided in social classes, torn by competition and based on an inherent growth impetus, bring an effective, socially just and democratic way out of the ecological crisis?

The green economy is undoubtedly an attractive perspective for many ecologically minded forces, certainly given the urgency of the ecological crises. Many people have doubts about the possibility to realise more fundamental changes, as it has become 'easier to imagine the end of the world than the end of capitalism', as Fredric Jameson famously stated (Jameson 2003). But green economy advocates will also be confronted with the limits of their project – ecologically, socially and politically. This necessitates a third position in the broad field of the struggle for hegemony. This is a position which not only radically questions fossil fuel capitalism, but also dares to break free from the limits of the green economy. This does not mean that advocates of the green economy suddenly become 'enemies'. They are legitimate defenders of a legitimate project, which is being contested on political grounds. Indeed, if we want to fight for just, democratic and effective answers to the ecological crises we are confronted with today, alternative social-ecological projects will have to be built which critically question the strategies and solutions of the green economy. It should not only focus on tackling the root causes of ecological destruction (including the seemingly indisputable axioma of economic growth), but in particular also stress the need for democracy and social justice in its vision for another social-ecological future.

Such a third pole, which is actually already emerging under the form of movements whose discourses are built around the nodal points of 'climate justice' and the 'commons', does not necessarily weaken the green camp in its struggle against fossil fuel capitalism. On the contrary, the stronger this third pole, the more pressure can be put on proponents of the green economy to live up to their promise to reconcile different concerns and deliver solutions which are ecologically effective and take social needs into account. Fundamentally, however, the goal of this third pole, which is currently still minoritarian, should not only, or in the first place, be to file off the sharp edges of the green economy, but also to fight for genuine social-ecological future alternatives.

In the framework of this concluding chapter, we will not provide an elaborated overview of all the alternative movements and approaches which emerged in opposition to the green economy, but we will delve into the question of what a repoliticisation of the ecological field can mean and how new movements can contribute to it. An increasing literature critically studies forms of depoliticisation and post-politics on a variety of ecological terrains (see e.g. Bettini 2013, Goeminne 2010, Kenis and Mathijs 2014b, MacGregor 2014, Machin 2013, Mason and Whitehead 2012, Neal 2013, Oosterlynck and Swyngedouw 2010, Pepermans and Maeseele 2014, Wilson and Swyngedouw, 2014). Far less scholarship exists, however, on exactly what repoliticisation could mean, or how it can be conceptualised. This question is crucial, however: repoliticising the ecological field is a condition for enlarging the political space of environmentalism, allowing socially just, ecologically effective and democratic alternatives to the green economy to emerge and get their voices heard.

Drawing especially on examples from the climate justice movement, this chapter will argue that repoliticisation happens in three moments. First comes a moment of critique. The veil of apparently neutral scientific, economic or technical representations should be pierced in order to reveal the political stakes and oppositions underpinning contemporary capitalism and its corrected, green version. What is at stake is a kind of ideology critique: it is a critique of post-political representations of the present. Mainly drawing on autonomist Marxism, we will develop an – admittedly succinct – 'political reading' of some core issues of current ecological debates in order to illustrate the significance of such a critique.

Second is a moment of subversion, which aims to expose and disrupt the very foundations of society, actually revealing it has no real foundation but is fundamentally contingent, and therefore changeable. We will especially make use of Rancière's political philosophy in order to conceptualise this moment, which disrupts existing ways of seeing, hearing and doing and opens a space for alternative practices. The third moment is a moment of construction, whereby alternative ideas, demands and projects are developed and brought together in a counterhegemonic discourse. Drawing on Laclau and Mouffe, we will shortly discuss some of the tenets of such a discourse, as it is already taking shape in the climate justice movement.

Our aim is not to delve into the philosophical assumptions which underpin these different theoretical frameworks. It is evident that the ideas of autonomist Marxists, Rancière and Mouffe and Laclau are philosophically speaking not always compatible, as their theories are grounded in divergent ontological and epistemological assumptions. However, this is not a conceptual exercise in political ontology and epistemology, but an attempt to give meaning to processes of repoliticisation carried out by actually existing movements. The practice of movements is not and ought not to be as theoretically consistent as a political philosophy tries to be. In this context, therefore, we think we can draw on these different sources, especially as actually existing movements already epitomise elements of the respective notions of political action and repoliticisation put forward by these different theories (Kenis and Mathijs 2014a). In what follows, we will first shortly discuss the three moments of repoliticisation we have distinguished, in order to subsequently illustrate these with the example of recent debates and struggles around the commons, which form an essential part of the discourse of the climate justice movement.

The moment of critique: piercing the veil of neutralisation

In Chapter 3, we described capitalism largely from the perspective of capital, analysing the latter's ecologically destructive features. But this is only one side of the story. The problem of this perspective is that it tends to portray capital as something characterised by strict laws, which can be scientifically studied, and can therefore be represented in neutral terms. However, as Harry Cleaver argued, these laws are not automatisms. Capitalism constantly attempts to impose the commodity form and its apparent laws on labour, whose struggle is fundamentally about rejecting and escaping from this form (Cleaver 1979). Capitalism is only a lawful system to the extent that it succeeds in imposing its forms upon society, labour and nature. As a consequence, the concepts expressing the commodity form, such as money, capital, price, etcetera, are far from neutral: they express a relation of power and antagonism, which they hide at the same time. Marx's aim, Cleaver states, was to reveal that behind economic categories, social and political power relations are hidden.

Fundamentally, that is also what his well-known attempt to reveal the 'secret' of commodity fetishism is about (Marx 1982, 163). Marx's argument that social relations are turned into things, and appear as fetishes (things which appear to have a life on their own), was precisely intended to show what lurks underneath the apparently neutral economic terms people use to describe apparently thing-like economic objects. The fetishism of the commodity precisely functions so as to make the political dimension of social relations invisible. What is actually a conflictual power relation appears as a thing with inherent qualities. 'Every reification is a forgetting,' Adorno and Horkheimer argue in their *Dialectic of Enlightenment* (Adorno and Horkheimer 1972, 230). It is a forgetting, and a rendering invisible, of social relations of power and conflict which lurk behind economic categories. Criticising conventional representations of the economy, which hide its dimensions of power and conflict, is therefore a crucial precondition for repoliticising the economy.

The 'political reading' of economic categories which autonomist Marxists propose attempts to develop such a critical perspective. It looks at the same phenomena, but then from the side of those people which capital seeks to control. The history of capitalism is also a history of resistance to that control, both through open confrontation and through subtle attempts to escape from its power. Think of workers' resistance, from strikes and factory occupations to less visible strategies against labour discipline. Or look at the strategies people develop to become less dependent on the market: from food collectives, such as community-supported agriculture, to sharing practices. Or the protest of citizens demanding a halt to pollution of fossil fuel industries: from petitions, demonstrations and boycotts to civil disobedience, from adbusting to sabotaging installations. Again and again, there are subjects resisting and escaping the control of capital, which has to invent a response, adapt and reorganise itself.

As we already showed in the first chapter, autonomist Marxists such as Mario Tronti and Antonio Negri have forcefully argued that many developments in capitalism cannot be understood if one disregards the importance of resisting subjects (Negri and Hardt 2000, Tronti 1977). Resistance and opposition are often the driving forces behind major transformations in capitalism. We have seen an example of such a complex dynamic of social change in Chapter 4, when we talked about Roosevelt's New Deal. It succeeded in transforming workers' wage demands into the catalyst for the development of a new type of capitalism, based on mass production for mass consumption. Another example is the trend towards 'corporate governance' and 'corporate social responsibility' that can be seen as multinationals' response to years of campaigning by social movements against human rights abuses committed by businesses (De Angelis 2003, 2007). Take for example the many campaigns for workers' and women's rights in sweatshops, such as the Clean Clothes Campaign. Although companies were able to rework the original goals of these forms of protest into their own hegemonic jargon (corporate social responsibility, stakeholdership, corporate governance, etcetera), these campaigns still had a significant impact.

As we argued already, the 'green economy' can be seen as the most recent major example of such a dynamic of change, whereby power and resistance have to be understood as a complex interplay of forces. It is a project which governments, international institutions, banks and think tanks have been developing out of concern about intensifying ecological crises, but also because appropriating and translating critical environmental ideas could help transform the ecological field and lay the groundwork for new economic opportunities.

The point is that we see the results of these dynamics of change, but not all the motive forces behind them. Forms of opposition, counterpower and resistance which played a role in forcing change upon capitalist powers largely remain invisible. That is precisely what allows these processes of change to be portrayed in post-political terms, as if they were merely a question of new forms of governance, management or policymaking. The change appears only to come from above, and we hardly realise that sometimes, massive movements from below were crucial to make it happen. This one-sided picture makes it very difficult to see the dynamics behind these changes and to envision how large-scale changes in the face of ecological catastrophes could happen in the future. If we want to envision how to repoliticise the present, we thus have to change our perspective. We have to see that there is often struggle and resistance where there only appears to be passivity and ignorance, conflict where there seems to be no more than economic mechanisms, and power relations where there merely appear to be market exchanges. Apparently neutral descriptions, in other words, hide underlying political realities.

Repoliticising climate change means looking at core features of our society through such a political lens, seeing how conflicts, power and resistance are present in a manifold of unexpected places. Such a perspective can help deconstruct apparently neutral, economic or technical terms. Take the concept of the externalisation of costs by capital, which we discussed in Chapter 3. The market offloads a number of its problems and externalises certain 'costs' onto society and the environment. But society is not a passive recipient of these externalised costs: there is friction involved in this process, sometimes even open resistance and opposition. Fundamentally, forms of social-ecological protest and resistance can be seen as obstacles for this process of externalisation. Even though very few protest movements completely win their case, their resistance against certain ecologically destructive practices (from mining via agrobusiness to the introduction of genetically modified organisms) pushes up the costs for corporations. Faced with resistance, companies have to invest in safety and public relations initiatives, set up advertisement campaigns to restore their tainted image, win back confidence of consumers, pay lawyers or even hire security firms. Furthermore, in so far as protest movements partly win their case, companies will be more limited in their capacity to externalise costs. This is not to suggest that this solves anything. The point is that by making visible the often hidden forms of power and conflict underlying the externalisation of costs, the resistance against the latter can be reinforced.

Significantly, companies try to externalise their environmental costs in particular onto those people who have less leverage to resist, because they live in difficult conditions, under oppressive regimes or lack information. If the 'externalisation of costs' meets opposition in Western Europe, many companies simply move their production processes or harmful practices to Africa, Asia or Latin America. It is no coincidence that much toxic waste ends up in the global South. But as soon as resistance and protest occurs there too, companies are faced with the same difficulty again. To give one example: in 2006, the *Probo Koala*, a ship chartered by shipping giant Trafigura, dumped 550 cubic meters of toxic waste in Abidjan, the capital of the Ivory Coast (Townsend 2009, 114). More than ten Ivorians died and thousands needed medical treatment. There was a massive protest, which was also picked up by environmental movements in Western Europe. With the help of NGOs, a lawsuit was successfully brought against the company. The latter thought it had found a cheap way to get rid of the waste, but thanks to the protest the cost of dumping waste was considerably increased.

Energy is political

Another interesting example is the energy sector. Energy is not just something technical that is necessary in the production process: it is also an instrument of capital's power over labour. Energy is the tool of choice to get rid of a stubborn workforce, as more machines powered by fossil fuels means less labour and therefore less (potential) resistance.

The process of mechanisation has continued unabated since the beginning of the nineteenth century. In Chapter 3, we explained that the competition between businesses plays a key role in this: companies try to outdo each other by using more productive machinery. But this analysis highlights only one side of the story.

Workers' protest may also have unintentionally been a driving force behind the mechanisation process. As autonomist Marxists have argued, the strategy to focus on the production of relative surplus value, driven by the introduction of machines, has been an important response to workers' resistance (Cleaver 1979). This not only enhanced productivity, but also made production less dependent on recalcitrant workers. Machines produce 24 hours a day, they do not become sick, do not go on holiday and, above all, they make business less dependent on the loyalty, skills and knowledge of the workers themselves. There is, of course, one key requirement: there must be cheap and reliable energy sources available.

In a paradoxical way, workers' struggles can thus push transformations in energy use, even though these transformations are ultimately often used against them, in order to control and discipline their labour. An example given by Kolya Abramsky can illuminate this (Abramsky 2010a, 95). After the Second World War, South African gold mines formed the backdrop of strong workers' resistance, which significantly drove up the cost of extraction. The management tried to stifle opposition, but ultimately chose a more intelligent solution: investing massively in mechanisation. The effect was significant. In 1950, ten people and 99,000 kWh of energy were needed to produce ten kilos of gold. In 1975, the number of workers needed was halved, while energy consumption almost doubled. Similar examples can be found all over the world: the most effective management ploy to counter workers' struggle is to mechanise production. This is not only the case in industry, as the service economy is also constantly looking for ways to replace workers with machines – in this case computers. This always results in an increase in energy intensity. The way in which capitalist enterprises respond to workers' resistance thus transforms the structure of production, and increases the ecological cost. This explains why access to cheap and reliable energy is an absolutely key factor for capitalism. It is not simply a means to keep the machines going, but also and above all a means to exercise power: energy is political. If you have energy, you have a key means to monitor and control labour and undermine overt or more subtle resistance. As energy becomes scarcer, more expensive or less reliable, this could have implications for companies' power strategies.

This analysis of the relation between labour resistance and the command of capital is, of course, also valid for the energy sector itself, which is the arena of very intense social and political struggles (Abramsky 2010b). Although it is central to the world economy, energy is one of the few sectors in which neoliberalism struggles (Midnight Notes Collective 2009). Even after the Iraq war, the largest industry in the world (oil and gas) remains largely in the hands of national oil companies and international cartels such as OPEC. Both are at odds with the fundamentals of the neoliberal doctrine. In countries such as Saudi Arabia, Russia, Venezuela and Iran, neoliberalism has not succeeded in fundamentally changing the ownership of the energy sector.

The role which social struggle plays in this should not be underestimated (Abramsky 2010b). From massive public movements on the streets to occupations of oil facilities and sabotage of pipelines, social struggles have played a crucial role in the development of the energy sector as we know it today. For instance, the nationalisation of oil companies in the Middle East and Latin America in the 1970s occurred due to pressure from mass demonstrations and strikes. The impact on the global energy market was immediately visible in the oil crises of the 70s. The more conflict drove up global oil prices, the more the global energy system came under pressure. It is interesting to note that in the context of these oil crises, the first timid steps were taken towards renewable energy and energy efficiency. However, at the moment when the prices decreased again, measures were turned back too (Verbruggen 2008).

Such examples show that it is important to analyse the energy sector through a political lens, and stop conceiving it merely in narrow technical terms. Energy is a form of power, and it is the object of struggle and resistance. As we already showed in the previous chapter, the way the energy sector is organised, the degree of its centralisation and decentralisation is politically highly significant. The way energy is discursively represented thus needs to be politicised. The same is valid for energy reserves. Steven Colatrella, who is part of the autonomous-Marxist Midnight Notes Collective, argues, for example, that there is such a thing as a 'political Hubbert curve' (Caffentzis 2008–9, 68, Midnight Notes Collective 2009). The Hubbert curve is a well-known graph that shows the consumption of raw materials and energy over time: usually the curve rises steadily until it reaches a peak, after which it begins to fall back. The Hubbert curve is very important in the debate about peak oil. Very often, however, this curve is understood in a depoliticised way, as if the moment of the peak depends only on the depletion of reserves, or the exhaustion of technical possibilities to extract the remaining oil (Cox 2011, Heinberg 2003, 2009). Looked at in this way, political struggles and forms of resistance become invisible. The point of the matter is that it is actually the cost of oil extraction that determines when we reach the peak. This cost not only depends on the technical costs of extracting oil (e.g. drilling in deep water is much more expensive than on land), but is significantly co-determined by struggles and resistance. Peak oil is therefore not something objectively determinable in a neutral, detached way. It is co-determined by political power relations, in the broadest sense of the term.

Resistance can have unintended but significant 'side effects': it can even considerably accelerate the transition to new energy systems, a transition which, again, is hardly merely technical or economic in nature. Resistance by coal miners was an important factor behind the shift towards surface mining and oil, Bruce Podobnik (2010) argues. Protest can thus have consequences far beyond its immediate demands. It can be the driving force behind processes of mechanisation, but also behind transformations in the energy system. Could this also mean that labour or environmental struggles, to the extent that they increase the costs and risks of fossil fuel exploitation, reinforce the tendency for companies to opt for renewable sources?

The moment of subversion: revealing a social order's lack of foundation

To repoliticise the present, it does not suffice to critically question fetishistic or reified representations. It does not suffice to argue that underneath seemingly neutral or scientific concepts such as capital, price or the externalisation of costs lurks a force field of powers and resistances. We have to go further. The fact that counterpowers and forms of resistance co-determine the concrete shape that capitalism adopts, including in its green variants, does not yet put into question the institutions of power and the principles they are based on. Moreover, as we have seen, forms of resistance or protests can be answered through the development of new investment strategies and business models which take the counterpowers into account, but at the same time render them invisible and translate their demands into something else. It might, for instance, be the case that protests push up the price of dumping waste for companies, but intelligent investors can respond by opening up new profit-making opportunities, such as industries in sorting, recycling or exporting waste (e.g. Burkett 2006). Some companies run into trouble, others find new markets, but the focus remains on profit rates and prices, concealing underlying political stakes.

Repoliticisation inevitably starts with making visible that society is a force field, and that there are counterpowers in society which can push economic and political powers in this or that direction. However, it also requires moving beyond this. One step further, it is about opening up the fundamental question about the very foundation of our social and political order. From the perspective of post-foundational political theory, repoliticisation is about revealing that in the end, society does not have an ultimate foundation (Marchart 2007). At best, it is grounded in the contingent foundations which political acts and decisions have created, but which can always be questioned and overturned.

When focusing on how critical social and environmental movements, such as the climate justice movement, can contribute to a repoliticisation, the work of Jacques Rancière is an indispensable help. His understanding of political action stresses not only the importance of making visible what remained invisible, but also the fact that in the end, society is based on a foundation which cannot possibly be a foundation, but subverts society when brought to the surface.

This might sound paradoxical, but an example Rancière gives in his book *Disagreement* can clarify a lot. He refers to a situation of someone giving an order to a subordinate, and asking him: 'Do you understand?' (Rancière 1999, 44). This is a very paradoxical question, Rancière shows. On the one hand, the one who gives the order actually means to say that "[i]t's not up to you to understand; all you have to do is obey" (Rancière 1999, 45). In other words, the question affirms the inequality between a superior and a subordinate. The question draws a line between the one who speaks and the one who remains silent, between what is to be heard and what remains unheard. On the other hand, however, the question assumes that the subordinate understands the order, and can apply it. It supposes that the superior and subordinate share an equal intelligence, namely the capacity to understand and interpret language. They both share a common language and intellectual capacity, even though this commonality is denied by the commander: the subordinate should not speak, but merely execute the order.

The point is that the most unequal of social relations, giving a command, is underpinned by and presupposes a fundamental equality of intelligence of speaking beings. Political action, according to Rancière, occurs when the subordinate contests this hierarchical state of affairs by bringing this fundamental equality to the fore and making it visible. She then reveals the egalitarian foundation of inegalitarian relations. This sparks a conflict of a very peculiar nature. The superior will deny that there is conflict, as there ought to be agreement around the fact that the order should simply be obeyed. The subordinate will bring forth that both parties are equal in their linguistic capacities, and that a discussion ought to take place. The crux of the matter is that making visible that this fundamental equality is the foundation of even the most hierarchic social relations undermines and even subverts the order of hierarchy. Equality is the foundation of an order which falls apart from the moment this foundation is rendered visible.

This example illuminates Rancière's broader political philosophy. One of its core concepts is the notion of the 'distribution of the sensible', which

> establishes at one and the same time something common that is shared and exclusive parts. This apportionment of parts and positions is based on a distribution of spaces, times, and forms of activity that determines the very manner in which something in common lends itself to participation and in what way various individuals have a part in this distribution.
>
> (Rancière 2007b, 12)

The distribution of the sensible refers to an order which is shared in a double sense: it is shared in common, and it is partitioned into unequal parts and positions which not only determine how people can participate in society, but also limit what is sayable, visible or hearable. The importance of this concept is that it helps one understand that exclusion is constitutive and inclusion can never be complete: each ordering of what is sayable, visible or hearable excludes certain things which are not. This means there is always a ground for conflict and contestation. Political action, therefore, is about disrupting this distribution of the sensible, and making something new visible or hearable.

Political action is something exceptional for Rancière, and this is especially the case in our current era. Rancière does not use the concept of 'post-politics' to describe this era, but he rather speaks about 'post-democracy' or 'consensual democracy' to refer to a situation where conflict is excluded, and consensus-seeking, integration, governance and partnership are constitutive of the distribution of the sensible (Rancière 1999, 2005). As a result of this, the situation is portrayed in such a way as if everybody is always already included, has a place, and is considered a partner: 'there are only *parts* of society – social majorities and minorities, socio-professional categories, interest groups, communities, and so on. There are only parts that must be converted into partners' (Rancière 1999, 14). In other words, post-democracy

> is a reasonable agreement between individuals and social groups who have understood that knowing what is possible and negotiating between partners are a way for each party to obtain the optimal share that the objective givens of the situation allow them to hope for and which is preferable to conflict.
>
> (Rancière 1999, 102)

In contrast to this, political action implies the emergence of a 'part of those who have no part' that unveils and contests exclusions and by doing so makes something new visible (Rancière 1999, 9). Post-democracy suggests that there is nothing beyond what is actually visible and sayable, that there are no exclusions and that all ought to be partners, or – to use the language of the green economy discourse – 'stakeholders'. Genuine politics, in contrast, shows that what exists is contingent. It makes something new visible or hearable. Crucially for Rancière, this happens when people act on the assumption that all are equal (Rancière

1999, 2007a). This does not necessarily mean that we are *actually* equal. But political action means acting under the *postulate* of equality, and this will have disruptive effects. It will reveal the hierarchies and exclusions of the existing social order, and thus make them contestable.

To sum up, political action is about bringing the presupposition of equality, which is the non-foundation of every social order, to the surface, in such a way that it subverts that very order. By doing that, the distribution of the sensible is bound to be transformed.

This approach sheds an interesting light on a whole range of social and environmental actions. An interesting example are the actions set up by the Climate Justice Action (CJA) movement during the 2009 climate summit in Copenhagen, as they had a very Rancièrian flavour (Kenis and Mathijs 2014a). Their aim was to denounce the 'false solutions' on the negotiation table (many of which would shortly afterwards become key ingredients of the green economy discourse), and to reveal the fact that certain voices and perspectives remained unhearable during the talks. Although UN Framework Convention for Climate Control (UNFCCC) summits are relatively inclusive, giving many stakeholders the right to access the conference venue, there are, of course, fundamental inequalities and exclusions, which is precisely what climate justice activists aim to reveal. One of the problems with such new forms of 'governance' or 'multistakeholder' approaches is that they fail to fully integrate the democratic values of equality and citizenship on which they (cl)aim to be built. The stakeholders they bring together are not *citizens*, but a variety of qualitatively different and unequal actors, ranging from politicians to companies, NGOs and academics (Lievens forthcoming). Compared with democratic elections, for example, where all citizens are, at least procedurally, equalised, the global governance architecture for climate change is structurally incapable of giving shape to values of equality, notwithstanding its discourse about inclusiveness and civil society participation.

This is one of the key issues which climate justice activists tried to reveal. Their explicit objective was to give a voice to those people who are neglected in the hegemonic discourse (such as indigenous people and small farmers), and to 'break' the consensus ideology of the climate summit. In this way, they tried to broaden the debate so as to include issues of social justice and more profound forms of democracy. Concretely, CJA organised a number of direct actions, the most important of which was the 'Reclaim power' action in which thousands of activists tried to get as close as possible to the Bella Centre, where the official UNFCCC conference took place. Just outside the building, they held an alternative 'people's assembly' where alternative voices were given centre stage and a socially just climate project was discussed. In this way, the movement especially tried to create a political space, a symbolic arena, which had to make clear for all to see via the world media that we are faced with political choices: about who speaks and who does not, about whose needs are taken into account and whose are not, and about which strategies and alternative societal projects could contribute to tackling climate change, not only in an effective, but also in a democratic and just way.

Interestingly, the action was not just a blockade or an occupation, but first and foremost a performance, and this is what made it outspokenly political in Rancière's sense of the term. Indeed, the activists acted under the postulate of equality: they did not just demand to be treated as equals, but acted *as if* they were equal to the negotiators inside and had as much right to participate in the conversation. As one spokesperson stated:

> We have no more time to waste. If governments won't solve the problem then it's time for our diverse people's movements to unite and reclaim the power to shape our future. We are beginning this process with the people's assembly. We will join together all the voices that have been excluded – both within the process and outside of it. We will be both non-violent and confrontational.[1]

Direct action, in the way CJA conceived it, is inevitably conflictual. It also aims at making something new visible or hearable. As Rancière states, acting politically entails the manifestation of a 'part of those who have no part', which discloses and contests exclusions and by doing so makes something new visible. The actions of CJA are examples of this *par excellence*: they actually intended to shift the lines of what could be seen or heard.

Other CJA actions during the summit also had a strong performative character. Armed with the slogan 'Hit the production', for instance, CJA activists intended to block the road to the Copenhagen harbour, as they considered the harbour to be a symbol of the destructive capitalist system causing climate change:

> In Copenhagen we will target the harbour with a mass blockade. The global shipping industry is at the heart of capitalism, a key symbol of an industrial system that is based on growth and the use of fossil fuels. We must show that the organisation of production in our societies is the *root cause* of climate change and must be changed.
>
> (CJA Leaflet 2009a)

Pointing explicitly to capitalism as one of the 'root causes' of climate change, CJA also aimed to reveal that society is changeable, establishing at the same time a clearly antagonistic relation to underlying power structures, claiming these should be radically transformed. Before they arrived in the harbour, however, the activists were all arrested.

From actions against tar sands exploitation and the Keystone Pipeline, to climate camps against the investment choices of banks or the construction of new runways or coal plants: the performative aspect of making visible what remained invisible and challenging inequalities is each time fundamental. Such actions open a space of conflict, while at the same time affirming the equality of each and everyone. That is what makes these acts political, as they contest the order of society by revealing its presuppositions.

The moment of construction

Revealing and contesting the (non-)foundation of social order is crucial in every attempt to repoliticise. But the act of subversion, however important, remains limited in its effects. It merely opens a space where something new can be imagined. It takes us outside of the parameters of what exists, revealing the latter's contingency. The problem with Rancière's philosophy, however, is that he radically rejects any attempt at building a new order, as this would inevitably install new hierarchies and invisibilities. In other words, politics for him is merely about contestation, not about the construction of a political project.

This is not the place to engage in a philosophical dialogue with Rancière (see Lievens 2014). Rather than focusing on the theoretical merits of his position, it might make sense to take a look at actually existing environmental movements. Even if their actions very often display core features of how Rancière conceives of political action, they always do more. They always also put forward certain demands, or at last produce discourses about possible social-ecological alternatives. Consider again the Climate Justice Action movement during the Copenhagen climate summit. While stating that '[w]e cannot trust the market with our future, nor put our faith in unsafe, unproven and unsustainable technologies,' and advocating 'climate justice' and 'system change', the movement advanced a number of alternatives, even though these were not developed in detail (Kenis and Mathijs 2014a):

> leaving fossil fuels in the ground; reasserting peoples' and community control over resources; relocalising food production; reducing overconsumption, particularly in the North; recognising the ecological and climate debt owed to the peoples of the South and making reparations; and respecting indigenous and forest peoples' rights.
>
> (CJA Leaflet 2009b)

This enumeration typically partakes of the logic of equivalence which we pointed to in Chapter 1 and which, according to Laclau and Mouffe, underpins (counter) hegemonic discourses. It is by establishing relations of equivalence between a whole series of demands that a political camp is demarcated in opposition to an adversary (Laclau and Mouffe 2001).

The movement's discourse was strongly articulated around the nodal point of 'climate justice'. Through this nodal point the movement attempted to bring together a wide range of people and movements ('from indigenous peoples to workers unions, from the landless to the european autonomous, from climate campers to youth from the suburbs of the metropolis, from anti-industrialists to anarcho-syndicalists') with the aim of developing a socially just and even anticapitalist form of climate politics (COP15zine 2009). 'Climate justice' thus functioned as the tendentially empty signifier under which a range of groups and demands were gathered in a chain of equivalence. As we already explained in the first chapter, hegemonic projects are built by appropriating discursive elements and integrating them into a coherent discourse. The essence of a hegemonic operation is the construction of nodal points that articulate as many available floating signifiers as possible. In the case of CJA, these signifiers originated in global justice struggles, indigenous movements, trade union struggles, peasant movements, etcetera.

Next to the nodal point of 'climate justice', CJA also constructed its discourse around the nodal points of 'system change' and 'direct action'. Together, they formed the cornerstones of its discourse (Kenis and Mathijs 2014a). 'System change not climate change' being its central slogan, CJA argued that the 'system' is the problem – not only as a root cause of climate change, but also as the reason why the climate crisis is not being solved. With 'system change' CJA refers to the need to fundamentally transform the way our society is currently organised, not only to ward off climate change, but as a desirable goal per se. Indeed, the movement rejoiced in the fact that 'the climate crisis seems to have opened the possibility of uniting a broad range of struggles against capitalism' (COP15zine 2009).

This process of (counter)hegemonic construction leads to the political field being divided into two or more camps, which challenge each other's hegemony or hegemonic pretensions. This division is the prerequisite, according to Mouffe, to making hegemony visible and contestable as such (Mouffe 2006). As she argues, the conflict between hegemonic and counterhegemonic projects is also of crucial importance for freedom and democracy: it makes it possible to see that there is a choice between different alternative visions of society.

Constructing alliances and chains of equivalences is therefore an essential ingredient for a movement of repoliticisation. Rancière is undoubtedly right to argue that whenever one starts to build new social relations and orders, new exclusions and hierarchies will be the result. Yet, movements such as the climate justice movement, which explicitly aim to repoliticise the climate debate, cannot and do not limit themselves to contesting and subverting. They have to build something, even during the actions themselves: organisations, networks, a logistic apparatus to provide activists with food and shelter etcetera. This infrastructure is inevitably part of the building of nascent counterhegemonies. The more democratic such a movement is, the more it will be able to deal with exclusions and hierarchies, although it will never be able to eradicate them completely. However, without the willingness to build counterhegemonies, the existing hegemony can never be made visible as such and repoliticised. In that sense, Rancièrian political action generates a space where conflict can appear, something new can be seen or heard, and the unnamed can be named, but it is not yet a space for what Swyngedouw calls 'the naming of different possible socio-environmental futures' (Swyngedouw 2010, 229).

A communism of the commons

If there is one idea that can be the nodal point of a counterhegemonic discourse beyond capitalism, it is the idea of the commons, which is already playing a key role in the climate justice movement. We touched upon the commons in Chapter 3 when we explained that the privatisation of common land, and of raw materials, minerals and other products of nature, was a key factor behind the historical emergence of capitalism. We have argued how capitalism undermines the commons by enclosing them and replacing them with private property. We have seen how this process has continued throughout the history of capitalism, to the present day, including in the green economy project. For example, carbon trading constitutes a kind of semi-privatisation of the atmosphere. Biomass is privatised in view of potential gains in a greener economy. New green technologies are patented, although no single invention is actually ever the product of an individual or a small group: each developer of a new technology stands on the shoulders of a large group of people, including previous generations of scientists.

Capitalism destroys many commons. Yet, new commons are constantly being (re-)created, from natural commons to digital commons and from new ideas to common spaces of encounter: things to which people have access without having to go via the market or without needing state authorisation. Commons are all those things, places, ideas and relations which people create together or inherit from previous generations in order to make them available for others. They include gifts of nature, such as the air, sea, raw materials, clean water, but also social creations such as public spaces, libraries, research, creative work, art, knowledge and values. We are not always aware of how diverse and important they are, but society simply could not function without the commons. From beaches and forests to the Internet, from philosophical insights to Wikipedia and even language: in a way, these are all commons. Furthermore, numerous studies point out that commons can make a very important contribution to the sustainable management of ecosystems (e.g. Wall 2014, Weston and Bollier 2014).

Capitalism has a peculiar relationship with the commons. On the one hand, it constantly threatens to undermine the commons by appropriating and privatising them (Wall 2014). On the other hand, however, capitalism cannot exist without the commons. There is a fundamental paradox here: commons are a condition of possibility of social life as such, including of capitalist society, while capitalism at the same time has an ingrained tendency to enclose and privatise commons. Commons are indeed crucial to the social fabric. What would society be without public spaces, freely accessible parks where people can meet, free access to knowledge and information, or the Internet? What would capitalism be without the free gift of nature, or without the educative practices through which ever new generations are raised?

Take the example of the so-called knowledge economy: it can only function optimally if knowledge is freely available (Casarino and Negri 2008, Negri and Hardt 2009). Yet, capitalism cannot function without patents and copyrights, which impede free access to knowledge and information. The paradoxical result is that this undermines the productivity of knowledge production, as knowledge becomes less accessible, especially for those without a large budget. The knowledge economy therefore constantly impedes its own development.

From the Paris Commune of 1871 to the actions of the Indignados and many environmental movements: whenever people organise themselves and take action against a particular type of wrong or injustice, new commons are produced. On Tahrir Square in Cairo during the Egyptian Revolution of 2011, activists started cleaning up the square and the streets around it, set up people's kitchens and organised information systems that were accessible to everyone. The square was an open communal space, where neither private property nor state authorities were in control. In times of crisis people often fall back on the commons. After Hurricane Katrina in New Orleans, hundreds of thousands of volunteers went to help rebuild the city, independently of the state or private companies. Since Greece was hit by the economic crisis in 2009, a lot of people were able to survive thanks to access to food or shelter outside the commercial circuit. But it is not only during crises that new commons are being created in the pores of capitalist society: community gardens, alternative media and communal spaces are created by citizens in many places of the world. Numerous forms of production and collective action are actually free associations of people in accordance with the logic of the commons.

However important forms of commoning and sharing are for society, it is striking that they often remain invisible. As Ugo Mattei, a legal scholar studying commons, argues:

> The current vision presents the opposition between 'the public' (the domain of government) and 'the private' (the domain of the market and of private property) as exhausting all the range of possibilities in a sort of zero-sum game. This gridlocked opposition [. . .] hides the commons from the public vision.
>
> (Mattei 2012, 38)

Increasingly, however, the occupation of the field of the visible by states and markets, or broader, by public and private spheres, is being questioned, both through contestatory practices of commoning and through critical research on the commons. Over the last years, and especially since the Nobel Prize for economics was given to Elinor Ostrom for her pioneering work on the commons, the amount of scholarship on the subject has increased a lot (Ostrom 1990, 2010). It almost appears as if the commons had to be saved from oblivion. In our view, this has something to do with how society is organised and how it withdraws certain things from the eye.

To put it in Rancièrian language: the distribution of the sensible is governed by the state and the market, in the sense that they are all there is to see or hear within that distribution. Putting forward the commons is then a subversive act, which disrupts that distribution. This is especially the case because the commons should not, in our view, be regarded as a third sphere next to or beyond the state and the market, as if there would be common goods next to public and private goods. Fundamentally, the commons, which encompass all forms of sharing which are not governed by private market principles or by state authorities, is a condition of possibility of society itself, including of the market and the state. Social life could not possibly exist without forms of commoning: without a minimal form of sharing (of language, morals, spaces, goods), social relations are impossible. Even markets can, at least to a certain extent, be considered communal spaces, even though they are also machines of privatisation, and the way the market is predominantly portrayed radically denies this communal dimension. Fundamentally, the market is a shared space: it is not private property nor is it completely controlled by the state. It can be accessed without having to pay or without needing state authorisation. Paradoxically, commons, sharing and free access underpin a social institution which appears to be radically at odds with these very principles, as the market is considered to be based on private interests and property. This remains unproblematic as long as this communal dimension of social life remains invisible. It is taken for granted, and predominant discourses through which society gives meaning to itself fail to take it into account. The way the market is usually portrayed, in other words, does not do justice to the forms of sharing which inevitably underpin it.

Bringing the commons to the fore, making it visible, is therefore *a critical act*, as it reveals a foundation stone of society. Such an act makes it possible to critically question the predominant economic and individualistic representations of society: even the individualism of market actors is not possible without some underlying forms of sharing. This critical act revealing the importance of the commons is at the same time a potential act of subversion. As we explained, according to Rancière, equality is the hidden condition of every hierarchical order and at the same time disrupts this order from the moment it is rendered visible. In a similar vein, the commons is a hidden condition of society, but from the moment the commons are made visible *as* a foundation of society, it threatens to put the predominant way in which key social institutions such as the market are portrayed into question. Therefore, making the commons visible *as* the condition of possibility of society disrupts the central and foundational role that markets and market principles have in currently predominant representations of society.

Precisely because the discourse on the commons emerges in contexts where commons are threatened to become privatised (when knowledge and information are enclosed, when public spaces are privatised, or when the air becomes a quasi-private good in emissions trading), making commons visible very often opens a space of conflict. Furthermore, the very demand of protecting the commons almost immediately confronts and repoliticises the green economy project.

To sum up, repoliticisation first requires a moment of critique, which makes the commons visible as a core dimension of society: society is about more than markets and states, it is about what we do and share together. Second comes a moment of subversion. Forms of commoning or sharing fundamentally underpin society, even those market and state institutions whose self-avowed mode of operation is at odds with the principles of commons. Revealing that commons are the non-acknowledged presupposition of apparatuses of privatisation potentially subverts these apparatuses. At least, their ideologies lose their plausibility: the market can no longer be understood in market terms, but is based on what these market terms exclude, namely sharing and commoning.

However, these critical and subversive moments are not enough to really repoliticise society in the name of the commons. As the above analysis already reveals, there are different types of commons. Repoliticising society through a discourse on the commons therefore requires making division visible about the types of commons that are desirable. Therefore, a positive, constructive project is required around the need to build and maintain democratic, socially just and ecological commons.

Indeed, if the commons is such a broad term that even the market can be considered a kind of commons, we need to make distinctions between different types of commons and engage in a political debate and struggle around them (De Angelis 2007, 94). To put it simplistically, from a democratic and social justice perspective, there are good and bad commons, commons which contribute to projects for climate justice and democracy, and commons which underpin market society. Negri and Hardt, for example, argue that the nation is a commons, but then of a corrupted kind. It is 'a social institution in which the common is both deployed and corrupted', as it engages 'the collective cultural, social and political expressions of the population', but it is also characterised by forms of exclusion and hierarchy which are at odds with the horizontal way commons are normally produced (Negri and Hardt 2009, 163). Similarly, David Harvey has pointed out that a gated community can also be considered as a kind of commons, but then an 'exclusionary commons' (Harvey 2012, 71). These are not the types of commons which can underpin a climate justice project.

Moreover, commons and principles of sharing are also increasingly being recuperated and turned into the object of new business strategies. Think, for example, about the so-called sharing economy, which has even sparked some enthusiasm in the international financial press (Dembosky and Bradshaw 2013, *The Economist* 2013). We do not want to reject the sharing economy, as it can surely help reduce the amount of raw materials and energy that are consumed. But it unfortunately has a similar effect as the green economy project: it translates the principle of sharing into something else, and thereby intensifies the hold which the market logic has on the world, including nature and people's life-worlds. The sharing economy is actually not about sharing, but about renting out. It is about letting another share in the use of a good against payment: think about successful but controversial initiatives such as Airbnb, which help people rent out free spaces in their house to tourists.

In this context, the slogan 'time is money' acquires a new significance. For the eighteenth- or nineteenth-century industrialist, it referred to the loss of income represented by each hour without production. In the sharing (or renting) economy, each hour an object is not shared or rented out equals a loss of income. In this sense, objects become financialised: they are not merely useful things which can be shared amongst people, but they are bearers of a potential income (and thus also of a potential loss of income when they are not rented out). Before the economic crisis in 2007, houses in the US were financialised: they became capital assets, which could yield new, financial incomes. Something similar is at stake in the sharing economy, but in this case a much wider range of goods become capital assets potentially yielding financial income. In this sense, the 'sharing economy' can represent a new type of 'colonisation of the life-world' whereby financial and monetary values invade daily life more deeply than ever before. One particular problem is that financial investors have found a new opportunity for rapid profit in the sharing economy, creating new power concentrations and even monopolies in this sector. This is not to dismiss the sharing economy as such: sharing and commoning are of essential importance in a climate justice strategy. But it is important to distinguish the different forms sharing can adopt, and develop forms of counterhegemony which integrate commons that point beyond the market society and refuse commodification. Sharing can be a practice that aims to move beyond a market society, but it can paradoxically also become the vehicle of an ever more profound marketisation and financialisation of all aspects of human life. Differentiating between both is a deeply political act.

Sharing and commoning can thus adopt very different forms. Even though the principles on which they are based radically question the way society is currently portrayed (as sharing is radically at odds with principles of private property), certain manifestations of the commons can also help reproduce our current society. In this sense, commons are in themselves not guarantees of a socially just or democratic society. Showing that the principle of sharing is a crucial condition for society has a critical effect on how society is predominantly represented, but the very existence of commons does not necessarily transform society beyond its market form, as commons can also underpin the market and new business models in the sharing economy. Four fifths of the Alpine region in Switzerland is in a certain sense communal property, but this does not mean that Switzerland is an egalitarian, let alone a post-capitalist, society (Ostrom 1990, 64; see also Wall 2014). Commons can perfectly well sit side by side with forms of exclusion and inequality. In a capitalist context, certain forms of exclusion are, of course, unavoidable. If the commons are not actively protected against capitalist profit hunters, for example, before long not much of them will remain. Think of the waters off the coasts of Africa that are fished by Western industrial fleets, or the Amazon forest that is cut clear for soy cultivation. In order to protect these commons, some form of exclusion is indispensable.

To repoliticise the present, we not only need to show that society is fundamentally based on communal principles which are at odds with private interests and property principles – we also need to distinguish those forms of commons which help reproduce the market, including its 'green' form, and those which move beyond it. In other words, climate justice movements need a politics of the commons advocating certain types of commons, while rejecting others. It needs a vision of democratic commons, whose political character is fully acknowledged. This requires a far-reaching notion of democracy. As Massimo De Angelis has argued, genuine commons actually assume three elements: a common good, an active community, and a continuous process of commoning or pooling (An Architektur 2010). There is a real commitment required of citizens to maintain the common goods, and democratic spaces and mechanisms to manage them as a community. In our view, this also presupposes a politicisation: an orientation to a common good, a collective identity, and a motivation to protect the common good against its opponents.

An alternative social-ecological project, based on a discourse centred around the nodal point of the commons, also needs a vision on the role of public authorities, if only because these can provide support for the principles of the common. On the one hand, the public sphere itself should become a sphere where forms of democratic commoning can take place: think about how protestors, from the Arab Spring to the Occupy movement, transform a public (state-controlled) space such as a square into a common space. In this sense, a democratic society is one which makes it possible that citizens transform public into communal spheres. On the other hand, public authorities can also play a role in supporting the commons.

It is difficult for governments to create real commons in a top-down way (although they can very easily destroy them).[2] Even the most democratic parliament cannot bring commons into existence. A movement from below is therefore always necessary, as the production of democratic commons requires the active involvement of citizens. At the same time, however, it is crucial that governments recognise certain commons and defend them against privatisation. In many countries there is legislation which recognises and protects forests or beaches as commons. Moreover, commons can be a foundational principle for policies, including in the environmental sphere. For example, considering the atmosphere as a commons could underpin specific climate mitigation policies which do not take the road of carbon trading. Emissions flowing from specific industrial processes could simply be banned, for example, in the name of the atmosphere as a common good. In contrast, considering the atmosphere as a dump is actually a way to privatise it. Prohibiting oil explorations in the arctic presupposes the principle that the arctic is a common good of humanity and should therefore be protected against private interests.

But what makes a counterhegemonic project around the commons particularly interesting is that it can not only be a core element to repoliticise the current environmental field, but also carry the seeds of a social-ecological project which could move beyond the constraints of capitalism. Making commons visible as a foundation of society, opposing its principles to those institutions which both rely on and deny the commons, and actively constructing democratic and socially just commons is, therefore, more than a key strategy beyond the limits of the green economy. As Nick Dyer-Witheford poetically summarises: 'If the cell form of capitalism is the commodity, the cellular form of a society beyond capital is the common' (Dyer-Witheford 2010).

Notes

1 http://climate-connections.org/tag/reclaim-power/
2 In his courses on governmentality, Foucault states that a socialist type of governmentality remains to be invented (Foucault 2004). The practice of governing the commons could point to the possibility of a specifically socialist form of governmentality: it

requires a self-limitation on the part of those who govern, similar to liberal governmentality, but the entirely different object that is governed, and the specific dynamics which characterise this object, will make this type of governmentality radically different from the liberal forms.

References

Abramsky, Kolya. 2010a. "Energy, Work, and Social Reproduction in the World-Economy." In *Sparking a Worldwide Energy Revolution. Social Struggles in the Transition to a Post-Petrol World*, edited by Kolya Abramsky, 91–101. Oakland, CA: AK Press.

Abramsky, Kolya, ed. 2010b. *Sparking a Worldwide Energy Revolution: Social Struggles in the Transition to a Post-Petrol World*. Oakland: AK Press.

Adorno, Theodor W., and Max Horkheimer. 1972. *Dialectic of Enlightenment*. New York: Herder & Herder.

Anderson, Kevin. 2013. *Why Carbon Prices Can't Deliver the 2°C Target*. http://kevinanderson.info/blog/why-carbon-prices-cant-deliver-the-2c-target/ (accessed 30 August 2014).

An Architektur. 2010. "On the Commons: A Public Interview with Massimo De Angelis and Stavros Stavrides." *E-Flux Journal* 17. http://www.e-flux.com/journal/on-the-commons-a-public-interview-with-massimo-de-angelis-and-stavros-stavrides/ (accessed 3 December 2014).

Bettini, Giovanni. 2013. "Climate Barbarians at the Gate? A Critique of Apocalyptic Narratives on 'Climate Refugees'." *Geoforum* 45:63–72.

Burkett, Paul. 2006. *Marxism and Ecological Economics. Towards a Red and Green Political Economy*. Leiden: Brill.

Caffentzis, George. 2008–9. "A Discourse on Prophetic Method. Oil Crises and Political Economy, Past and Future." *The Commoner* 13:53–72.

Casarino, Cesare, and Antonio Negri. 2008. *In Praise of the Common. A Conversation on Philosophy and Politics*. Minneapolis: University of Minnesota Press.

CJA Leaflet. 2009a. "Hit the Production." Copenhagen.

CJA Leaflet. 2009b. "Reclaim Power: Pushing for Climate Justice!" Copenhagen.

Cleaver, Harry. 1979. *Reading Capital Politically*. Brighton: The Harvester Press.

COP15zine. 2009. *Dealing with Distractions. Confronting Green Capitalism in Copenhagen and Beyond*. http://dealingwithdistractions.files.wordpress.com/2009/12/dealing_with_distractions_read-2.pdf (accessed 3 December 2014).

Cox, Roger H. J. 2011. *Revolutie met recht*. Maastricht: Stichting Planet Prosperity Foundation.

De Angelis, Massimo. 2003. "Neoliberal Governance, Reproduction and Accumulation." *The Commoner* 7. http://www.commoner.org.uk/07deangelis.pdf (accessed 3 December 2014).

De Angelis, Massimo. 2007. *The Beginning of History. Value Struggles and Global Capital*. London: Pluto Press.

Dembosky, April, and Tim Bradshaw. 2013. "Start-ups: Shareholder Societies." *Financial Times*, 7 August.

Dyer-Witheford, Nick. 2010. "Commonism." In *What Would It Mean to Win?* edited by Turbulence Collective, 105–112. Oakland, CA: PM Press.

Foucault, Michel. 2004. *Sécurité, territoire, population. Cours au Collège de France, 1977–1987*. Paris: Gallimard/Seuil.

Goeminne, Gert. 2010. "Climate Policy Is Dead, Long Live Climate Politics!" *Ethics, Place and Environment* 13 (2):207–214.

Gramsci, Antonio. 1998. *Selections from the Prison Notebooks.* London: Lawrence & Wishart.

Harvey, David. 2012. *Rebel Cities. From the Right to the City to the Urban Revolution.* London: Verso.

Heinberg, Richard. 2003. *The Party's Over. Oil, War, and the Fate of Industrial Societies.* Gabriola Island, British Columbia: Society Publishers.

Heinberg, Richard. 2009. *Blackout. Coal, Climate and the Last Energy Crisis.* Gabriola Island, BC: New Society Publishers.

Jameson, Fredric. 2003. "Future City." *New Left Review* 21:65–79.

Kenis, Anneleen, and Erik Mathijs. 2014a. "Climate Change and Post-Politics: Repoliticizing the Present by Imagining the Future?" *Geoforum* 52:148–156.

Kenis, Anneleen, and Erik Mathijs. 2014b. "(De)politicising the Local: The Case of the Transition Towns Movement in Flanders (Belgium)." *Journal of Rural Studies* 34:172–183.

Laclau, Ernesto, and Chantal Mouffe. 2001. *Hegemony and Socialist Strategy: Towards a Radical Democratic Politics.* London: Verso.

Leaton, James. 2012. "Unburnable Carbon – Are the World's Financial Markets Carrying a Carbon Bubble?" *The Carbon Tracker Initiative.* http://www.carbontracker.org/wp-content/uploads/2014/09/Unburnable-Carbon-Full-rev2-1.pdf (accessed 3 December 2014).

Leaton, James. 2014. "Oil and Gas Majors: Fact Sheets." *The Carbon Tracker Initiative.* http://www.carbontracker.org/wp-content/uploads/2014/09/CTI-Oil-Gas-Majors-Company-Factsheets-August-2014-FULL.pdf (accessed 3 December 2014).

Lievens, Matthias. 2011. "Gramsci over de passieve revolutie." *Vlaams Marxistisch Tijdschrift* 45 (4):56–64.

Lievens, Matthias. 2014. "Contesting Representation. Jacques Rancière on Democracy and Representative Government." *Thesis Eleven* 122 (1):3–17.

Lievens, Matthias. 2014. "From Government to Governance. A Symbolic Mutation and Its Repercussions for Democracy." *Political Studies.* Article first published online: 28 October 2014, http://onlinelibrary.wiley.com/doi/10.1111/1467-9248.12171/abstract.

MacGregor, Sherilyn. 2014. "Only Resist: Feminist Ecological Citizenship and the Post-Politics of Climate Change." *Hypatia* 29 (3):617–633.

Machin, Amanda. 2013. *Negotiating Climate Change. Radical Democracy and the Illusion of Consensus.* London: Zed Books.

Marchart, Oliver. 2007. *Post-Foundational Political Thought: Political Difference in Nancy, Lefort, Badiou and Laclau.* Edinburgh: Edinburgh University Press.

Marx, Karl. 1982. *Capital. A Critique of Political Economy. Volume 1.* Harmondsworth: Penguin Books.

Mason, Kelvin, and Mark Whitehead. 2012. "Transition Urbanism and the Contested Politics of Ethical Place Making." *Antipode* 44 (2):493–516.

Mattei, Ugo. 2012. "First Thoughts for a Phenomenology of the Commons." In *The Wealth of the Commons*, edited by David Bollier and Silke Helfrich, 37–44. Amherst: Levellers Press.

Midnight Notes Collective. 2009. "Promissory Notes: From Crises to Commons." http://www.midnightnotes.org/Promissory%20Notes.pdf (accessed 3 December 2014).

Mouffe, Chantal. 2006. *On the Political.* London: Routledge.

Mueller, Tadzio, and Nicola Bullard. 2011. "Beyond the 'Green Economy': System Change, Not Climate Change? Global Movements for Climate Justice in a Fracturing World." UN Research Institute for Social Development conference, Geneva, 10–11 October.

Neal, Sarah. 2013. "Transition Culture: Politics, Localities and Ruralities." *Journal of Rural Studies* 32:60–69.

Negri, Antonio, and Michael Hardt. 2000. *Empire*. Cambridge, MA: Harvard University Press.

Negri, Antonio, and Michael Hardt. 2009. *Commonwealth*. Cambridge, MA: The Belknap Press of Harvard University Press.

Oosterlynck, Stijn, and Erik Swyngedouw. 2010. "Noise Reduction: The Postpolitical Quandary of Night Flights at Brussels Airport." *Environment and Planning A* 42 (7):1577–1594.

Ostrom, Elinor. 1990. *Governing the Commons. The Evolution of Institutions for Collective Action*. Cambridge: Cambridge University Press.

Ostrom, Elinor. 2010. "Beyond Markets and States: Polycentric Governance of Complex Economic Systems." *American Economic Review* 100 (3):641–672.

Pepermans, Yves, and Pieter Maeseele. 2014. "Democratic Debate and Mediated Discourses on Climate Change: From Consensus to De/politicization." *Environmental Communication* 8 (2):216–232.

Podobnik, Bruce 2010. "Building the Clean Energy Movement: Future Possibilities in Historical Perspective." In *Sparking a Worldwide Energy Revolution. Social Struggles in the Transition to a Post-Petrol World*, edited by Kolya Abramsky, 72–80. Oakland, CA: AK Press.

Rancière, Jacques. 1999. *Disagreement: Politics and Philosophy*. Minneapolis: University of Minnesota Press.

Rancière, Jacques. 2005. *Chroniques des temps consensuels*. Paris: Seuil.

Rancière, Jacques. 2007a. *On the Shores of Politics*. London: Verso.

Rancière, Jacques. 2007b. *The Politics of Aesthetics*. London: Continuum.

Roberts, David. 2013. *World's Top Industries Shown to Be Unprofitable* . . . http://www.greeneconomycoalition.org/know-how/world%E2%80%99s-top-industries-shown-be-unprofitable (accessed 30 August 2014).

Swyngedouw, Erik. 2010a. "Apocalypse Forever?" *Theory, Culture & Society* 27(2–3): 213–232.

The Economist. 2013. "All Eyes on the Sharing Economy." 9 March.

Townsend, Terry. 2009. "Capitalism's Anti-ecology Treadmill." In *The Global Fight for Climate Justice*, edited by Ian Angus, 110–120. London: Resistance Books.

Tronti, Mario. 1977. *Ouvriers et capital*. Paris: C. Bourgois.

Trucost. 2013. *Natural Capital at Risk: The Top 100 Externalities of Business*. TEEB for Business Coalition.

Verbruggen, Aviel. 2008. *De ware energiefactuur*. Antwerp: Hautekiet.

Wall, Derek. 2014. *The Commons in History. Culture, Conflict, and Ecology*. Cambridge, MA: MIT Press.

Weston, Burns H., and David Bollier. 2014. *Green Governance. Ecological Survival, Human Rights, and the Law of the Commons*. Cambridge: Cambridge University Press.

Weyzig, Francis, Barbara Kuepper, Jan Willem van Gelder, and Rens van Tilburg. 2014. "The Price of Doing Too Little Too Late. The Impact of the Carbon Bubble on the EU Financial System." In *Green New Deal Series*. Brussels: Green European Foundation.

Wilson, Japhy, and Erik Swyngedouw. 2014. *The Post-Political and Its Discontents. Spaces of Depoliticisation, Spectres of Radical Politics*. Edinburgh: Edinburgh University Press.

Epilogue
Beyond the green economy

The 'transition to a green economy is already underway,' we can read in the United Nations Environment Programme's green economy report (UNEP 2011, 7). Its optimism is heartening. But is it not also disarming? Is such optimism a 'moral duty', as the saying goes, or is it taking away the feeling of unrest which can lead to indignation and revolt? UNEP's optimism is apparently not shared by many climate justice movements, which advocate different and further-reaching transformations, beyond growth, free trade and principles of private property, in favour of real democracy and just commons.

As we stated in the first chapter, the more the green message becomes mainstream, the more 'being green' acquires different and even divergent meanings. More than ever, it is becoming clear that widely divergent pathways can be followed when attempting to tackle climate change and other major ecological crises. Mostly remaining under the radar, but sometimes appearing on the surface, a hegemonic struggle is ongoing about what the transition to an alternative social-ecological future could mean.

Uncovering this hegemonic struggle, one aim of this book has been to show that social-ecological change will inevitably be confronted with 'the political', and that this is something which should not be avoided, but embraced. It is only by recognising the political dimension of every process of social-ecological change that the full spectrum of possible strategies and trajectories can become the object of a public debate, that values such as justice and democracy can take centre stage, and that people can become actively involved. Indeed, the mobilisation of citizens paradoxically requires the acknowledgement of the fact that the community to which they belong is fundamentally divided. When disagreement and division are recognised and given a place in the political sphere, citizens can identify with one of the *camps* engaged in political struggle within the political arena. Representing society in consensual terms, misrecognising conflicts and exclusions, in contrast, risks alienating many citizens: politics, or 'governance', then becomes an issue for elites.

This is not merely a theoretical argument – it can be empirically verified. Which are the issues that lead to large mobilisations, a growing political awareness amongst large parts of the population and the creation of novel spaces of democratic debate and conflict? These are always the issues which divide, and around which genuine political conflicts involving diverging societal projects have been able to arise.

Moreover, it is by concretely experiencing how important it is to be able to freely express one's opinions, engage in struggles and take sides that one identifies not only with one's own camp in the struggle, but also with the democratic arena which makes this struggle possible in the first place. Engaging in conflict, in other words, paradoxically also helps produce community: democratic conflict stimulates citizens to develop a common attachment to a shared democratic space, despite their disagreements. Moreover, it helps them become aware of how important the cause is around which the conflict has emerged. Similarly, to really involve citizens in the struggle against climate change, we need to fully recognise that the process through which a different social-ecological future is realised is deeply conflictual. By openly recognising the plurality of possible social-ecological projects, and by creating a space where different conceptions of what it means to be 'green' can clash, a manifold of social groups can come to identify with one of those conceptions, and even with the need for social-ecological change as such. By allowing conflict and disagreement on an issue such as climate change to emerge, the issue can start to occupy a central place in society, challenging citizens to develop an opinion about it and take sides. Only then can it become clear to citizens that they have to consciously choose between different social-ecological futures, and that the stakes of this decision are very high.

In contrast, if tackling climate change is portrayed in terms of consensual governance and leaves fundamental parameters of our current society unaffected, it not only risks remaining insufficient in view of the challenge ahead, but it will also fail to have a mobilising and democratising effect. This risks being the destiny of the green economy project, at least as it is given shape today. To go beyond its limits, we will have to ask more fundamental questions. By asking these questions, conflicts of interests, social struggles and ideological oppositions will inevitably pop up.

'The stone age did not end for lack of stones, and the oil age will end long before the world runs out of oil,' the former Saudi oil minister Zaki Yamani once stated. The point is: we will have to end it ourselves, and this will not happen without conflict and struggle. It will require fundamental social changes and real political acts, which, as Slavoj Žižek states, are not about 'something that works well within the framework of the existing relations, but something that changes the very framework that determines how things work' (Žižek 2000, 199). A real transition is always at least a bit of a revolution.

References

UNEP. 2011. *Towards a Green Economy: Pathways to Sustainable Development and Poverty Eradication.* http://www.unep.org/greeneconomy/Portals/88/documents/ger/GER_syn thesis_en.pdf (accessed 3 December 2014).

Žižek, Slavoj. 2000. *The Ticklish Subject. The Absent Centre of Political Ontology.* London: Verso.

Index